STARFISH AQUATICS INSTITUTE

StarGuard

FIFTH EDITION

Best Practices for Lifeguards

Jill E. White

HUMAN KINETICS

Library of Congress Cataloging-in-Publication Data

Names: White, Jill E., 1955- author.
Title: Starguard : best practices for lifeguards / Jill E. White, Starfish
  Aquatics Institute.
Description: Fifth edition. | Champaign, IL : Human Kinetics, [2017] |
  Includes bibliographical references.
Identifiers: LCCN 2016014955 (print) | LCCN 2016028605 (ebook) | ISBN
  9781492523987 (print) | ISBN 9781492543947 (ebook)
Subjects: LCSH: Lifeguards--Training of--Handbooks, manuals, etc.
Classification: LCC GV838.74 .W45 2016 (print) | LCC GV838.74 (ebook) | DDC
  797.2/00289--dc23
LC record available at https://lccn.loc.gov/2016014955

ISBN: 978-1-4925-2398-7 (print)

This publication is written and published to provide accurate and authoritative information relevant to the subject matter presented. It is published and sold with the understanding that the author and publisher are not engaged in rendering legal, medical, or other professional services by reason of their authorship or publication of this work. If medical or other expert assistance is required, the services of a competent professional person should be sought.

The web addresses cited in this text were current as of March 2016, unless otherwise noted.

Acquisitions Editors: Tom Heine and Michelle Maloney; **Senior Managing Editor:** Amy Stahl; **Copyeditor:** Bob Replinger; **Permissions Manager:** Dalene Reeder; **Graphic Designer:** Denise Lowry; **Cover Designer:** Keith Blomberg; **Photograph (cover):** Jill E. White; **Photographs (interior):** © Jill E. White, unless otherwise noted. Photo on page 11 Rafael Ben-Ari/Fotolia. Photo (a) on page 12 © Tom Griffiths. Photos on pages 15, 17, 21, 23, 24, 25, 40, 41, 53, 54, 74, 75, 79, 80, 82, 83, 84, 86 (photo d), 100 (photos b, c, and bottom photo), 102, 103, 104, 105, 106, 115, 128 (photos a and b), 129, 137, 140 (photos d and e), 141, 143, 144, 145, 148, 151, 152, 153, 154, 155, 168, 177, 180, 181, 182, 188, 195, 199, 242, and 245 © Human Kinetics. Photos on page 128 (top) provided by American Safety & Health Institute. Photos on pages 85, 86 (photos a and c), 87, and 159 © Starfish Aquatics Institute. Photo on page 198 MileA/iStock/Getty Images. Photo on page 201 Wibit Sports, Germany. Photo on page 202 © evgenyb/Fotolia.com. Photo on page 206 © Justin S. Padgett. Photo on page 227 provided by Rich Irish. Photo on page 234 © iStock International Inc.; **Photo Asset Manager:** Laura Fitch; **Visual Production Assistant:** Joyce Brumfield; **Photo Production Manager:** Jason Allen; **Art Manager:** Kelly Hendren; **Illustrations:** © Human Kinetics; **Printer:** Sheridan Books

We thank the following StarGuard Training Centers for assistance in providing the locations for the photo shoots for this book: Crystal Lake Park Family Aquatic Center, Urbana, IL; Chatham County Aquatic Center, Savannah, GA; Sunsplash Family Waterpark, Cape Coral, FL; City of Scottsdale, Scottsdale, AZ; Charleston County Parks & Recreation Commission, Charleston, SC; Lee County Parks & Recreation, Ft. Myers, FL; Mundelein Park District, Mundelein, IL; Elmhurst Park District, Elmhurst, IL; and Indy Parks & Rec, Indianapolis, IN.

The video contents of this product are licensed for educational public performance for viewing by a traditional (live) audience, via closed circuit television, or via computerized local area networks within a single building or geographically unified campus. To request a license to broadcast these contents to a wider audience—for example, throughout a school district or state, or on a television station—please contact your sales representative (**www.HumanKinetics.com/SalesRepresentatives**).

Printed in the United States of America   10 9 8 7

The paper in this book is certified under a sustainable forestry program.

Human Kinetics
P.O. Box 5076
Champaign, IL 61825-5076
Website: www.HumanKinetics.com

In the United States, email info@hkusa.com or call 800-747-4457.
In Canada, email info@hkcanada.com.
In the United Kingdom/Europe, email hk@hkeurope.com.

For information about Human Kinetics' coverage in other areas of the world, please visit our website: **www.HumanKinetics.com**

E6719

CONTENTS

Part I   Prevention Strategy   1

Chapter 1   Foundation of Best Practices 3

Chapter 2   Reducing Risks at an Aquatic Facility 7

Chapter 3   Managing Bodily Fluids and Fecal Matter Contamination 21

Part II   Surveillance   33

Chapter 4   Recognizing Distress and Drowning 35

PREFACE

Water hides and suffocates people who are beneath its surface in minutes. This inherent danger of water is the reason for the StarGuard training program. This text is designed to prepare you to earn a StarGuard course completion certificate. When you become a lifeguard, you will never be able to eliminate the risk, so you cannot guarantee that a person will be safe. But you will have an important role in making people safer through your vigilance and by being ready to save lives. Others play a role as well. The goal is to reduce risk at an aquatic facility by using a team approach that also includes parents or caregivers, facility patrons, facility managers or supervisors, and your employer. This approach will help us return to having reasonable expectations for the role of a lifeguard without diluting high-performance mandates.

In this edition, we continue to focus on the StarGuard Risk Management Model, which includes five components:

1. prevention strategy,
2. surveillance,
3. response and rescue,
4. emergency care, and
5. workplace environment.

One part of this text is devoted to each component. After you understand the model, learning best practices for applying that knowledge is the next step. The StarGuard training program continues to be unique in its experiential methodology and integrated approach, combined with a team and leadership development foundation. The experiential approach is especially important to prepare you to perform high-quality CPR as a member of a coordinated team.

What's New in the Fifth Edition and Its Organization?

The fifth edition of *StarGuard: Best Practices for Lifeguards* and its web resource continue to include evidence-based practices streamlined to be practical and easy to learn and apply.

Part I: Prevention Strategies. This section contains three chapters of fundamental concepts about how to reduce the risk inherent at a recreational aquatic venue. Chapter 1 identifies misconceptions about lifeguarding and the need for best practices. Chapter 2 offers strategies to reduce the risk of aquatic emergencies by providing updated information about preventing underwater blackout, skills screening, and use of life jackets. Chapter 3 explains how to prevent exposure, for yourself and others, to potentially disease-causing bloodborne and waterborne pathogens by offering updated guidance on managing fecal and vomit incidents from the U.S. Centers for Disease Control and Prevention's Model Aquatic Health Code.

Part II: Surveillance. This section examines the concepts and techniques that underlie what you will do for almost every minute you are on active lifeguard duty. Chapter 4 has updated, simplified victim recognition information with focus on the three critical areas of importance and the latest information about the drowning process and correct use of drowning terminology. Chapter 5 gives you strategies for learning to look for distress and drowning. The chapter has been streamlined for clarity and emphasis on active engagement and targeting any person who is underwater for more than a few seconds combined with a look-for-life approach.

Part III: Response and Rescue. This section describes the planning and skills necessary to respond effectively during an emergency. Chapter 6 stresses the importance of deciding to act and gives steps for taking action when an emergency is identified. An updated chain of survival specific to aquatic rescues has been added, emphasizing early rescue breathing. Consistent with the 2015 CPR guidelines, the information about calling EMS identifies appropriate use of cell phones and the development of a response plan that considers the circumstances. Chapter 7 focuses on skills for land-based assists and water rescue for distressed or drowning persons, using a streamlined presentation and updated photos.

Part IV: Emergency Care. This section looks at the skills necessary if a drowning, injury, or illness occurs. The goal is to prepare you to provide care until emergency medical services (EMS) arrives. Chapter 8 introduces the most recent evidence-based protocols that are revolutionizing the approach that lifeguards and EMS have traditionally used to manage a person with a suspected spinal injury. Chapters 9 (Basic First Aid) and 10 (Basic Life Support) include content provided by the Health and Safety Institute (HSI) through its American Safety and Health Institute (ASHI) brand updated to 2015 International Consensus on Cardiopulmonary Resuscitation and Emergency Cardiovascular Care Science With Treatment Recommendations, 2015 American Heart Association Guidelines for Cardiopulmonary Resuscitation and Emergency Cardiovascular Care, and 2015 American Heart Association and American Red Cross International Consensus on First Aid Science With Treatment Recommendations. Chapter 11 considers the unique circumstances and hypoxic nature of drowning and details the latest evidence-based protocol for responding to an unresponsive drowning person developed by SAI's medical directors.

Part V: Workplace Environment. The section explores key concepts that affect how effective and safe you will be on the job. Chapter 12 provides strategies for minimizing the risk of workplace injury, including updated terminology related to safety data sheets. Chapter 13 identifies common professional behavior and performance expectations for both you and your employer and reinforces the need for accountability and ongoing training. Chapter 14 identifies site-specific and situation-specific considerations with expanded information about the need for a safety plan when lifeguarding at single-guard facilities, ways to direct bystanders to help, and strategies for lifeguarding swim practices. Chapter 15 explains how to adapt your knowledge and skills for the waterpark setting, including expanded waterpark information and slide dispatch best practices. Chapter 16 provides information specific to a nonsurf waterfront setting with a new reminder about the need for site-specific training when inflatables, trampolines, or floating platforms are present.

The appendix provides information about using supplemental emergency oxygen. It is presented as an optional training module for use in facilities that have emergency oxygen equipment.

Features of the Book

The fifth edition of *StarGuard: Best Practices for Lifeguards* includes several new or revised features designed to streamline your learning experience:

- **Chapter objectives.** Learning objectives for each chapter appear at the beginning of the chapter rather than at the beginning of each part, as in the previous edition.
- **Visit the web resource.** This element encourages you to visit the web resource and lists the learning exercises and resources you'll find there for each chapter. Use the instructions and key code in the letter bound into the front of the book to access the web resource.
- **Key points and on-the-job best practices.** This summary table at the end of each chapter helps reinforce important information and identifies performance expectations and competency requirements found in most international lifeguard qualification standards.

Assistance in Meeting National and International Standards

The fifth edition continues to include content that is at the forefront of national and international standards. The curriculum meets or exceeds standards for lifeguard competencies and qualifications as outlined in numerous guidance documents, including but not limited to the Model Aquatic Health Code (MAHC) sponsored by the U.S. Centers for Disease Control and Prevention (CDC), Abu Dhabi Quality and Conformity Council (QCC) Abu Dhabi Occupational Terms for Pool Lifeguard, Dubai Corporation for Ambulance Services, the minimum competencies recommended by the International Life Saving Federation (ILS), and many others.

Terminology

The terms used in this text for *drowning* are based on definition guidelines developed at the World Congress on Drowning (WCD), approved at a meeting of the International Liaison Committee on Resuscitation (ILCOR), and adopted by the World Health Organization (WHO).

The term *lifeguard* generally refers to a person primarily responsible for monitoring patrons in an aquatic environment by providing constant, dedicated surveillance; enforcing the facility's risk reduction strategies; and responding during an emergency.

The terms *swimmer, patron, bather, guest,* and *person* are used interchangeably to refer to people who are in or near the water at an aquatic venue.

The terms *rescuer* and *responder* generally refer to a person responding to, and providing care during an emergency either in or out of the water. The terms may refer to a lifeguard as well as to other personnel, bystanders who are assisting, or emergency medical services.

Compliance and Constraints

This text is intended to be used solely as a resource for lifeguards enrolled in a StarGuard training course delivered through an authorized instructor affiliated with an independent approved training center. The information is furnished for that purpose and subject to change without notice. Recommendations in this text do not replace those of local authorities having jurisdiction. When an emergency occurs, the circumstances of each incident will vary, and guidelines for aquatic safety and emergency care that apply exactly in all cases do not exist. The publisher and authors make no representations or warranties with respect to any implied future performance by persons using this text or completing StarGuard training.

Lifeguard training and certification is only the first step in becoming a competent lifeguard. The documentation you receive upon successfully completing the course verifies that you had certain skills and understanding at that time. The responsibility for future performance lies with you, your supervisor or manager, and your employer.

How to access the supplemental web resource

We are pleased to provide access to a web resource that supplements your textbook *StarGuard: Best Practices for Lifeguards, Fifth Edition*. This resource offers interactive and multimedia learning activities covering lifeguarding aspects from surveillance techniques and prevention strategies to first aid and emergency care as well as quizzes for each module.

You can access the web resource through StarGuard ELITE's Lifeguard Portal at: http://www.lifeguardportal.com

If you do not have a login for the portal, please contact customer support at info@ starguardelite.com or call (573) 207-5087.

Part I

Prevention Strategy

Foundation of Best Practices

CHAPTER OBJECTIVES

This chapter

- identifies what is important in saving lives,
- explores some misconceptions about lifeguarding,
- introduces the concept of best practices, and
- explains the need for a team approach to best practices.

Identifying What Is Important in Saving Lives

There are two kinds of lifeguards: those who get it and those who don't. Those who get it are lifeguards for life.

What is *it*? The understanding that drowning can happen quickly, silently, with deadly consequences in a matter of minutes, and that it can happen to anyone, even in a facility where nothing has happened in decades. And that being a lifeguard (who gets it) is one of the most valuable and demanding jobs you'll ever have.

Let's contrast this attitude and understanding with lifeguards who don't get it. They may not understand how quickly and silently drowning can occur, and they may work within a culture of complacency that has built up over the years. Complacency is being content and satisfied with the way things are while being unaware or uninformed of potential dangers or defects. In an aquatic setting becoming complacent is easy because drowning does not happen frequently. Lifeguards can perform poorly and never have to meet a challenge because no person has drowned at that facility. These people don't want to be bad lifeguards—they just don't know what they don't know. The goal of the StarGuard program is to counteract complacency and help you understand the importance of what you will do as a lifeguard.

Aquatic facilities can and should be fun, and working there should be, too. But you need to know what your job may entail.

Misconceptions About Lifeguarding

When you think about your lifeguarding job, what comes to mind? Do you have any of these misinformed ideas about lifeguarding?

- Easiest job ever—I'll be paid for hanging out at the pool with my friends and getting a tan.
- Nothing bad has ever happened at the pool where I'll work, so I shouldn't be expected to have to save people.
- Drowning will be easy to see, and I know rescue skills, so I am completely prepared.

Drowning is a leading killer of children worldwide, and one of the ten leading causes of death for people ages 1-24 years (World Health Organization 2014). The majority of drowning deaths occur in bodies of water without lifeguards, but having a lifeguard is not a guarantee of safety.

Lifeguard training, education, and standards have changed significantly over the years. Gone are the days when a coach, teacher, or attendant could be expected to serve as a lifeguard while performing other duties. Today, the role of a lifeguard is extremely proactive, involving constantly and exclusively watching the water and the patrons in it. In the past, the role of a lifeguard was more reactive, which meant being available to make a rescue when notified that someone was in trouble.

Lifeguarding can be one of the best and most rewarding jobs you can have. It can also be the worst experience of your life if you don't understand the risks. The goal of the StarGuard training program is to help you understand these risks and know the actions you can take—best practices—to develop a high level of competency.

Need for Best Practices in Lifeguarding

What is a best practice? This term can have many meanings, but for the purpose of this text it refers to actions you can take to develop and perform with a high level of competence. *Best* does not mean exclusively the only "right" practice. The intent in identifying best practices is to give you a framework so that you can focus on the behaviors and skills that can make the most difference in saving lives. Best practices on the job are described at the end of each chapter throughout this book.

Identifying causes, obstacles, and challenges to vigilance, and understanding the importance of ongoing training and how these contribute to provide a safe swimming environment is difficult (Branche and Stuart 2001).

Age and experience vary widely among lifeguards. Often, lifeguarding is the first job that a person has in the teen years. The excitement of entering the workforce usually creates a highly motivated person ready to accept responsibility. But in some circumstances, the workplace culture, and even the attitudes of society, changes the lifeguard who came out of training as someone who gets it into someone who becomes complacent and doesn't get it, which can be a recipe for disaster.

StarGuard training will help you identify and focus on the three critical things that can save a life when someone is drowning and within minutes of dying, and the program prepares you to do these things extremely well:

- Recognize
- Respond and rescue
- Resuscitate

Each of these actions is important, but 100 percent of your time as a lifeguard may be spent searching for high risk situations. You will be scanning to recognize distress or drowning, enforce rules, and make interventions to change patron behavior. The interventions you will do every day are valuable and important components of saving lives.

Lifeguarding can be one of the most rewarding jobs you will have.

You must realize the importance of interventions and not equate lifeguarding only with the hero stuff of response, rescue, and resuscitation.

Need for Best Practices From Management and Patrons

You will play an important part in saving lives, but you can't do everything. Your employer and supervisors will have crucial responsibilities in allowing you to do your job to the best of your ability. The guests who come to your facility should also share in the responsibility for their actions. This team approach should create a recipe for safety and reduce the risk present at every aquatic facility.

▶ VISIT THE WEB RESOURCE

The activities in the web resource will help you reinforce your learning. Follow the instructions on the key code form bound into the front of the book to access the web resource, where you will be able to navigate to the module designed specifically for each chapter, including the following interactive online learning activities based on chapter 1:

- ◆ Listen to lifeguards talk about what motivated them to become a lifeguard and reflect on your personal motivators.
- ◆ Take a survey to distinguish between your perceptions of lifeguarding and the reality of being a lifeguard, and examine your personal expectations.
- ◆ Test your knowledge and receive feedback.

CHAPTER SUMMARY

Key points	Best practices on the job
• Best practices are actions you take to perform with a high level of competence. • Proactive interventions to change patron behavior can reduce risk. • Your ability to recognize, respond, rescue, and resuscitate are important. • Everyone should share in the responsibility for safety. • What you do matters.	Avoid complacency and understand the demands of being a lifeguard.

Reducing Risks at an Aquatic Facility

CHAPTER OBJECTIVES

This chapter

- introduces the StarGuard Risk Management Model,
- describes the importance of a prevention strategy and layers of protection,
- identifies high-risk behaviors and policies to control them,
- provides methods for inspections and hazard identification,
- suggests methods for effectively enforcing rules and minimizing risk of injury, and
- identifies the need to watch for threatening behaviors and the way to do so.

Aquatic risk management includes all the components in place at an aquatic facility to reduce the chance that an emergency will happen. As a lifeguard, you are part of the risk management system, so you need to know preventive strategies and the factors that contribute to drowning, illnesses, and injuries.

StarGuard Risk Management Model

The StarGuard Risk Management Model has five components:

Figure 2.1 The StarGuard Risk Management Model.

1. **Prevention strategy.** This element includes all the components in place to reduce the risk of patrons drowning or becoming ill or injured.

2. **Surveillance.** Watching guests in the water, monitoring their behavior, and recognizing emergencies play a large role in reducing risk.

3. **Response and rescue.** You must understand what you and others need to accomplish, have a plan, and use best practices to respond to and manage the emergency.

4. **Emergency care.** If an illness, injury, or drowning occurs, you must be prepared to provide emergency care until EMS arrives.

5. **Workplace expectations.** The site-specific training, supervision, and culture at your workplace play a significant role in your future performance and ability to follow best practices.

Each component of the StarGuard Risk Management Model is separate from but dependent on the others—just like the appendages of a starfish, as illustrated in figure 2.1. If any part is weak or missing, your ability to minimize overall risk will be reduced.

Let's look more closely at a realistic concept of prevention and the way that it relates to your job as a lifeguard.

Prevention Strategy

Prevention is at the heart of your job. If you see dangerous or risky behavior, you can intervene and reduce the chance of an accident. Despite your best reasonable efforts, however, accidents can happen, and you can't watch everyone all the time. You can't prevent accidents if patrons choose to disregard your warnings or don't use common sense, such as when caregivers leave children unattended, nonswimmers choose to enter the water without a life jacket, or people dive into shallow water where "No Diving" signs are posted. In these instances, patron actions can cause an emergency.

Rather than thinking that prevention is solely the job of the lifeguard, you and the facility managers where you work should focus on your mutual responsibility for implementing prevention strategies. Having a strategy implies that several layers of protection are in place, all designed to help reduce the chance of injury, illness, or drowning. Patrons should share in this responsibility as well.

Layers of Protection

Most risk reduction efforts will be the responsibility of the owners, operators, or managers of the facility where you work. These people make the decisions about the safety features, warnings, rules, policies, and other procedures that are in place. But you will be responsible for enforcement and need to understand the elements that should be in place and some of the reasons behind what you will do on a day-to-day basis. The layers of protection that make up a prevention strategy, as illustrated in figure 2.2, are the following:

- **Design (safety) features and barriers.** The way that a facility is designed (e.g., layout and barriers) and the type of materials used (e.g., nonslip flooring) can help reduce the risk of injury and control access.
- **Warnings.** Signs can help reduce injury by warning patrons of dangerous conditions or communicating important information.
- **Rules.** Rules should spell out the behavior expected at all times of everyone at a facility, and they should be posted in a visible location. Examples of two common rules are no running and no diving in shallow water.
- **Policies and procedures.** Policies help guide decisions and outline rules for specific circumstances that may not apply to all users. Well-designed policies that are strictly enforced can be one of the most effective layers of protection. Examples of policies include defining the age at which children may enter a facility unattended, identifying the types of flotation devices allowed, restricting nonswimmers to certain areas, requiring the use of life jackets, and restricting the use of play

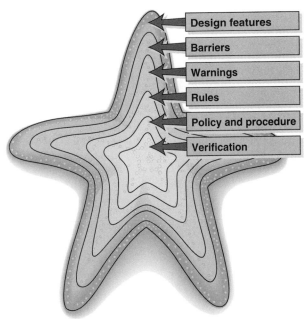

Figure 2.2 Layers of protection that make up a prevention strategy.

features to patrons of certain heights. Procedures describe actions to be taken in specific circumstances, including responding to emergencies. Procedures provide the framework for managing incidents and handling problems.

- **Verification and inspections.** The verification of zones to determine location and number of lifeguards and the vigilance strategies expected of the lifeguards are a significant layer of protection. Regular and frequent inspections can either verify that the swim area, mechanical room, locker rooms, common areas, and facility exterior are in good condition or identify problems that need to be fixed.

Most policies have been developed to try to control dangerous patron behavior. You need to understand what kinds of behaviors can contribute to accidents so that you understand how enforcing a policy can help reduce risk.

Controlling High-Risk Behaviors

Many known factors influence drowning risk (CDC 2016). This section describes the most common patron behaviors that contribute to injury, drowning, as well as injury and recreational water illness at an aquatic facility, along with suggested policies to reduce the likelihood of these behaviors. The suggestions are not all-inclusive and may not be feasible or appropriate in all situations. The facility where you work may have different policies based on site-specific needs, so be sure you are aware of what regulations you are expected to follow. More information about prevention of recreational water illness can be found in chapter 3, and suggested strategies for reducing risk at waterpark and waterfront facilities are provided in chapters 15 and 16.

The following are the most common patron behaviors that cause injury:

- Running, causing slips and falls
- Rough play
- Collision with another patron
- Diving into shallow water
- Striking the wall, diving board, or other equipment

Dangers of Headfirst Entry Into Shallow Water

In particular, diving or entering headfirst into shallow water cause severe injury and lifelong paralysis. A person may be paralyzed from the waist down (paraplegia) or neck down (quadriplegia) and be unable to walk again.

Suggested policies or strategies for reducing the risk of injury include the following:

- Restrict the use of starting blocks to those diving under the direct supervision of an instructor or coach. When not in use, mark starting blocks with warning signs or put covers on them to prevent patrons from having access.
- Restrict all headfirst entries (dives) to deep water and require entry with a hands-above-the-head body position. Restrict divers from performing any technique that takes them back toward the board or side, or diving off starting blocks, unless under the supervision of a coach or instructor trained in safe diving technique and teaching progressions.
- Train any person responsible for dispatch at the top of a waterslide in correct dispatch instructions and timing. Details about dispatch methods are described in chapter 15.

- Control access to any jumping or diving attractions to reduce the chance of collisions.

The following are the most common patron behaviors that contribute to drowning:

- Lack of close and dedicated adult supervision for children
- Extended or repeated breath-holding activities or breath-holding contests
- Bobbing or wading into deeper water and then being unable to lift the mouth or nose out of the water to breathe
- Being a nonswimmer or weak swimmer in the water without a life jacket
- Slipping off a flotation device such as a noodle or raft
- Having a seizure, heart attack, or other medical condition while in the water
- Not resting and becoming exhausted
- Being under the influence of alcohol or drugs

Dangers of Unsupervised Children and Weak Swimmers

Suggested policies or strategies for reducing the risk of drowning include the following:

- Require that all children under a certain age be accompanied and supervised by a responsible person of a certain age (required ages will vary from facility to facility). Lifeguards are not babysitters, and lifeguards can't watch all children at all times.
- Parents and guardians should not leave children unattended. An even stronger policy requires that all preschool children or nonswimmers be directly supervised, within touching distance, by a responsible adult. Posting signs that clearly state the responsibility of the parent or caregiver and the way that this standard relates to the responsibility of the lifeguard can help you enforce a supervision policy.

Active adult supervision within arm's reach helps prevent drowning.

- Require that nonswimmers stay in water that is less than waist deep. Deep water is relative to the height of a swimmer and can be considered anything above chest level for that person. A policy that requires nonswimmers to stay in waist-deep water can reduce the risk of drowning. Placing buoyed ropes across areas to define a depth change or using buoyed ropes to enclose areas of specific depths can help keep nonswimmers and children in waist-deep water.

- Prohibit nonswimmers from using attractions that enter into deep water, such as diving boards and jump platforms.

- When feasible conduct swim skill tests to screen for and then identify nonswimmers (see Conducting Skim Skill Tests section later in this chapter).

- Require that nonswimmers or weak swimmers wear a life jacket or swimming flotation suit in the appropriate size approved by the U.S. Coast Guard (USCG) or International Organization for Standardization (ISO) Personal Flotation Device (PFD) Standard. Looseness in the shoulder area or body means that the device is too large. A life jacket policy can reduce the risk of drowning because the life jacket will keep the person wearing it on the surface. A life jacket, however, may not keep a struggling person faceup. In the United States, a vest style (figure 2.3a) and flotation suit style (figure 2.3b) are the most functional for swimming (versus boating) activity and provide the best comfort and mobility.

- Consider offering lifejackets for use by guests. Create a method for distribution that provides the correct size, and use instructions (Aquatic Safety Research Group 2011).

- Restrict the use of flotation devices (such as noodles, rafts, and float toys) to certain activities or areas to help reduce the risk of drowning if a nonswimmer or weak swimmer falls off a device. Restricting the use of large float toys also helps keep your underwater view clear.

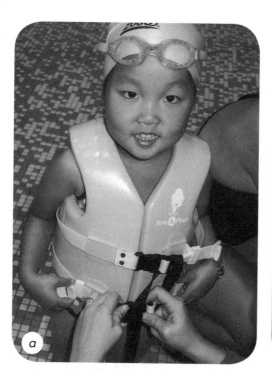 

Figure 2.3 (a) USCG-approved vest style life jacket; (b) USCG-approved swim flotation suit.

- Request physician approval in writing before allowing patrons to participate in certain activities, such as strenuous exercise classes or competitive programs. This policy may reduce the risk that a medical emergency will happen at your facility.

- Require a rest break by clearing the water on a prescribed schedule. Rest breaks can help reduce the risk that swimmers, particularly children, will become overtired.

- Have a procedure for evicting patrons suspected of being intoxicated or using drugs. This policy reduces the risk of injury and of impaired swimmers being in the water.

Conducting Swim Skill Tests

If a policy at your aquatic facility allows only swimmers with demonstrated swimming skills to use certain areas of depth or requires nonswimmers to wear life jackets, you must have a way of determining skill level. Swim skill tests will determine whether someone can meet the requirements. Conducting swim skill tests on every patron who enters an aquatic facility is impractical, but a testing method should be in place to screen users as needed. Screening for nonswimmers may be prioritized to include the following:

- First: any child under age 12 that is part of a group such as camps, field trips, or parties
- Second: all children under age 7 and anyone under 48 inches (120 cm) tall
- Third: children ages 8 to 12

A swim skill test places a person with unknown and untested skill in a high-risk situation. Therefore, you must minimize the risk and provide constant and dedicated attention to the swim test participant. You can accomplish this by doing the following:

- Be aware that a person's self-assessment of her or his swimming ability may not be accurate.

- Test in water no more than waist deep for the participant.

- Test along a wall or dock if possible and walk along the edge to watch the swimmer. Allow only feetfirst entry during the test—no diving.

- Test no more than two swimmers at a time, except when testing swimmers of known skill for endurance (completing a distance swim of a predetermined length).

- Make sure that rescue equipment is ready.

- Keep a written record of all swim skill evaluations that you conduct. Include the date, time, and swimmer's name and age. Detail which skills were evaluated, including the distance and time (e.g., swim 30 feet [9 m], tread water for 1 minute). Indicate the skill assessment outcome, such as passed or failed, or satisfactory or unsatisfactory, according to the criteria set up at your facility.

After the results of the screening have been noted, you should have an action plan for those who are nonswimmers or those who do not pass your criteria. One effective method is to float nonswimmers by requiring them to wear a life jacket. An additional step to identify those who should be wearing a life jacket is to issue a wristband of a certain color or style that can be seen by lifeguards or those responsible for supervising groups. See the chapter 2 bibliography and resources section in the back of this book for more information on life jackets.

Dangers of Extended and Repeated Breathing-Holding Activities

Prohibit breath-holding contests, underwater swimming contests, and underwater hypoxic training drills (breath holding while swimming). These policies reduce the risk that swimmers will pass out while underwater because of lack of oxygen and drown. This condition is known as sudden underwater blackout, also sometimes called shallow water blackout (although it can happen in any depth).

More recently some organizations have begun using the term "hypoxic blackout," but this term isn't completely accurate or helpful in raising awareness of the danger in the water (Griffiths 2016, Morgan et al. 2015). Regardless of the term used, repeated and extended breath-holding can be especially dangerous if a person has been hyperventilating (breathing abnormally fast and deep several times) before attempting a breath-holding activity.

The following are the most common patron behaviors that can contribute to recreational water illness:

- Swallowing recreational water (treated water in pools, spas, waterparks, or spray parks)

High Risk of Parties and Group Outings

A high number of rescues and drowning incidents occur during events such as day-camp trips, group outings, and birthday parties.

Group leaders and party hosts should understand that they are responsible for the direct supervision of the participants and should be required to maintain a reasonable leader-to-participant ratio. Group leaders or party hosts often inappropriately view a trip to the pool as a chance to relax and turn over responsibility to the lifeguards. They also may be unaware of the swimming ability of the children in attendance and may not understand the need to make sure that nonswimmers wear life jackets. The energy level of the participants is often high, and peer pressure can encourage children to try activities that would not be allowed under parental supervision. A badge or vest that identifies the adults with the group as "child watchers" can help you know who the group leaders are as well as communicate a sense of responsibility to those assigned the identification.

Conducting a group orientation and safety briefing before the participants enter the water helps reduce the risk during these events. The orientation should include the following:

- Identifying group leaders
- Defining the responsibilities of the leaders
- Identifying the deep and shallow areas of the facility
- Explaining the rules and policies
- Locating and sizing life jackets
- Explaining restrictions and supervision requirements for nonswimmers
- Identifying nonswimmers

- Swallowing freshwater that contains contaminants such as wildlife feces, fertilizer runoff, or pesticides
- Fecal accidents in the water
- Diaper changing near recreational water
- Not showering before entering the pool

Additional policies and patron education efforts that can help prevent waterborne illnesses are described in detail in chapter 3. The most effective are to require the use of swim diapers by anyone who does not have bowel control and to prohibit changing diapers on the pool deck.

Conducting Inspections and Identifying Hazards

Part of your job as a lifeguard is to watch for hazards or conditions at your facility that might threaten patrons' safety. You have this responsibility whether you are working at an indoor or outdoor facility. In addition, your employer may expect you to conduct inspections on a regular basis as part of an ongoing risk management system, so you need to know the types of hazards you might encounter. Examples of hazards at swimming pools include equipment defects; fall-causing hazards; security risks; air, water, or chemical hazards; and missing items. Hazard identification specific to waterparks may be found in chapter 15 and specific to waterfronts in chapter 16.

Equipment Defects

- Broken or nonfunctioning equipment
- Loose bolts
- Rust on support beams
- Loose railings or handrails
- Loose stairs or footholds
- Broken grates
- Cracked or broken lane-line floats
- Broken fixtures
- Sharp edges or protrusions
- Leaks
- Cracks
- Exposed wires or overloaded plugs

Inspect your facility for hazards daily.

Fall-Causing Hazards

- Loose carpet
- Debris
- Standing water
- Obstructions
- Inadequate lighting

Security Risks

- Damaged locks
- Doors that do not latch or open properly
- Suspicious people

Air, Water, or Chemical Hazards

- Poor air or water quality
- Unsanitary conditions
- Improperly stored chemicals or cleaning products

Missing Items

- Missing signs or markings
- Missing equipment or supplies

If you find a hazard that can't be immediately removed or fixed, you should limit access to the area and point out the dangerous condition to patrons. When possible, post warning signs and use barricades or rope off the area to keep people away. Report hazards to your supervisor or follow the procedure at your facility.

Electrical Safety

Besides the physical hazards in an aquatic facility, electricity can pose a risk. Electricity is present in the wiring used to power the pool pumps, lights, and other systems as well as in the outlets used for equipment. Electricity can also be present in the form of lightning, so you should understand the strategies for electrical safety and procedures for monitoring thunderstorms.

Water and electricity can create a deadly mix. Take these precautions to prevent electrical shock:

- Keep electrical devices away from the edge of the water.
- Elevate cords or cover cords on the ground with a mat or tape to prevent tripping.
- Know the location of the main power switch for your facility so that you can shut off power in the event of an injury from electrical shock. If the power cannot be turned off, use something that does not conduct electricity, such as wood, to remove the source of voltage from contact with the victim.

Severe Weather

To reduce the risk of injury from severe weather, closely monitor the weather and be prepared to direct swimmers out of the water and the surrounding area. Here are ways to monitor the weather:

- Emergency weather radios are inexpensive and provide warning signals when severe weather statements are issued.
- Live satellite and radar images and local forecasts are available on the Weather Channel and on weather information websites.
- Lightning detectors provide an early warning of approaching lightning. These devices measure the lightning strike distance, track the storm direction, and sound an alert when lightning is within a dangerous range. Lightning detectors, shown in figure 2.4, come in two forms: (1) a device permanently mounted to a pole attached to a building and (2) a portable device that can be clipped to a belt or carried.

Be familiar with weather unique to your location. Knowledge of local weather patterns, such as where storms usually form and which direction they move, can be useful in making safety decisions. To determine whether a storm is approaching your location, do the following:

- Watch the movement of the clouds; a storm may move in a direction different from the wind at ground level.

- Note abrupt changes in wind direction and speed as well as a sudden drop in temperature; both can be signs that you are in the path of a storm.

Emergency action plans (EAPs) are needed for severe weather as well as for aquatic emergencies. Learn the steps in your facility's EAP for severe weather. The EAP should detail evacuation procedures for a tornado warning and lightning-generating storms.

Instruct swimmers who are outdoors to exit the water and patrons to leave the surrounding area whenever storms are approaching. Lightning can develop a great distance ahead of a storm cloud and may appear to come out of clear blue sky. Consider yourself in striking distance whenever you can hear thunder from an approaching storm.

Keep swimmers out of the water until a passing storm is at least 10 miles (16 km) away. In most instances, the storm has moved on and threat is minimal when 30 minutes have passed since the last lightning or thunder.

If an electrical storm approaches and you are outdoors, direct patrons out of the water and to the closest safe location. A primary safe location is any enclosed building that people normally occupy. A secondary safe location could be any vehicle with a hard metal roof and rolled-up windows. If an electrical storm approaches and you are at an indoor aquatic facility, follow the EAP for severe weather at your facility. There are different professional opinions on whether or not an indoor pool should be cleared of patrons when a storm is near (Langendorfer 2010). When patrons are out of the water and located in a primary shelter, they should not use landline telephones, take a shower, or touch surfaces exposed to the outside, such as metal doors, windows, electrical wiring, cable, and plumbing. Electricity can travel indoors through these paths and could cause injury to people in these situations.

The most dangerous hazard in an aquatic facility is the behavior of the people who use the facility. Rules are made to help control dangerous behavior and actions. Because enforcing the rules will be an important part of your job, let's explore some ways to communicate the rules effectively to patrons.

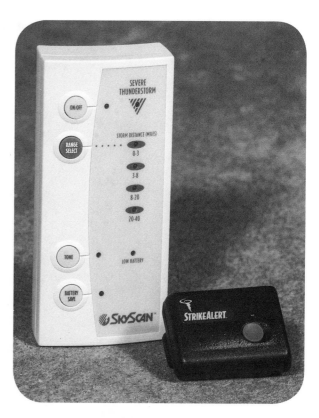

Figure 2.4 Portable lightning detectors.

Enforcing Rules and Policies

First, you need to know the rules at your facility and the reason for each rule. Make sure you understand each rule and that your fellow lifeguards understand it in the same way. Then, you need to enforce the rules effectively. You will have the most success getting patrons to follow the rules at your facility if you take a positive, professional approach. To be effective when enforcing a rule, follow these steps:

1. Signal to get a patron's attention, using the method designated at your facility. If your facility is crowded and noisy, you may need to blow a whistle or speak into a megaphone to attract attention; if it is less crowded, you may be able to speak directly and more discreetly to the patron.

Enforce rules in a positive manner.

2. Use verbal or nonverbal communication to indicate to a patron that what he or she is doing is not acceptable. If the person does not understand or does not respond, then ask the person to come talk to you.

3. After the patron comes to you, keep watching the water and explain to the patron that you are required to keep your attention on the swimmers in the water while you are talking. That way the patron won't mistake your lack of eye contact for a lack of respect or poor customer service.

4. Be courteous and positive when you talk to the patron. Use phrases such as "Please walk" instead of "Don't run" or "We allow only plastic bottles" instead of "You can't have glass in here." Briefly explain that the reason for a rule is to keep patrons safe, not to restrict their fun or enjoyment.

5. Use the "sandwich approach" when discussing a rule or policy infraction. Say something positive to the patron, state what you want the patron to do, and then say something positive again. Here's an example: "Ma'am, we're glad you are enjoying our pool today with your children. I want you to be aware that we have a policy that all small children need to be within arm's reach of an adult when they are in the water, so please stay in the water with your children. Thank you. We want everyone to be safe while having fun."

Whenever you are guarding, be consistent; enforce the same rule or policy the same way for everyone, each time. If a patron refuses to comply with a rule or policy, notify your supervisor, using the communication system in place at your facility.

Identifying Threatening Behaviors

Besides knowing how to reduce hazards and enforce rules, you also must watch for behaviors that might be harmful to others. Aquatic facilities are usually open to the public, and although the aquatic playground setting attracts people who want to enjoy themselves, it can also attract people with other intentions. For example, child predators go where children go. The threat of gang violence, terrorism, sexual predation, and other antisocial acts is present in any public location that attracts large crowds. If you notice suspicious behavior or activity, report it immediately to your supervisor. This behavior may include the following:

- Leaving unidentified packages unattended and where they should not be left
- Videotaping children without their knowledge
- Making frequent physical contact, especially in the water, with children in a crowd, or "by accident"
- Using and the toilet or changing areas frequently or for prolonged periods
- Loitering or interacting with children without any apparent relation
- Loitering in a facility and not being dressed in swimwear
- Congregating outside the fence
- Talking about violence or showing off a weapon
- Indecent exposure
- Sexual activity, gestures, intimate contact, or harassment

Most of these behaviors by themselves are not threatening. You will need to consider the circumstances as you notice behaviors. If the behavior of another person makes you uneasy, further evaluation by others is a reasonable next step.

If you encounter serious disturbances such as violence among patrons, follow the emergency action plan of your facility for these incidents. When a behavior is suspicious enough for concern, notify your supervisor, call for police assistance, and have them address the situation.

Performing Proactive Interventions

Every time you enforce a rule, discourage high-risk behavior, control admission of nonswimmers or weak swimmers into deeper water, or talk to a patron to educate her or him about risks, you have performed a proactive intervention and potentially stopped an emergency from occurring. Watching your zone and performing interventions are the critical skills you will use the vast majority of the time you are a lifeguard. Rarely (hopefully) will you use rescue skills. Recognize that every time you perform an intervention, you are saving lives.

▶ VISIT THE WEB RESOURCE

You can reinforce your learning by visiting the web resource, where you can do the following in the interactive online learning activities based on chapter 2:

◆ Build the StarGuard Risk Management Model.

◆ Conduct a swim skills test.

◆ Evaluate risk reduction scenarios.

◆ Evaluate virtual weather conditions and determine if it's safe for patrons to continue swimming.

◆ Test your knowledge and receive feedback.

CHAPTER SUMMARY

Key points	Best practices on the job
• Unattended children and nonswimmers are at high risk of drowning. • Repeated and prolonged underwater swimming or breath holding activities can result in sudden underwater blackout and drowning. • Parties, camps, and group outings to pools are high-risk events. • Every time you reduce risk or perform an intervention you are saving lives. • The five components of the StarGuard Risk Management Model are prevention strategy, surveillance, response and rescue, emergency care, and workplace expectations. • A prevention strategy has several parts, known as layers of protection.	• Enforce rules and provide interventions in a consistent, positive manner; especially prohibit repeated and prolonged breath-holding activities or contests and diving into shallow water. • Know how to inspect for and recognize hazards. • Monitor severe weather and know the evacuation procedures at your facility. • Take precautions to prevent electrical shock. • Watch for threatening or suspicious behaviors and, if observed, notify your supervisor. • Develop mutual responsibility between you, your facility, and patrons for following prevention strategies. • When feasible, implement a swim skills screening and lifejacket program. • Conduct orientation and safety briefings for groups.

Managing Bodily Fluids and Fecal Matter Contamination

Based on information from American Safety & Health Institute with Human Kinetics, 2007, *Complete emergency care* (Champaign, IL: Human Kinetics), 1-18.

CHAPTER OBJECTIVES

This chapter

- defines bloodborne pathogens,
- explains what to do in case you are exposed to bloodborne pathogens,
- defines recreational water illness (RWI),
- introduces a model for cleaning up bodily fluid spills on pool surfaces, and
- introduces a model for in-water vomit and fecal incident response.

This chapter explains how to prevent workplace exposure to potentially disease-causing pathogens and how to reduce the risk of exposure to waterborne pathogens. When lifeguarding, you may come in contact with blood, vomit, or fecal matter that can contain pathogens. When lifeguarding, you need to be aware of patron behaviors and incidents in or around the pool that can contaminate the water.

The information regarding bloodborne pathogens and infection control is licensed from the American Safety and Health Institute (ASHI 2016) and is also consistent with the recommendations of the International Lifesaving Federation (ILS 1999).

Bloodborne Diseases

Bloodborne pathogens are disease-causing microorganisms that are present in blood or other bodily fluids such as semen. Blood presents the highest risk of infection.

You may have contact with blood or bloody bodily fluids when caring for someone, or performing cleaning duties at the aquatic facility where you work. While the risk of contracting a disease is very low, it is wise to take simple measures to avoid exposure in the first place. In these circumstances, you need to use infection control guidelines to minimize the risk that you and others will become ill. Infectious bloodborne diseases include hepatitis B, hepatitis C, and human immunodeficiency virus (HIV), the virus that causes acquired immune deficiency syndrome (AIDS).

Exposure can occur through the direct contact of infectious material with an open wound or sore, or when absorbed through the membranes of the mouth, nose, and eyes. Exposure can also occur through a skin puncture with a contaminated, sharp object.

Standard Precautions

Reducing exposure lowers the chance of infection. Standard precautions (also sometimes knows as universal precautions) is a set of protective practices used whether or not an infection is suspected. To be effective, your approach is the same for everyone, regardless of relationship or age. Whether or not you think the victim's blood or other bodily fluid is infected, you act as if it is.

Hepatitis B (HBV) Vaccine

The HBV vaccine is delivered by injection and is used to prevent infection by the hepatitis B virus. The vaccine works by causing your body to produce its own protection (antibodies) against the disease. The vaccine is made without any human blood, blood products, or any other substances of human origin. It cannot give you the hepatitis B virus (HBV) or the human immunodeficiency virus (HIV).

In the United States and many other countries, occupational safety regulations require that an employer make the hepatitis B vaccination available if you are assigned to a job with occupational exposure to blood or bodily fluid and have not previously been vaccinated. In the United States you may decline the hepatitis B vaccination but decide to accept it later. If you decline the vaccine, you must sign a declination document.

Reducing Exposure to Bloodborne Pathogens

You can prevent transmission of bloodborne pathogens by isolating yourself and others from contact.

Personal Protective Equipment

Personal protective equipment (or PPE) describes protective barriers worn or used to prevent exposure to infectious diseases. The minimum personal protective equipment available for your use while lifeguarding should include disposable gloves, protective eyewear, protective footwear, and a barrier mask for use during resuscitation and CPR.

Removing Contaminated Disposable Gloves

Use disposable, single-use gloves to protect your hands. If a glove is damaged, don't use it! Wearing two pairs of gloves can provide an additional barrier and further reduce the risk of transfer of bloodborne pathogens.

When taking off contaminated gloves, do so carefully. Don't snap them, which may cause blood to splatter.

Grasp First Glove Without touching the bare skin, pinch the glove at the base of either palm, pulling it slightly away from the hand *(a)*.

Remove Inside Out Gently pull the glove away from the palm and toward the fingers, turning the glove inside out as you remove it. Gather the removed glove inside the palm of your gloved hand *(b)*.

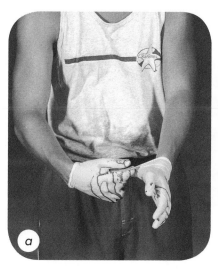
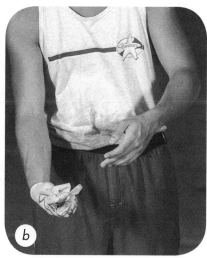

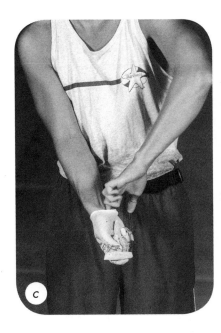

Slide Finger Under   Without touching the outside of the contaminated glove, slide the bare index finger inside the wristband of the gloved hand. Gently pull outward and downward so that the glove comes off inside out, trapping the first glove inside *(c)*.

Throw Gloves Away   Throw away both gloves in an appropriate container to prevent any further contact. Wash your hands immediately with warm running water and soap, or use an alcohol-based hand rub *(d)*.

Never wash or reuse disposable gloves. Make sure that you always have a fresh supply of gloves in your first aid kit. If you find yourself in a first aid situation and you don't have any gloves handy, improvise. Use a towel, plastic bag, or some other barrier to help you avoid direct contact.

Some people are allergic to natural rubber latex, which can be a serious medical problem. You may be at risk for developing latex allergy if you use latex gloves frequently. Allergic reactions may include skin rashes; hives; nasal, eye, or sinus symptoms; asthma; and (rarely) shock.

If you are allergic, take steps to protect yourself from latex exposure and allergy in the workplace. Taking simple measures such as using nonpowdered latex gloves and nonlatex gloves can stop the development of latex allergy symptoms and help you prevent new cases of sensitization (CDC 1997).

Putting on Gloves With Wet Hands

Putting dry gloves onto wet hands is difficult, especially when you are in a hurry. If your hands are wet and you are near water, it may help to fill your glove with water and then slip your wet hand into the wet glove.

Get Gloves   When possible, carry gloves with you *(a)*.

Fill Glove With Water   Open the wristband and scoop in water *(b)*.

Insert Hand Line up your fingers with the water-filled glove *(c)*.

Lift Hand Repeat with the other glove and hand *(d)*.

Protective Eyewear and Footwear

Bloodborne viruses can be transmitted through the mucous membranes of the eyes from blood splashes or from touching the eyes with contaminated fingers or other objects. In the presence of large amounts of spurting blood or spewing vomit, wear some type of covering for your eyes to reduce the risk that bodily fluids will splash into your eyes and enter your body.

Goggles or glasses with solid side shields or a chin-length face shield provide the most reliable practical eye protection from blood splashes and sprays. Regular prescription eyeglasses and contact lenses are not considered eye protection. Contact lenses, by themselves, offer no protection against infection.

Whenever you are cleaning up bodily fluids, you also need to wear some type of footwear to prevent contact with your bare feet. At a minimum, wear sandals. When large amounts of bodily fluids are present, consider footwear with more coverage and protection.

CPR Barrier Devices

Barrier devices (pocket masks, face shields, or bag-valve mask devices) must be made readily available to employees who are designated or can reasonably be expected to perform resuscitation (CPR) procedures.

Your employer must provide you with proper training in the specific type, use, and location of the devices present where you work, according to the manufacturer's instructions or acceptable medical practice.

Barrier devices are available in several styles (see figure 3.1):

- A shield-style device provides a minimal barrier and is compact enough to be carried on a keychain or in a pocket. This type of barrier is designed for use by laypeople and is not the best choice for use in the aquatic workplace.

- CPR pocket masks designed for professional rescuers have a large mouthpiece and a one-way valve. They create a seal over the mouth and nose of a person who is not breathing. You place your mouth on the mouthpiece to deliver rescue breaths.

Figure 3.1   Different examples of CPR barrier devices.

- Bag-valve mask devices (also known as BVMs) provide the most protection because you never make mouth-to-mask contact and instead squeeze the bag to provide ventilations to a person who is not breathing.

When you are protected by personal protective equipment (PPE), your risk of transmission is greatly reduced. But incidents may occur when you are unexpectedly not protected by PPE. If a *significant amount* of blood or bodily fluids comes in contact with your unprotected skin or eyes or you have been stuck with a needle, you may be considered exposed and should follow specific steps after the incident.

Exposure Incidents and Follow-Up

You may be exposed to blood or bodily fluids when you provide first aid and do not use PPE or when you are cleaning up around your facility if syringes are discarded in the trash or on the grounds. If you or others have a sharps injury such as an accidental needle stick or are exposed to blood or bodily fluids at work, immediately follow these steps:

1. Wash cuts and needle sticks with soap and water.
2. Flush splashes to the nose, mouth, or skin with water.
3. Irrigate eyes with clean water, saline, or sterile irrigants.
4. Report the incident to your supervisor.
5. Immediately seek medical treatment.

After a report of an exposure incident (and after initial first aid), an employer in the United States must make a confidential medical evaluation and follow-up immediately available to you. If you work outside the United States, follow your employer's guidance.

Disease Transmission and Swimming Pools

The information in this section is provided by the U.S. Centers for Disease Control and Prevention (CDC), a leading authority on recreational water illnesses (RWI), and is consistent with the CDC's Model Aquatic Health Code. RWIs are illnesses caused by germs and chemicals found in the water we swim in. Contrary to popular belief, chlorine does not kill all germs instantly. Some germs today are extremely tolerant to chlorine, and they were not known to cause human disease until recently. When these germs get in the pool, it can take anywhere from minutes to days for chlorine to kill them. Swallowing just a little water that contains these germs can make people sick.

If vomit or fecal matter gets into the water, germs may possibly remain long enough before being killed by the sanitizing agent such as chlorine for a patron to become ill by swallowing contaminated water. With outbreaks on the rise, you need to understand how the risk for transmitting these diseases can be reduced.

Recreational water illnesses are caused by germs spread by swallowing, having contact with, or breathing in mists or aerosols of contaminated water in swimming pools, hot tubs, waterparks, water-play areas, interactive fountains, lakes, rivers, or oceans. RWIs can also be caused by chemicals in the water or chemicals that evaporate from the water and cause indoor air quality problems.

RWIs encompass a wide variety of infections, including gastrointestinal, skin, ear, respiratory, eye, neurologic, and wound infections. Patrons who are most at risk for getting sick from an RWI include children, pregnant women, and those who have an immune system deficiency caused by HIV, chemotherapy, or other conditions.

Germs that cause RWIs generally enter the water when a swimmer has a fecal incident while in the water. When swimmers are ill with diarrhea, their stool can contain millions of germs and contaminate the water. In addition, on average people have about .14 gram of feces on their bottoms that, when rinsed off, can contaminate recreational water. Germs are less likely to be present in a small amount of vomit, which is a common occurrence when a child swallows too much water, especially right after eating. Viruses are more likely to be present in vomit when it contains more than just regurgitated pool water, which may indicate that a person is sick. Germs that may be present in blood don't survive in chlorinated water and do not pose a threat.

The most common cause of RWI is diarrhea, which can contain germs such as the following:

- *Crypto* (KRIP-toe, which is short for *Cryptosporidium*)
- *Giardia* (gee-ARE-dee-uh)
- *Shigella (shih-GEHL-uh)*
- Norovirus
- *E. coli* (ee-CO-lye, which is short for *Escherichia coli*)

Keeping chlorine in swimming pools and hot tubs at recommended levels is essential to maintain a healthy pool. Chlorine in recreational pool water kills germs that can contaminate water, but the chlorine does not work immediately on some types of pathogens. For example, in swimming pool water treated with chlorine at levels that meet most health regulations, *E. coli* can live for less than a minute, and some viruses will live for about 16 minutes. Parasites can be harder to kill. *Giardia* survives about 45 minutes, and *Cryptosporidium* can survive for almost 11 days.

Reducing Exposure to Waterborne Pathogens

When people swim, they always ingest a small amount of water. Therefore, germs should be kept out of the water in the first place, and chemicals in the pool water should be adequate to kill germs that are present. The aquatic facility where you work should have several strategies for reducing exposure to waterborne pathogens, including patron education, water testing, and fecal and vomit response procedures for both land-based and in-water incidents.

Patron Education

Educating patrons about how to avoid contaminating the water is the first step in reducing the risk of RWIs. Your employer should post signs and distribute information for patrons about how to reduce the spread of recreational water illnesses. The CDC has established a list of healthy swimming behaviors for protection against RWIs that should be included as the foundation to educate patrons. Make sure you can explain, in a way that is inoffensive and acceptable to parents, why behaviors such as using public chairs and tables for diaper changing is a health risk.

Steps of Healthy Swimming for All Swimmers

- Stay out of the water if you have diarrhea.
- Don't swallow the water.
- Shower before you get in the water and wash your hands after using the toilet or changing diapers.
- Don't pee or poop in the water.

Steps for Parents of Young Kids

- Take your kids on hourly bathroom breaks and check diapers often. Waiting to hear "I have to go" may mean it's too late.
- Change diapers in a bathroom or diaper-changing area, not at poolside. Germs can spread in and around the pool.
- Wash your child thoroughly (especially the rear end) with soap and water before swimming. Invisible amounts of fecal matter can end up in the pool.

Water Quality

Treated water should be tested several times per day using a test kit designed for measuring the chlorine level as well as the pH. The authority having jurisdiction at your location will determine how often during a day these tests must be conducted. A free chlorine level of 1 to 3 mg/L or parts per million (ppm) and pH of 7.2 to 7.8 maximize germ-killing power.

If you are responsible for adjusting chemical levels, adding chemicals to the water, or backwashing to clean the pool filters, you must obtain additional training and certification in pool operation and safety procedures for handling chemicals. You will need to know how your employer wants you to respond if the chemical levels are not adequate.

Incident Management

Fecal or vomit incidents are a concern and an inconvenience for both pool staff and patrons. A written contamination response plan will help you respond more efficiently to any problems. You may not have control over the occurrence of an event, but you do have control over how you respond to it and document it.

Contamination Response on Pool Surfaces

Your workplace should have a specific plan for how to clean up and dispose of bodily fluids or fecal matter that is found on the pool deck or other surfaces. A cleanup procedure should consist of at least these key components:

1. Block off the area of the spill from patrons until clean up and disinfection are complete. Use universal precautions and wear your personal protective equipment.
2. Put on disposable gloves and wear shoes to prevent contamination of hands and feet.
3. Remove the substance. Among the many effective methods for removing a liquid substance are soaking it up with an absorbing material and scooping up the material into a container. Then use paper towels to wipe up any remaining substance. Commercially packaged biohazard cleanup kits usually

include single-use packets of absorbing material; such material is also available in large containers. As an alternative, you can use other high-absorbing materials (such as cat litter) effective for the type of contaminant, the type of surface to be cleaned, or the area within the facility. Remove a solid bodily substance by scooping it up or picking it up inside a plastic bag.

4. Gently pour or spray a bleach solution of one part household bleach to nine parts of water on the area.

5. Leave the bleach solution on the area for at least 20 minutes or as otherwise directed on the label or by your regulatory agency.

6. Wipe up any remaining bleach solution with paper towels and allow the area to air dry.

7. Saturate any nondisposable cleaning tools such as mops and brushes with the bleach solution and air dry.

8. Remove gloves and place in plastic garbage bags with all soiled cleaning materials.

9. Double-bag and securely tie up plastic garbage bags and discard.

10. Thoroughly wash your hands with soap and water.

11. Report the incident on the body fluid contamination response log for your facility.

Contamination Response in Chlorinated Recreational Water

The way you respond to a potential contamination incident in the water depends on the type of bodily fluid or fecal matter.

A formed stool can act as a container for germs. If the fecal matter is solid, removing the feces from the pool without breaking it apart will limit the degree of pool contamination. Formed stool, however, also protects germs inside from being exposed to the chlorine in the pool, so prompt removal is necessary.

Diarrhea is a higher-risk event than a formed-stool incident. With most diarrheal illnesses, the number of infectious germs found in each bowel movement decreases as the diarrhea stops and the person's bowel movements return to normal.

Vomit may contain norovirus, which can be killed in the same manner as a formed stool.

Blood contamination of properly maintained water in an aquatic venue does not pose a public health risk to swimmers, because the types of viruses or bacteria in blood are easily killed by chlorine and lack the routes needed to spread the pathogens to other people.

Your facility should have a detailed contamination response plan that follows the guidelines established by the authority having jurisdiction in your location. If your job function includes water testing, handling of pool chemicals, and water dosing, follow the guidelines and safety procedures in place at your facility. Otherwise, follow the plan established by your employer to notify those who can make water adjustments.

For the most recent disinfection guidelines suggested by the CDC, go to www.cdc.gov/healthywater/swimming/residential/index.html. A sample remediation plan is found in table 3.1.

The information about fecal, vomit, and blood contamination and disinfection guidance is based on the recommendations of the CDC's Model Aquatic Health Code, but it does not replace the regulations that may be in place in your location. The recommendations are revised when new research or information becomes available.

TABLE 3.1   Contamination Response Plan

Formed stool, vomit, or diarrhea		Blood
1. Close the pool to swimmers, including all areas that share the same recirculation system. 2. Remove the material from the pool using a net, scoop, or bucket and dispose of it in a sanitary manner. Do not use aquatic vacuum cleaners. 3. Test the water. pH should be 7.5 or lower and water temperature 77 degrees Fahrenheit (25 degrees Celsius) or higher. Adjust if necessary and confirm that the filtration and circulation systems are operating.		Blood contamination of a properly maintained aquatic venue's water does not pose a public health risk in swimmers.
Formed stool or vomit	**Diarrhea**	
1. If necessary, raise the free chlorine residual to 2.0 ppm (mg/L). 2. Reopen the pool after the free chlorine residual has reached and been maintained at 2.0 ppm (mg/L) for 25 minutes.	1. Raise the free chlorine residual to 20 ppm (mg/L) and maintain this level for at least 12.75 hours. 2. Reopen the pool after the free chlorine level has dropped to below the maximum allowed by your local health authority.	

Report the incident on the body fluid contamination response log at your facility.

Freshwater Contamination

Freshwater swimming areas in lakes, streams, ponds, and rivers can also contain pathogens and germs that cause RWIs. Contamination from human bodily fluids or feces is possible, but the bacteria and other pathogens found in freshwater usually come from wildlife feces or wastewater runoff. Freshwater is not chemically treated with chlorine, so no mechanism is in place to kill pathogens. A common testing schedule for freshwater is weekly or more frequently if required by the local health authority or if bacteria levels are above a certain point. The usual procedure is to obtain a water sample in a sterilized container and take it to a laboratory for testing. If the test results are not within the acceptable range, the swimming areas are closed until nature takes its course and the bacteria levels drop.

▶ VISIT THE WEB RESOURCE

You can reinforce your learning by visiting the web resource, where you can do the following in the interactive online learning activities based on chapter 3:

◆ Demonstrate proper procedure for handling situations involving recreational water illness in an RWI simulation.

◆ Provide protective equipment to a virtual lifeguard.

◆ Decide how to minimize your risk of exposure to bloodborne illnesses in virtual scenarios.

◆ Test your knowledge and receive feedback.

CHAPTER SUMMARY

Key points	Best practices on the job
• Standard precaution is to treat any bodily fluid as if it is infected.	• Keep a body fluid contamination response log.
• Personal protective equipment (PPE) are devices worn or used to provide a barrier against exposure.	• Follow standard precautions and use PPE.
• Bloodborne pathogens are disease-causing microorganisms present in blood or other bodily fluids, such as semen.	• Know how to put on disposable gloves with wet hands and how to safely remove contaminated gloves.
• Recreational water illness (RWI) are illnesses caused by germs and chemicals found in the water we swim in.	• Report exposure incidents.
• A diarrheal incident is more likely than a formed stool to contain germs that can cause RWI.	• If you are responsible for water testing, make sure you understand how your employer wants you to respond if the disinfectant levels are not adequate.
• The best source for up to date recommendations for cleanup of fecal matter or vomit in or around a pool can be found at www.cdc.gov/healthywater/swimming/residential/index.html.	• Follow the contamination response plan for fecal and vomit water contamination cleanup in accordance with requirements set by the facility where you work or the authority having jurisdiction.
	• Provide education to patrons about healthy swimming behaviors and how to reduce RWIs.
	• Know how to explain, in a way that is inoffensive and acceptable to parents, why using public chairs and tables for diaper changing is a health risk.

Part II

Surveillance

Recognizing Distress and Drowning

CHAPTER OBJECTIVES

This chapter

- differentiates between distress and drowning,
- explains the drowning process,
- describes what a person in distress or drowning may look like,
- explains why time is critical when a person is drowning, and
- identifies why drowning victims are hard to recognize when under the water.

One of the most important skills you must develop as a lifeguard is the ability to recognize when a swimmer needs help so that you can intervene quickly. A drowning person does not look like the stereotype portrayed in movies or drawings—someone frantically waving arms or shouting for help. A distressed or drowning person exhibits behaviors that are much more subtle and difficult to detect. You should also understand that all people in the water are at risk of distress or drowning—from nonswimmers to world-class athletes and everyone in between.

Distress

A person in distress is still on the surface of the water but is struggling to stay afloat. The person's mouth or nose or both are above the surface, and he or she is still able to breathe (see figure 4.1). Some behaviors that indicate a person is in distress include the following:

- Head back and body low in the water
- Arms extended from the sides and moving up and down
- Minimal use of the legs, with little support from a kick
- Bobbing up and down

Sometimes, a person in distress will try to remain upright and turn to face the nearest source of assistance, for example, toward a lifeguard stand, the pool wall, or shore. If this is the case and the person is relatively close, you may be able to recognize a fearful, wide-eyed look on her or his face. But you cannot rely only on facial expression to indicate distress because a person may be facing away from you or blocked from your view by other people.

If distress continues, the person's mouth and nose will sink below the surface of the water, and he or she will begin to drown. How quickly a person progresses from distress to drowning varies depending on many circumstances. A person who cannot keep her or his mouth and nose out of the water and breathe will die unless someone intervenes. The earlier the person receives help, the better the chance is of keeping a distress situation from becoming a fatal drowning.

Figure 4.1   Person in distress with mouth and nose above the surface.

Note that not everyone experiences distress first, before drowning. Many drowning victims are not upright or on the surface of the water to start with and therefore never exhibit any of the observable instinctive responses to try to stay on the surface. Examples include people who submerge underwater and never surface, especially children. Chapter 5 provides more detail about the circumstances that often surround drowning without observable distress.

Drowning Process

A person's first response to the drowning process is to hold his or her breath, followed shortly by a laryngospasm. A laryngospasm is a physical reaction to water droplets at the back of the throat that causes the top of the larynx (the windpipe that carries air from the mouth to the lungs) to close. At this time the victim tries to breathe but cannot and instead may swallow large amounts of water.

As the person's blood oxygen level falls, the laryngospasm relaxes and the victim may breathe a small amount of water into the lungs. The amount inhaled is different for each person. Studies have shown the average amount of water inhaled during drowning to be relatively small, typically less than 30 ml (Sempsrott and Schmidt 2012). A person does not drown because of water in the lungs, but because of lack of oxygen.

If the person does not return to the surface and start breathing, either on her or his own or after being resuscitated, the heart will stop, brain damage caused by lack of oxygen will occur, organs will stop functioning, and the person will die. The heart and brain are the organs at greatest risk for permanent damage during drowning, even if someone interrupts the drowning process and resuscitates the person.

The length of time that passes before interruption of the drowning process is crucial to the victim's survival.

Definition of Drowning

Lack of agreement on a definition of *drowning* has made analysis of drowning studies difficult. The official universal and correct definition of drowning is "the process of experiencing respiratory impairment from submersion or immersion in liquid." A person who has experienced a drowning will have one of three outcomes:

1. Survive the drowning with complete recovery.

2. Survive the drowning with permanent brain damage. The brain damage can range from mild to severe. Many drowning survivors must be placed on a ventilator and fed through a tube. These drowning survivors live in what is called a vegetative state, and they cannot function without the aid of machines to keep them alive.

3. Die. A person who dies because of a drowning incident is considered a drowning fatality. The death may occur at the scene or may occur later at the hospital because of lack of oxygen to the organs or infections such as pneumonia.

Any person who has experienced drowning should be evaluated and monitored by a health care professional. This advice applies to even those individuals who were submerged for a short period and appear to have complete recovery on scene, as symptoms may worsen within a few hours of submersion.

The term *near drowning*, although once popular, should not be used. Because drowning is a process, a person can't partially have the experience. Just as a person can't have a near heart attack—the heart attack occurs and the person either recovers completely, lives but has complications, or dies—a person can't have a near drowning. In addition, use of the terms *secondary drowning*, *dry drowning*, or *delayed drowning* are inaccurate and confusing and should not be used (Van Beek et al. 2005).

Water Depth and Drowning

A person is drowning if the face and airway are covered with water and the head cannot be lifted or brought to the surface to breathe. Drowning can occur through either just the face being covered with water or the entire body being underwater. Recognize that drowning can occur in a small amount of water, such as if a child is trapped in a bucket or toilet or is unable to get up after falling facedown in a puddle or in the shallow water of a beachfront or stairs entry area. Remember that shallow water is relative to a person's height. What may be considered shallow to an adult would be deep to a toddler.

Time Factors

You can interrupt drowning at any time by making a rescue and opening the person's airway so breathing can resume. The person may breathe spontaneously, or you may need to give rescue breaths as soon as possible. The earlier you interrupt the process, the better the victim's chances are for survival without brain or organ damage.

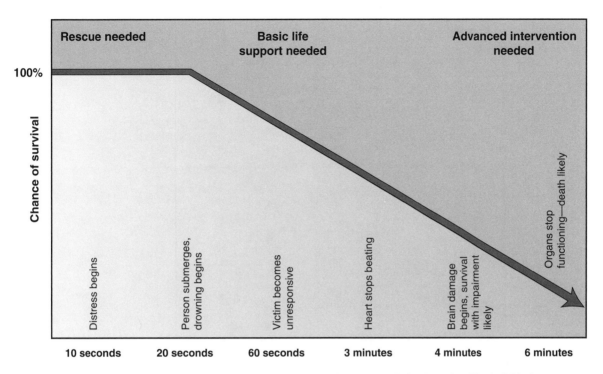

Figure 4.2 Time is critical in chances for survival.

The length of time a victim is submerged is the most important predictor of survival. Unless the water is very cold (less than 50 degrees Fahrenheit, or 10 degrees Celsius), brain damage and death generally occur within several minutes after the person submerges under the water and starts drowning, although this varies from person to person. Figure 4.2 shows how the length of submersion relates to survival outcomes.

To intervene quickly in an emergency, you must rely on your observation skills and understand what a person in distress or who is drowning might look like.

Drowning Recognition

A person in distress or drowning may have certain movements or behaviors that you can observe, but you need to realize that drowning will not look like the frantic splashing and waving often portrayed in movies (see figures 4.3 and 4.4).

A person in **distress** can still breathe and may look like she or he is

- struggling to stay on the surface, mouth at water level;
- making back-and-forth or up-and-down movements just under the water;
- trying to swim but not moving forward;
- scared, with a wide-eyed panic-stricken look or with the eyes squeezed shut;
- bobbing, alternately at or below the surface;
- gasping for air with head back;
- struggling to get to the side of the pool; or
- struggling to grab something to stay afloat.

Figure 4.3 A drowning person may still show movement in the water.

Figure 4.4 A drowning person may float on the surface with his or her head facedown in the water or may be faceup.

A person who is **drowning** cannot breathe and may look like he or she is

- bobbing;
- floating on or near the surface of the water, either horizontal or vertical;
- floating underwater on or near the bottom; or
- laying on the bottom.

An unresponsive person who is submerged and drowning is often described as looking like a shadow, a blur, a towel on the bottom, or the drain. The movement caused by others in the water may make an unresponsive person's body move as well. This movement is often mistaken for "playing" underwater.

Not all drowning symptoms can be seen. The properties of the water can interfere with the ability to see a victim who has submerged under the surface (see figure 4.5). Bobbing or floating face down at or under the water surface may mean the person is drowning. An unresponsive person may even be faceup.

Figure 4.5 Close-up view of a submerged drowning victim who is difficult to see through the surface of the water.

How the Water Hides a Drowning Person

You might think that in a pool with clear water you would easily be able to see something on the bottom. Although this might be the case when no one is in the pool and the water is still, the circumstances change when the water begins to move. Realize that water hides and suffocates its victim.

As soon as people enter the water, the water begins to move. Movement of the water causes the surface to become filled with ripples and undulations. Even a breeze can cause the water surface to become impossible to see through. Add glare caused by the sun angle or reflection off windows, and your vision underwater can be completely obscured. Figure 4.6 shows a sequence of how a simulated drowning victim can completely disappear from view as the surface water moves.

Figure 4.6   (a) Visible simulated drowning victim; (b) water movement begins to hide the victim; (c) victim is almost invisible.

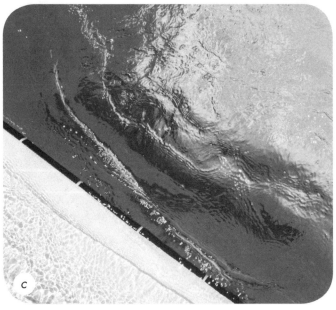

Because distress and drowning symptoms may be subtle and silent and the water can hide a victim, you need to know how to look to give you the best chance of seeing a victim early in the drowning process. This topic is discussed in chapter 5.

▶ VISIT THE WEB RESOURCE

You can reinforce your learning by visiting the web resource, where you can do the following in the interactive online learning activities based on chapter 4:

◆ View video of actual rescues to learn to quickly identify a person in distress.

◆ View video to become familiar with the way the water hides people.

◆ Test your knowledge and receive feedback.

CHAPTER SUMMARY

Key points	Best practices on the job
• Recognizing a distressed or drowning person early gives the best chance for survival. • A person in distress is at or near the surface and can still get the mouth or nose out of the water to get an occasional breath. • A drowning person is under the surface of the water and cannot breathe. • Drowning will have three outcomes: survival without brain damage, survival with mild to severe brain damage, or death. • Bobbing or floating at or under the water surface may mean the person is drowning. • Movement of the water can make it very difficult to see a person under the surface.	• Know how to recognize a person in distress. • Know how to recognize a person who is drowning. • Understand that drowning can happen quickly and silently. • Use correct drowning terminology. • Participate in ongoing victim recognition training and assessment of your ability to recognize a drowning victim quickly.

Looking for Distress and Drowning

CHAPTER OBJECTIVES

This chapter

- identifies critical lifeguard observation skills,
- explains the RID factor,
- describes lifeguard zones of patron surveillance,
- provides strategies for scanning,
- provides strategies for remaining vigilant,
- describes a rotation system including methods for maintaining surveillance during rotations, and
- explores the potential of drowning detection technology.

It is widely accepted that one effective drowning prevention intervention is to provide trained, professional lifeguards to conduct patron surveillance and supervision at aquatic facilities and beach areas (Branche and Stuart 2001). Constant visual contact with the water, as a dedicated and only task, should be your primary responsibility while on station. The two key words in this statement are *constant* and *dedicated*. *Constant* means that you are not distracted while you are watching the water. *Dedicated* means that you don't have any other duties while watching the water.

Observation Skills

To recognize distress or drowning, you must continuously perform three crucial observation skills: scan, target, and assess. To *scan* means to search the water to identify anything unusual. *Target* means to look more closely. *Assess* means to evaluate the situation, determine if the person needs help, and decide your course of action.

While it is important to know the specific behaviors of distress and drowning, it is also important (and may be more effective) to search for critical events that can lead to drowning (Lanagan-Leitzel 2012). The following scenarios illustrate how you might use your observation skills:

- While you scan a crowded pool, you notice a man holding a young child. He is standing in shoulder-deep water, and they are located near a gradual slope into deeper water. Neither exhibits distress behaviors. But you notice several things about the situation that could indicate a potential problem, so you briefly target your attention on the father and child.

- You target the father and child for closer examination for the following reasons: The father's bobbing movements are gradually pushing him toward deeper water. The child does not appear comfortable in the water. The crowded conditions may prevent the father from quickly changing position and moving toward shallow water.

- You assess the situation and realize that with one more step the father could quickly become submerged just enough to be unable to breathe or to recover to a standing position. You decide to take action and intervene to get the attention of the father, directing him to move back toward shallower water.

Let's consider another example. While you scan you notice a child is playing in the shallow area of the pool, which for him is water that is chest deep. He and a friend decide to move out a bit from the edge, pushing off the bottom and bobbing or maybe "wall walking" (holding on to the side) a short distance into slightly deeper water. The water is just deep enough that when the child pushes up off the bottom to get to the surface for a breath, his mouth does not clear the water. The child gulps a mouthful of water instead of air. In this situation, the child is not able to cry out for help because he is already underwater. The child's movements may make him appear to be swimming underwater, and you may not notice anything extraordinary during your scan.

If you can see under the water where the child is located, you notice the child has not returned to the surface for air. In this case you were able to recognize the critical event of the child getting too deep, which is what causes you to target the situation for further examination, assess it as an emergency, and begin a rescue.

Scanning is your primary job function.

In many instances a nearby patron with a clear view may notice the victim first. Whenever someone in the water requests your attention and has concerns about another person in the water, respond immediately and check it out.

RID Factor

Each year, people drown in swimming pools with lifeguards on duty. The first question people usually ask is, "How could this happen?" In many cases, the drowning was a result of a medical or environmental condition. The factors of recognition, intrusion, and distraction—known as the RID factor (Pia 1984)—have been identified as major contributors to drowning in guarded venues.

The following are the three factors:

- **Recognition**. The lifeguard did not recognize that the person was in distress or drowning. A lack of recognition could occur because the lifeguard didn't know what to look for or the lifeguard was not scanning. In some instances the lifeguard could not recognize drowning because the person silently slipped beneath the water without struggle, and it was not possible to see under the surface of the water.

- **Intrusion**. The lifeguard was not attentive and did not watch patrons closely because other nonsurveillance tasks, such as water testing, maintenance, or cleaning, intruded on his or her ability to scan.

- **Distraction**. The lifeguard was distracted because she or he was bored, engaged in conversation with peers or patrons, or involved in some other activity that affected vigilance.

The RID factor explains why it is important to know what distress or drowning may look like, to scan constantly as your only dedicated responsibility when you are on station, and to use vigilance strategies to remain alert and keep from being distracted. You may not be physically able to see every instance of distress or drowning, but understanding the RID factor will help you perform to the best of your ability and meet your lifeguard responsibilities.

Lifeguard Zones of Patron Surveillance

A *zone* is the area of the water you are assigned to provide patron surveillance by scanning. A zone is three-dimensional and includes the water surface, the bottom, and everything in between. No matter where patrons are located or how many patrons are in your zone, the physical area that you scan does not change. A zone may also include monitoring of adjacent decks or monitoring activities on a structure such as a waterslide, play element, or other aquatic feature.

You should be able to describe the exact boundaries of your zone of patron surveillance and focus on that area. With proper coverage, all water areas in a facility are assigned to one or more lifeguards. If you work at a facility with several lifeguards, the water area is divided into multiple zones with overlapping coverage. If you are the only lifeguard at your facility, your zone is the entire pool. The size of the zone you are responsible for may change with the conditions at your facility. You also must be aware of transition zones and know how to handle zone coverage during a rotation and during an aquatic emergency.

Zone Size and Zone Charts

A zone should be of a size so that it is physically possible to scan and respond to rescue within about 30 seconds. You should be able to

- scan the three-dimensional (3D) area within 10 seconds and
- get to the farthest part of the zone within 20 seconds.

Zone size and assignments at your facility may change based on the number of patrons, the nature of pool activities, the time of day, or other conditions. For example, as more patrons enter your zone, you may need more time to scan or swim across it because of the crowded conditions. If you can't scan the zone in 10 seconds or if you don't think you could get to the farthest area of the zone within 20 seconds, the zone should be made smaller by adding another lifeguard and reassigning the zones.

Zone charts that clearly mark the location of each site-specific protection zone should be posted in the lifeguard office or on the stands. A common method to indicate specific zones is to assign each zone configuration a color code and post zone charts for each. For example, zone assignments when two lifeguards are on duty may be code yellow. Later in the day, when the facility is more crowded and additional lifeguards are on duty, the zone assignments switch to code red.

Zone Coverage During Rescues

When a lifeguard enters the water to make a rescue, surveillance must continue. Another lifeguard must immediately take over that person's zone, in addition to his or her own. The lifeguard to the rescuer's left usually takes over the zone, but you should follow the plan in place at your workplace.

If you have taken over a zone during a rescue, watch for a signal for assistance from the lifeguard making the rescue. If she or he needs help and other lifeguards cannot take over surveillance, clear the zone of swimmers according to the plan in place at your facility.

Now that you understand the concept of zones of patron surveillance, let's look at the placement of lifeguards and at scanning methods for effectively monitoring your zone.

Zone Verification to Determine Location of Lifeguards

For the purposes of maintaining effective surveillance, the zones are generally set up based on the location of the lifeguards and their ability to see the entire zone.

The ideal location for scanning is a place where you can see your entire zone. This position may be from an elevated lifeguard stand, but another location may be better if the stand has blind spots or a glare problem from the sun during certain times of day. In some conditions, the only way you are able to cover your zone is by roaming the deck and scanning the water while you walk.

Depending on the features at your facility, some lifeguard locations may be in the water, such as at the bottom of a waterslide or on floating docks. Chapters 15 and 16 describe strategies for determining locations and surveillance strategies at site-specific attractions.

Before establishing or changing a zone plan for a facility, zones should be tested at various times of day and in different patron-level conditions to verify the ability to see the entire zone (no blind spots) from the lifeguard location. One method of zone verification is to station a lifeguard in the stand and have a person submerge to the bottom in various places of the zone. Start under the lifeguard stand and continue in a grid-like pattern, being sure to verify all corners and potential blind spots. Another method is to use a submersible mannequin to conduct the zone verification.

Besides verifying the absence of blind spots, verify that the submerged person or mannequin can be viewed within 10 seconds as the eyes scan from the farthest area of the zone back to the area of submersion. Then place the submerged person or mannequin in the farthest area of the zone and verify that the rescuer can reach the area from the lifeguard stand within about 20 seconds.

Scanning Strategies

Effective scanning is a combination of eye movement, head movement, body position, alertness, and engagement.

- **When to scan.** Sweeps of your entire zone with your eyes every 10 seconds will be effective in most circumstances. The timing of your scans may vary based on the zone, the number of people you look at as you sweep your eyes, and other factors such as the need to stop scanning for brief periods to enforce rules or other interventions. In general, effective scanning should be timed to allow you to be engaged in searching for signs of life and symptoms of distress or drowning when you can't see that a person is alive and breathing above the surface of the water. If you scan too fast, you will not be able to assess what you see.

- **Where to scan.** Scanning should be 3-dimensional. Look at every area of water in your zone—bottom, middle, surface, in corners, below your feet. Your job is to scan the water in the zone, not just watch the people. *Triage* your scanning by first looking for anything out of the ordinary on the bottom and under the surface (vitally urgent). Then scan the surface looking for distress or drowning indications (urgent) and for behavior that may require rule enforcement (important).

- **How to scan.** Move your eyes and your head when you scan. As you sweep your eyes, pause occasionally to focus on a segment of the zone and target (focus on) anything out of the ordinary.

- **What to look for.** While you are scanning, look for life! Active swimmers with faces above the water are OK. Target anyone whose face is under the water, either at the surface, just below, or along the bottom. Verify that the person comes to the surface within a few seconds, including anyone who is bobbing up and down, appears to be swimming or playing underwater, or appears to be floating facedown.

Scanning is simply searching the water in a systematic way.

Strategies for Maintaining Vigilance

Vigilance means to be watchful, attentive, alert, and aware. When you are vigilant you have a sense of urgency and understand why it is important to focus on your task. You are expected to be vigilant when you are on station, but maintaining vigilance can be difficult, especially in conditions of heat and during times of low activity in your zone. Consider these strategies to help you remain vigilant and keep your attention from drifting.

- **Make frequent changes (about every 5 minutes) in posture or position (Griffiths 2007).** The goal is to keep you alert through physical movement and variation. The exact timing and the changes you make are not as important as the fact that you are doing something. One way to make significant position and posture changes is by switching from sitting to standing or strolling. For example, during the first 5 minutes of your rotation, sit. During the next 5 minutes, stand. Then stroll for the next 5 minutes. The goal is to do some type of movement rather than sit in the same place and position for a long period.

If your facility has elevated lifeguard stands with only a small step for your feet, standing or strolling may not be practical. In this instance, you will have to identify other ways to meet the objective of keeping alert through physical movement.

- **Keep your mind fully engaged in active scanning, targeting, and assessing during your time on station.** If you are moving your head and sweeping your eyes but your mind is thinking about things other than the behaviors of the patrons, you may not be vigilant enough to effectively search your zone.

- **Rotate frequently to get a break from surveillance.** Research from other professions that require high vigilance, such as air traffic control and the military, has shown that the ability to remain focused starts to decrease significantly after about 30 minutes (United States Lifeguard Coalition 2011). When feasible, the rotation schedule at your facility should be established so that you are not in any one location for a long time. The short break from surveillance to move from station to station will help you be vigilant. Alternating periods of nonsurveillance duties helps as well, as does taking breaks when you can get out of the sun or go to the bathroom.

- **Use the vigilance voice technique.** Vigilance voice is a method to help you explore your zone by putting a voice to what you see (Smith 2006). It is similar to commentary drive techniques used by emergency response teams when teaching driving skills. By talking through every detail of what you see while you scan, you will remain focused and be able to identify problem areas you may not have noticed before.

- **Get adequate sleep, stay hydrated, and try to stay cool.** Not being fully rested, being dehydrated, and being exposed to hot temperatures can all impair vigilance (United States Lifeguard Coalition 2011).

- **Participate in victim recognition training (VRT) assessments**. Another common method that facilities use to maintain lifeguard vigilance and help you learn to identify a submerged drowning victim is mannequin or shadow drops. This type of site-specific training activity is feasible at facilities where a small waterproof training mannequin or a body outline that lies flat on the pool bottom can be placed into the water without attracting the notice of a lifeguard (see figure 5.2). These unexpected

Figure 5.2   A silhouette in the shape of a drowning victim can be used to help you learn what a body on the bottom of the water may look like. *(a)* View from a distance. *(b)* View from right above.

scenarios help you to practice actually seeing something on the bottom. They are also a good way to test and develop zones by verifying that the item can be seen in any location within the zone. Besides doing assessments that simulate a victim on the bottom, management staff should create a way to assess VRT by having a person simulate an unresponsive drowning victim floating on the surface.

- **Participate in shadow guarding**. Learning from others is sometimes helpful. Shadow guarding pairs up two lifeguards, one usually more experienced than the other. The less experienced lifeguard shadows the other and learns by observing and discussing (such as through the vigilance voice activity) the best strategies for scanning the zone. If you are assigned to a shadow guard position, remember that your conversations and attention should remain on being vigilant, not on socializing.

- **Participate in a lifeguard audit program**. Your facility may have a system in place to conduct unannounced lifeguard reviews, also known as audits. These reviews may be conducted by a member of the management staff (internal) or by someone not affiliated with your facility (external). Reviews keep your vigilance high because you never know whether someone is watching and documenting your performance while you are on station.

You can't provide constant and dedicated surveillance for one zone for an extended period because doing so becomes physically and mentally too difficult. To give you breaks from surveillance responsibilities, your facility should have a system for frequently moving lifeguards from one location to another. When another lifeguard comes to take over your zone, the change is called a *rotation*.

Proactive Rotations

Having a sound lifeguard rotation plan and rigorous procedures is crucial to your ability to be effective in patron surveillance. During the rotation, a lapse of patron surveillance can occur if the switch is not done correctly. Therefore, the rotation system must be practiced and evaluated to eliminate or minimize the lapse of patron surveillance time. Heat, humidity, and high bather counts are stresses for qualified lifeguards that may warrant more frequent breaks.

Rotations help you keep your attention level high. The shorter your time at a zone is and the more frequent your rotations are, the more attentive you are likely to be. Rotations generally involve the lifeguard on break coming back into a lifeguard zone and the other lifeguards moving in sequence to new locations. Rotation timing varies from facility to facility, but it generally occurs every 15 minutes to every hour. Rotation charts should be present at your facility to diagram the movement of the lifeguards from station to station.

The lifeguard taking over a zone is known as the incoming guard, and the lifeguard who has been scanning the zone is the outgoing guard. A well-performed rotation presents a professional image and does not compromise the level of surveillance for the zone. A well-executed rotation

- occurs quickly,
- involves limited conversation, and
- provides a systematic transfer of responsibility.

A proactive rotation begins the minute you begin to proceed to your station. Depending on the features at your facility, your station may be a lifeguard stand of some type, a slide tower, an in-water location, or a roving position. Scan the water as you walk toward the zone so that you can get a feel for the activity level and begin to prepare yourself mentally for your scanning responsibility. Scanning the zone before you take it over assures that you are becoming responsible for a clean zone—one that does not have a drowning victim on the bottom that the previous lifeguard missed.

If you don't have your own rescue tube as you rotate into a station, the outgoing lifeguard will have to transfer one to you. The lifeguard with the rescue tube during a rotation is responsible for scanning and would be the person to make a rescue, if needed.

The zone-sweeping procedure is for a traditional lifeguard stand with several stairs along the back or front, with one rescue tube. In this procedure the rescue tube is transferred twice. If your facility has lifeguard stands that allow a side, front, or back walkout, you can modify the rotation system so that the rescue tube is transferred once. If both lifeguards have a rescue tube, perform the rotation in the same manner except for the transfer of the rescue tube.

Incoming Guard Sweeps the Zone

The incoming lifeguard performs a full sweep and scan of the bottom of the pool and then says, "Bottom clear" *(a)*.

Passing the Rescue Tube

The outgoing lifeguard passes the rescue tube to the incoming lifeguard *(b)*.

Incoming Guard Takes Over Zone

The incoming lifeguard positions the rescue tube, begins scanning, and says, "I have the zone." The outgoing lifeguard climbs down *(c)*.

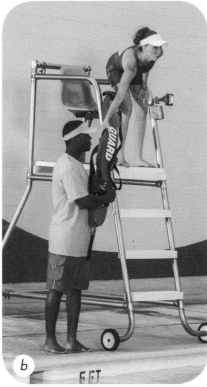

Exchanging the Rescue Tube

Both lifeguards scan. The rescue tube is passed back to the outgoing lifeguard, who positions the rescue tube and assumes responsibility by saying, "I have the zone" *(d)*.

Incoming Guard Climbs Up

The incoming lifeguard climbs up into the chair *(e)*. The outgoing lifeguard passes the rescue tube back up to the incoming lifeguard, who positions the rescue tube, begins scanning, and says, "I have the zone."

Outgoing Guard Sweeps the Zone

The outgoing lifeguard does a complete sweep and scan of the bottom, says (or signals), "Bottom clear," and leaves the zone *(f)*.

- If both of you have a rescue tube, perform the rotation in the same manner except for the transfer of the rescue tube.
- Be careful not to slip while climbing up or down a chair ladder, and use the 3 points of contact.

A proactive rotation does not end when you leave the lifeguard stand. Scan the zone as you walk away. Remember that the eyes of the patrons are on you any time you are in public view, so you should maintain your professionalism.

Drowning Detection Technology

We've identified the difficulty in being able to see a victim who is submerged under the water, even in a pool with clear water. In locations with turbid (dark) water, seeing under the surface is impossible. Crowds, glare, ripples, blind spots, dark water, or floating rafts and tubes can make it difficult for you to see beneath the surface to scan the area you know is vitally important. Advances in technology are resulting in the development of systems to help counter these surveillance difficulties.

Although it may not be feasible to have such a system at all aquatic venues, you may work at a location that uses this technology, so you may need to be familiar with the concept. You will need to obtain site-specific training on the equipment where you work.

Underwater Camera Systems

Underwater cameras can be linked to a small monitor on your guard chair that gives you a real-time view under the surface to include in your scanning pattern. Do not sit and watch the screen; rather, look at the monitor about every 10 seconds as part of your regular scan. Some monitors can be programmed to sound a reminder beep at a designated interval and to track compliance when you push a button to verify that you have looked at the underwater view on the screen.

This technology greatly enhances your ability to see under the water and scan without the limitations of surface movement or glare. In some facilities, reliable and user-friendly technology may be the only answer to full and effective water surveillance.

Alarm Systems

One type of alarm system emits a warning signal if a swimmer has been submerged under the water for a predetermined threshold of time. A system of receivers and detection devices is installed that covers the swimming area. Some systems can sense a body on the bottom. Other systems require swimmers to wear a tracking sensor device, usually inside a headband or wristband. If the sensor submerges past a certain depth for a dangerous length of time, the alarm sounds.

The use of technology should not de-emphasize your role as a lifeguard. Nor should these devices be allowed to create a culture of complacency because they are in place. Instead, technology should supplement your skills and reduce your limitations. Even with a diligent staff the risk of drowning is always present at an aquatic venue.

▶ VISIT THE WEB RESOURCE

You can reinforce your learning by visiting the web resource, where you can do the following in the interactive online learning activities based on chapter 5:

- ◆ View video of actual scanning patterns and lifeguards performing effective scanning.
- ◆ Participate in virtual activities to place lifeguards in zones and create zone charts.
- ◆ Watch a demonstration of how to verify a lifeguard zone.
- ◆ Evaluate rotations of actual lifeguards.
- ◆ Test your knowledge and receive feedback.

CHAPTER SUMMARY

Key points	Best practices on the job
• Zones are areas of assigned responsibility. • RID stands for recognition, intrusion, and distraction. • Zone size and assignments at your facility may change based on the number of patrons, the nature of pool activities, the time of day, or other conditions. • Surveillance should be your only duty while on station and responsible for a zone. • Effective scanning is a combination of eye movement, head movement, body position, alertness, and engagement. • Remaining alert, vigilant, and engaged with the zone are critical to early drowning recognition. • The concept of "look for life" can help you identify critical events for targeting and assessment.	• Stay actively engaged with your zone. • Know your zone of patron surveillance. • Scan to search the zone about every 10 seconds. • Target and assess anything unusual and any person submerged for more than about 10 seconds. • Rotate positions frequently, using a proactive systematic transfer of care for the zone. • Stay well-rested, hydrated, and cool. • Provide surveillance during a rotation. • Change your posture in the lifeguard stand about every 5 minutes.

Part III

Response and Rescue

Deciding to Act and Emergency Response

CHAPTER OBJECTIVES

This chapter

- examines legal considerations and barriers to action,
- presents a drowning chain of survival,
- explains the importance of deciding to act and communication signals,
- presents the STAAR aquatic rescue model,
- identifies how and when to contact emergency medical services (EMS) and what to expect when you call,
- describes an effective emergency action plan (EAP),
- explains how to manage an emergency scene including providing directions to a crowd and coordinating bystander involvement, and
- identifies considerations when activating the EAP for a water rescue.

An emergency, such as a sudden illness, injury, or drowning, can happen at any time. A coordinated response by the people and agencies that provide care offers the best chance for a good outcome.

When an emergency happens, responders may provide different levels of care. Responders may have certain legal obligations depending on the severity of the event and their training.

Legal Considerations

During an emergency, certain legal principles apply regarding what you are expected to do in the United States. These principles include the following:

- **Duty to act**. If you are a lifeguard expected to give emergency medical care, including CPR, you almost certainly have a duty to act. But emergency care that you perform voluntarily on a stranger in need while you are off duty is generally considered a Good Samaritan act.

Duty to act is a requirement to act toward others and the public with the watchfulness, attention, caution, and prudence that a reasonable person in the same circumstances would use.

- **Good Samaritan principle**. Because governments encourage people to help others, they pass Good Samaritan laws (or apply the principle to common laws). These laws prevent a rescuer who has voluntarily helped a stranger in need from being sued for wrongdoing. You are generally protected from liability as long as you are reasonably careful, act in good faith (not for reward), and do not provide care beyond your skill level. If you decide to help an ill or injured person outside your job, you must not leave that person until someone with equal or more emergency training takes over (unless it becomes dangerous to stay).

- **Consent**. A responsive adult must agree to receive care. To get consent, first identify yourself. Then tell the victim that you are a lifeguard and ask whether it's OK to help. People over the age of 18 may give oral or written consent or give consent by gesturing.

  - **Implied consent** means that permission to perform care on an unresponsive victim is assumed. This principle is based on the idea that a reasonable person would give permission to receive lifesaving first aid if he or she were able.

  - **When caring for children**, you should gain consent from a parent or legal guardian. But when a life-threatening situation exists and a parent or legal guardian is not available, give first aid care based on implied consent.

  - **When caring for older adults**, you must keep in mind that if they are suffering from a disturbance in normal mental functioning, such as Alzheimer's disease, they may not understand your request for consent. Consent must then be gained from a family member or legal guardian. Again, when a life-threatening situation exists and a family member or legal guardian is not available for consent, give first aid care based on implied consent.

- **Confidentiality**. A person has the right for her or his name and medical history to remain confidential among care providers. Care providers may share only information pertinent to medical care. The regulation in the United States that governs confidentiality is the Health Insurance Portability and Accountability Act, commonly referred to as the HIPAA law.

- **Standard of care**. This is the level of emergency care that you are expected to provide, based on the level of your training and with a response that a reasonable person in the same circumstances would use. If a person's actions do not meet this standard, then the acts may be considered negligent, and any damages resulting may be claimed in a lawsuit for negligence.

- **Negligence**. This occurs when an injured or ill person incurs proven damage from a trained person who has a duty to act and the person does not uphold the standard of care.

- **Refusal of care**. A person older than 18 can refuse treatment and care if he or she is alert and oriented to the surroundings.

- **Advance directives, living wills, and do not resuscitate (DNR) orders**. These documents are authorized by law and are usually witnessed or notarized. The documents allow a person to appoint someone as her or his representative to make decisions on resuscitation and continued life support if the person has lost decision-making capacity (e.g., if the person is in a coma). Advance directives are statements about what victims want done or not done if they can't speak for themselves. The DNR is a type of advance directive. This document is a specific request not to have CPR performed. In the United States, a doctor's order is required to withhold CPR. Therefore, unless the victim has a DNR order, emergency care providers should attempt resuscitation. Victims who are not likely to benefit from CPR and may have a DNR order include those with terminal conditions from which they are unlikely to recover. Outside the hospital, rescuers should begin CPR if reasonable doubt exists about the validity of a DNR order or advance directive, the victim has changed his or her mind, or the victim's best interests are in question.

- **Documentation**. Emergency care provided should be recorded in writing.

Legal Liability

The legal system in the United States and most countries allows a lawsuit to be filed any time there is a perceived wrong. Filing a lawsuit puts into motion a series of events to determine the details of the alleged wrongdoing. The person filing the lawsuit, called the plaintiff, must prove that the other person, called the defendant, caused the injury either through action or inaction and that the injury could have been anticipated and therefore could have been prevented.

Only a judge or jury can decide whether the people named in the lawsuit were guilty of negligence. Before going to trial, a judge may determine that the evidence of wrongdoing is insufficient or refuse to hear the case. Alternatively, the parties involved may settle the case. In any event, simply naming someone in a lawsuit does not mean she or he is guilty; she or he must be found to be so in a court of law.

The legal process is time consuming, emotionally draining, and expensive. If an injury or drowning event happens while you are lifeguarding and a lawsuit is filed, it would likely name your employer, and possibly you and others as defendants. In most instances, your employer would cover the legal costs to defend you. In some locations, if you work for a governmental agency, you cannot be held liable.

But if you are working as an independent contractor or for someone other than your primary employer (such as at an after-hours party for which the host is paying you directly), you can be held liable and may not be covered under an insurance policy. You should understand the different types of employment status and the possible consequences in the event of legal action. If you are unsure of your status, be sure to ask and consider obtaining legal advice.

In most countries, to be considered an employee, you are required to fill out government withholding tax forms. In the United States, legitimate employers follow state and federal labor laws as well as occupational safety regulations, pay employment tax, and provide worker's compensation insurance in case you are injured on the job. All these provisions are designed for your protection. If you are asked to work without filling out employment tax forms, the person hiring you may be considering you an independent contractor and you will likely not be covered by worker's compensation or liability insurance should you get injured or should a lawsuit be filed against you. In this instance, you should consider purchasing liability insurance. Be sure you understand your employee status and the possible consequences before accepting any lifeguarding job.

Distress and Drowning Chains of Survival and Prehospital Response

The chain of survival concept has been included in CPR training for a number of years. However, it does not account for the unique circumstances of distress or drowning. A drowning chain of survival has been created to guide important life-saving steps for rescuers (Szpilman et al. 2014). The steps of the chain are

1. prevent drowning,
2. recognize distress,
3. provide flotation,
4. remove from water, and
5. provide care as needed.

While these steps are important, the chain needs to be modified for situations when a drowning person is unresponsive to include early recognition, early rescue breathing, early activation of EMS, early CPR and defibrillation, and early advanced life support. You'll learn more about this in chapter 11.

You, as a lifeguard, are the first link in this chain of survival, and considered part of the prehospital system of care, along with other responders. Emergency medical responders consist of people with various types of training who respond when an emergency number such as 9-1-1, 0-0-0, or 1-1-2 is called. EMS units are usually staffed with emergency medical technicians (EMTs) or paramedics. Emergency medical technicians have completed extensive hours of advanced training, particularly in advanced cardiac life support (ACLS), and they can perform additional emergency medical procedures under the authorization of a physician designated as a medical director for the local EMS unit. Paramedics are additionally trained to use specialized equipment, administer medications, and perform medical procedures under the direction of a physician.

The care that you and any of these people provide is prehospital care because it takes place either at the site of the emergency or in an ambulance on the way to the hospital. The EMS responders decide whether or not to transport an ill, injured, or deceased person to a hospital. If a person is transported to the hospital, the emergency department medical team can provide advanced life support care if necessary. This medical team may determine that additional specialized care is necessary and transfer the injured or ill person to another hospital, such as a regional trauma center.

A coordinated response is important in prehospital emergency care, let's look at communication signals that should be established at an aquatic facility.

Communication Signals and Activating the Emergency Action Plan

Clear communication signals are vital to the operation of an aquatic facility and are the first step in a coordinated response in prehospital emergency care.

Your facility should have a system of communication signals that allow you to indicate that a rescue is in progress, call for help, request coverage of your zone, and activate the emergency action plan (EAP).

Most communication signals are based on a combination of whistle and hand movements, such as the signal shown in figure 6.1. At a minimum, you should have a whistle with you at all times. Know and practice the communication signals designed for your workplace. Following is a list of communication signals that should be in place and some of the most common signals used:

- Standard rescue: long whistle blast or air horn blast
- Major rescue (e.g., unresponsive person): two long whistle blasts or air horn blasts
- I need help: raised fist
- I need another lifeguard's attention: two short whistle blasts
- Cover my zone: two short whistle blasts; tap top of head
- Clear the pool: series of whistle blasts
- Zone clear and covered, resume activity: thumbs-up

When you activate the emergency action plan for an aquatic rescue, you put into motion a system of backup and support. Your whistle signal or other

Figure 6.1 A system of communication signals between lifeguards is important.

Figure 6.2 A whistle signal or other site-specific communication device activates the emergency action plan for your facility.

site-specific communication device alerts others that a rescue is taking place (see figure 6.2). In multiguard facilities, a rescue team will respond.

The members of a rescue team vary from facility to facility, but generally the lifeguards on break from surveillance and supervisors on site respond to the EAP signal. This plan of response allows the lifeguards on station to continue to supervise their own zones during a rescue or coordinate clearing patrons from the area. The ability of your rescue team to make a successful rescue is only as strong as your weakest rescue team member and is directly related to your team's ability to work together. Therefore, you and your rescue team must simulate real-life situations when practicing the emergency action plan. Rescue team members should be prepared to provide the following assistance:

- Cover your zone while you make the rescue or clear the zone.
- Enter the water and assist with the rescue if you signal for help.
- Bring rescue equipment to the pool edge, beach entry, or other designated point.
- Call EMS if necessary.
- Provide crowd management.
- Help remove the person from the water.
- Assist with follow-up care or basic life support on deck or on the shore.

Emergency Action Plans

Each person plays an important role in the event of an aquatic emergency. The role you will play depends on many factors, including your training, government regulations, local guidelines, and the decisions the managers of your facility have made.

An emergency action plan (EAP) is a written document detailing who does what and when in the event of an emergency, which must be practiced regularly. An EAP should be

- posted in key areas for quick reference;
- simple and easy to follow;
- practiced using realistic and appropriate scenarios;
- designed to include everyone who will respond; and
- developed for various types of emergencies, not just drowning but also other situations such as injury, severe weather, or fire.

Some of the duties to be defined for an emergency at your facility may include, depending on the emergency and site-specific considerations, responsibilities such as the following:

- Calling EMS
- Signaling for equipment and help
- Maintaining surveillance
- Removing or controlling dangerous conditions (e.g., shutting off gas and electricity or neutralizing chemicals)
- Evacuating patrons
- Bringing equipment to the scene
- Attending to the victim and providing care
- Meeting EMS personnel, leading them to the scene, and unlocking gates or doors, as necessary
- Notifying parents or relatives
- Obtaining and securing the victim's personal belongings
- Obtaining witness statements
- Writing reports
- Notifying supervisors
- Serving as a spokesperson and providing information to the media

An example of an emergency action plan for an unresponsive drowning victim when three lifeguards and one supervisor or manager are on duty is included in chapter 11. This plan is an example only; you must follow the EAP specifically designed for the facility where you work.

STAAR Aquatic Rescue Model

When an aquatic emergency occurs, having a systematic method for responding is helpful. The StarGuard program uses the acronym STAAR (scan, target, assess, alert, rescue; see figure 6.3) to maximize the key elements you will perform in an aquatic emergency to activate your emergency action plan, call EMS, and make a rescue.

Figure 6.3 The StarGuard aquatic rescue model.

Adapted, by permission, from K. Tyson and R. Ogoreuc, 2002, "S.T.A.R.R.: Method for responding to aquatic emergencies," *American Lifeguard Magazine*, Winter: pages 15, 17, 18.

Regardless of whether the person to be rescued is on the surface of the water or submerged, is responsive or unresponsive, or is facing toward you or away from you, the steps you follow are the same:

Scan the zone.

Target the area with your eyes if you recognize distress or drowning behavior or if something abnormal catches your attention.

Assess the situation and decide whether to take action.

Alert others with a whistle or other device.

Rescue the person; decide what action to take.

When the rescue has been accomplished, the two final steps are to *remove* the person from the water and to complete a rescue *report*. After the person is out of the water, your role is to monitor her or his condition. If necessary, provide first aid or, if the victim becomes unconscious, basic life support care until EMS responders arrive. Fill out the rescue report after all necessary emergency care has been provided and before the injured person leaves your facility. If the person is being transported by EMS, obtain as much information as possible and complete the report later.

Deciding to Act

Providing help in an emergency may involve acting in the face of uncertainty. You may have to force yourself to take action even though you are not sure the situation is a real emergency or when the sick or injured person actively denies that he or she needs help. Never be afraid to call EMS just because you are unsure that a real emergency exists. Let the dispatch center and emergency service professionals help you in times of confusion or doubt. That's what they are there for.

The signs and symptoms of a medical emergency or a person in distress or drowning may also be vague or unusual. During your assessment of the situation, you will always come to a point when you will need to decide whether or not to take action and then what action to take. "When in doubt, check it out!" and "If you don't know, go!" are helpful phrases to help you decide to act.

Early Activation of Emergency Medical Services

Early activation of EMS is a critical component in the chain of survival. Knowing how to call EMS from the facility where you work is an important component of your lifeguard responsibilities. Most countries have a single three-digit emergency telephone number that allows a caller to contact local EMS for assistance. Most communities in the United States use 9-1-1 as the emergency number for calling EMS, although a few still use special seven-digit emergency numbers. The 9-1-1 number is used by many countries worldwide. In the European Union, 1-1-2 is the common emergency call number. The emergency number in Australia is 0-0-0. For successful early activation, the following should occur:

- All staff members must know how to dial out if your facility requires special access to an outside line. For example, in many situations you must first dial 9 to get a line before dialing the emergency number.
- The name, address, and phone number of your facility should be posted next to all telephones.
- If the emergency number is something other than 9-1-1 (or other than the local emergency number in your area), all staff members must memorize the number and the dialing instructions, and the emergency number should be posted next to all phones.

Many EMS agencies have enhanced computerized systems that instantly provide the dispatcher with the address and telephone number of the caller if the person is calling from a landline phone. But this system does not work with all wireless or cell phones, so when calling on a cell phone you need to identify your location by a street name, a street number, a landmark, or directions. If you do not know your location, the dispatcher will work with you to help determine what your exact location is or where to send help.

When to Call EMS for Help

Research has shown that people have difficulty recognizing a medical emergency or underestimate the seriousness of an emergency and fail to call for help. Remember, if you *think* you or someone you know is experiencing a medical emergency, call for help immediately. If someone experiences any of the following, you should call 9-1-1 (or your local emergency number):

- Bleeding or spurting blood that you can't stop
- Difficulty breathing or cessation of breathing
- Gasping for air or turning blue or purple or very pale
- Choking and the inability to clear the obstruction
- Altered mental status: unresponsiveness, fainting, lack of alertness, and emission of strange noises
- Chest pains, chest pressure or constriction, or crushing discomfort around the chest (even if the pain stops)
- Unusual numbness, tightness, pressure, or aching pain in the chest, neck, jaw, arm, or upper back
- A temperature of 105 degrees Fahrenheit (41 degrees Celsius) or higher (heatstroke)
- Severe stiff neck, headache, and fever
- A snakebite
- A bee sting that causes a reaction
- An allergic reaction of any kind
- A seizure or convulsion
- Uncontrollable jerking movements
- Burns over an area larger than the palm of your hand
- Electrical burn or shock
- Severe injury, trauma, or an attack

What to Expect When You Call 9-1-1 in the United States

Typically, a professional emergency dispatcher with specialized training to deal with crises over the phone will answer your 9-1-1 call. Be prepared to explain your situation briefly and accurately. Many dispatchers today are trained to provide real-time instruction in CPR and lifesaving first aid while simultaneously dispatching emergency medical service professionals to your location. Listen to the dispatcher and follow her or his instructions.

Most public safety agencies have access to a variety of highly trained personnel and specialized equipment and vehicles. To ensure that the right people with the right equipment are sent to the correct location, the 9-1-1 dispatcher must ask you specific questions. At times, the dispatcher may seem to be asking these questions to determine whether or not you need help. In actuality, he or she is asking questions to determine the level of help you need. Remember, trained dispatchers never ask unnecessary questions.

The dispatcher will always ask you to state the address of the emergency and your callback number for verification. You must state this information (or state it twice if a computerized 9-1-1 screen is unavailable) to be sure that the dispatcher hears it and copies it down correctly. The dispatcher knows how important it is to do it right and not just fast. The dispatcher asks four universal questions to put her or his knowledge and experience to work for you quickly and effectively after she or he has verified the address and callback telephone number at the emergency site:

1. Exactly what happened (person's problem or type of incident)?
2. What is the victim's approximate age?
3. Is the victim responsive?
4. Is the victim breathing?

Getting this critical information from you typically takes less than 30 seconds. After that, you may be asked to do nothing, to get out of an unsafe environment, or to stay on the line and assist in providing care for the ill or injured person. Working with 9-1-1 callers, emergency medical dispatchers (EMDs), professionals trained to provide telephone instruction in CPR and lifesaving first aid, have helped save thousands of lives during the 5 to 10 minutes it usually takes EMS professionals to arrive at the scene of an emergency. If you are calling from a cell phone, it may be helpful to put the call on speaker mode while you return to the scene to help.

In all cases, remember that the most important thing you can do when calling 9-1-1 is to *listen carefully*. Always do whatever the dispatcher asks you to do. Don't tell him or her to hurry; the dispatcher already knows that. Every question from the dispatcher is asked for an important reason; that's why it's in the protocol.

Crowd and Bystander Management in an Emergency

During crowded conditions or emergencies, your ability to manage large groups of people will be extremely important. You may have to deal with a crowd to communicate safety information, make emergency announcements, provide direction, control violence, or evacuate the facility.

Providing Direction

First, get the crowd's attention and make sure that patrons can hear you. Use a microphone or megaphone if available. Then give directions in short phrases, spoken in a loud, clear voice. Repeat the announcement several times. Provide information that is accurate but simple; skip unnecessary detail or explanation. An example of poor communication might be the following announcement: "May I have your attention. We've just been notified by the National Weather Service that a tornado warning has been issued for Clark, Wayne, and Green counties until 7:30 p.m. A tornado has been sighted near Eldorado and is heading this way. Please get out of the water, gather your belongings, and seek shelter. If you don't have transportation, go to the locker rooms. If you have questions, see the pool manager." A better way to communicate this information would be like this: "Attention. Severe weather is approaching, and a tornado warning has been issued. Please clear the pool immediately." Additional details or assistance could be provided by staff as people leave or seek shelter.

Make announcements in the language of the majority of patrons. If large groups of patrons speak other languages, make announcements in more than one language. In a multiple-language environment, signage at your facility should be in more than one language or use descriptive pictures to illustrate safety and emergency instructions.

Evacuating the Pool or Facility

The emergency action plans for your facility should include predetermined evacuation routes or shelter areas for emergency hazards such as fire, chemical spills, or inclement weather. You should also have a predetermined method of evacuating patrons from the water during a rescue involving a suspected spinal injury or unresponsive drowning victim. If you need to evacuate patrons, first scan for obstacles and then initiate your EAP. Announce clearly the need to move from the area. Calmly direct patrons along the prepared evacuation routes or direct them to walk to a designated shelter area. When possible, position staff between the crowd and the pool area to monitor and control access during the evacuation period.

Bystander Involvement

During an emergency, bystanders often attempt to help. You will need to be familiar with the policy for bystander involvement at your facility. In some locations, bystanders are not allowed to assist for legal or other reasons. In other circumstances, you may need to solicit help from bystanders and tell them specifically and clearly what to do.

▶ VISIT THE WEB RESOURCE

You can reinforce your learning by visiting the web resource, where you can do the following in the interactive online learning activities based on chapter 6:

- ◆ Create an emergency action plan.
- ◆ Evaluate scenarios and decide if EMS should be called.
- ◆ Explain how to activate EMS and communicate with an EMS dispatcher.
- ◆ Listen to EMS to dispatch communication.
- ◆ Test your knowledge and receive feedback.

CHAPTER SUMMARY

Key points	Best practices on the job
• If you are a lifeguard expected to give emergency medical care, including CPR, you almost certainly have a duty to act. • Lifeguards are part of the prehospital and EMS chain of survival. • The chain of survival for a person in distress includes prevent drowning, recognize distress, provide flotation, remove from water, and provide care as needed. • The chain of survival for an unresponsive drowning person includes early recognition, early rescue breathing, early activation of EMS, early CPR and defibrillation, and early advanced life support. • Communication signals are the first step in a coordinated response in prehospital emergency care. • Deciding to act is an important part of response. • When you activate the emergency action plan for an aquatic rescue, you put into motion a system of backup and support. Your whistle signal or other site-specific communication device alerts others that a rescue is taking place and help is needed. • An emergency action plan (EAP) is a written document detailing who does what and when in the event of an aquatic emergency, which must be practiced regularly. • The five actions that are the StarGuard aquatic rescue model include scan, target, assess, alert, and rescue. • During an emergency, bystanders often attempt to help.	• Regularly practice scenarios to assess the emergency action plans (EAPs) at the facility where you work. • Understand and use the communication signals and equipment for your facility. • Know how to call EMS from your facility. • Effectively manage crowds and bystanders during an emergency. • Appropriately assess an emergency and decide to act. • Understand the legal considerations of working as a lifeguard. • Know the policy of bystander involvement at your facility. • Participate in coordinated training and scenario practice with the EMS system that would respond to your location at least once per year.

Assists and Rescues

CHAPTER OBJECTIVES

This chapter

- describes the benefits of using a rescue tube,
- identifies methods of land-based assists,
- describes entry and approach skills,
- describes skills for rescue on the surface and under the surface of the water,
- considers special-situation rescues and emergency escape skills, and
- explains responsibilities after the rescue.

A person who is in the water and needs to be assisted or rescued will be

- either on top of the water or submerged,
- either facing you or facing away from you, and
- either responsive (still conscious and breathing) or unresponsive (not breathing).

In this chapter we discuss how to perform assists and water rescues for people who are in distress or drowning but are still responsive. Chapter 11 provides details about rescues for a drowning person who is unresponsive. We start with land-based assists and then discuss the details of how to enter the water, approach and execute a rescue, remove the person from the water, provide safety and other instructions, release her or him from the scene, and report the incident.

Rescue Tubes

Always wear and use a rescue tube when lifeguarding. The only exception would be when you are in a zone of extremely shallow water. Wear the strap diagonally around your chest and keep the tube between you and the person at all times when making a water rescue. A rescue tube is a length of dense foam or similar buoyant material fitted with a strap. An effective rescue tube is usually 42 to 54 inches (107 to 137 cm) long, and thick enough to hold firmly with a wide grasp (see figure 7.1). The rescue tube will do the following:

- Provide flotation support for you
- Provide flotation support for the distressed swimmer or drowning person
- Eliminate body-to-body contact with the distressed swimmer or drowning person
- Improve the likelihood of a successful rescue

Rescue tubes have revolutionized the ability of lifeguards to make safe and effective water rescues in a wide range of conditions. These devices provide an excellent means of flotation and can support more than one person at one time. Rescue tubes level the playing field by making it possible for a small lifeguard to manage a large

Figure 7.1 Rescue tubes provide flotation support for you and the person in distress or drowning.

drowning person, for a lifeguard to manage more than one person at a time, and to provide support for rescue breathing in the water.

A rescue tube should be worn with the strap diagonally across the body. Gather any extra dangling strap in your hand or tuck it behind the rescue tube to avoid a trip hazard while standing and reduce the chance that the strap will be caught on the lifeguard stand when you enter to make a rescue. While sitting, place the rescue tube across your lap. While walking, hold the tube across the front or along the side of your body so that you are rescue ready at all times. You're now ready to put everything you've learned so far into a system for making an effective rescue. You know how to scan, target, and assess to recognize a distressed swimmer or drowning person. You have some type of communication device to alert others that you are making a rescue and to activate your facility's emergency action plan. You know how to use the available equipment. The next step is to respond and take action.

Land-Based Assists

If a distressed swimmer is responsive and within reaching distance, extending your rescue tube to the person and helping from land may be faster and just as effective as helping from the water. The swimmer must be able to

- see or feel the rescue tube as you extend it,
- follow your directions to grab the tube, and
- have the strength to hold on to the rescue tube while being pulled to safety.

When you extend a rescue tube to a person in the water, keep your legs apart and turn your body sideways to create a stable base, and shift your weight back to avoid being pulled in (see figure 7.2). Be careful not to injure the person with the device as you place it within his or her reach.

Water Entry

Entering the water to make a rescue is often the most effective way to manage a conscious distressed swimmer or drowning person. Before you make a water rescue, however, follow the steps of the STAAR aquatic rescue model: scan, target, assess, alert, *and then* enter the water to make a rescue.

To begin a rescue from the side or a lifeguard stand, enter the water using either a compact jump or an ease-in entry.

Compact Jump

A compact-jump entry is useful in a wide range of water depths and circumstances. Because you enter the water in a compact position, your risk of back, leg, or foot injury is lower than it is with other techniques.

A compact jump is best performed into water that is at least as deep as the distance from your takeoff point to the surface of the water where you will enter. For example, if you jump from a lifeguard stand platform that is 5 feet (1.5 m) above the water, the water should

Figure 7.2 When using a rescue tube for a land-based assist, keep your legs apart to create a stable base.

be at least that deep. Depending on the water depth and the height of your lifeguard stand, climbing down from the lifeguard stand and entering from the deck or another safe point of action might be best.

Hold the rescue tube tightly across the front of your body and gather the strap in your hand or tuck it behind the tube *(a)*.

Jump forward and pull your knees up so that your body is in a compact position, almost like a cannonball jump *(b)*. Lift your toes up so that your feet enter the water in a flat position.

Keep yourself in the compact position until you enter the water *(c)*. You may submerge momentarily, but the rescue tube will bring you to the surface quickly.

Ease-In Entry

An ease-in entry won't create a splash and reduces the risk of collision. This entry should be considered if you are very close to a person, if the area is crowded, or you suspect that a person has an injury.

Sit on the pool edge. Slip into the water feetfirst. Control the speed and depth of your entry by holding on to the side.

Run-In Entry

You'll use a run-in entry from a beach or zero-depth venue.

Lift your knees high as you run to lift your feet above the waves and water surface. When you are too deep to run, lean forward on to your belly and begin to swim.

Approach Strokes

After you are in the water, the objective is to use any combination of arm strokes and leg kicks to make rapid progress toward the person. For example, you may be able to swim faster using a freestyle arm stroke and kick, or you might prefer a breaststroke or a combination of the two strokes. Swim with your head up to maintain visual contact while you approach.

Tube Across Chest

You can use a freestyle kick with a freestyle pull to approach the person.

Or you can use a freestyle or breaststroke kick with breaststroke pull to approach the person.

Trailing Tube

Keep the strap across your chest and allow the tube to trail behind. When you are about 10 feet (3 m) from the person, pull the strap to bring the rescue tube into position across your chest.

Keep the rescue tube under your arms and across your chest if the person is responsive and is just a few yards or meters away. This position is safer for you, because it keeps the tube between you and the active person who is in distress or drowning.

Because the position of the rescue tube across your chest creates drag, swimming with the tube trailing behind you is usually faster. If you anticipate swimming more than a few yards, use this approach stroke. You should also consider swimming with the tube behind you when a person is unresponsive and time is critical. Your goal in this situation is to get to the person as quickly as possible.

As you swim toward the person you are rescuing, assess the situation to determine which type of water rescue will be best. Depending on the location of and condition of the person, you may decide to use a front, rear, two-guard, or leg-wrap rescue technique. If more than one person needs assistance, you will manage a multiperson rescue.

Water Rescue on the Surface

The first objective of a water rescue is to minimize body-to-body contact between you and the person being rescued. Other objectives include the following:

- To keep your head and the head of the person you are rescuing above water so that you both can breathe

- To make progress toward a safe point of exit, such as a wall, ladder, or zero-depth entry area
- To provide safety instructions before releasing the person from the scene to reduce the risk that the incident will happen again

A responsive person in distress or drowning on or near the surface will be either facing you or facing away from you. Use the front rescue if the person is facing you and the rear rescue if the person is facing away from you or if you feel more comfortable making a rescue from behind. Use the two-guard rescue if you need help with a large or very active person.

Front Rescue

When making a front rescue you can see the other person's face, which provides you the ability to communicate with him or her. Also, when you push the rescue tube into the other person's chest and keep kicking, you drive the person backward, minimizing the risk that he or she will grab you.

Analysis of rescues show that after a person in distress is holding on to the rescue tube and realizes that it provides flotation, she or he stops struggling and panic subsides. But if a person refuses to grab the rescue tube, back away and try the rescue again. If the person still will not grab the rescue tube, swim to a position behind her or him and use the rear-rescue technique.

Swim to a position about an arm's length in front of the person *(a)*.

a

Push the rescue tube firmly into the person's chest by quickly extending your arms and locking your elbows. Encourage the person to grab the tube. Keep your arms straight and extended so that the person is at least an arm's length away from you and on the other side of the rescue tube *(b)*.

Keep kicking to continue your forward motion while pushing the person backward *(c)*. When the person is calm and maintaining contact with the rescue tube, change direction (if needed) toward the closest wall or exit point.

Rear Rescue

To perform a rear rescue, you hold the person securely on the rescue tube from behind, which reduces the chance that the person will grab you. You'll learn how to modify a rear rescue for an unresponsive drowning person in chapter 11.

Keep the rescue tube at your chest and move directly behind the person. Turn your head to the side to avoid injury *(a)*.

Reach under the person's arms and around his or her chest and then pull the person slightly back on to the tube. Hold the person securely on the tube *(b)*.

Kick to make progress toward the safe point of exit. If the person is calm and secure on the rescue tube, consider maintaining your grasp around the tube and person with one arm, and pulling with the other.

Two-Guard Rescue

The two-guard rescue allows you to manage an uncooperative, large, or uncontrollable person effectively and safely. This technique combines the front and rear rescues and requires two rescuers.

If you are the initial rescuer and need assistance, back away from the person and signal for help by raising a clenched fist *(a)*.

Position one lifeguard in front of the person and the other behind the person. If you are behind, perform a rear rescue and make a target with your open hands. If you are in front, perform a front rescue, aiming for the target. Communicate with your corescuer so that you both perform the front rescue and rear rescue techniques at about the same time *(b)*.

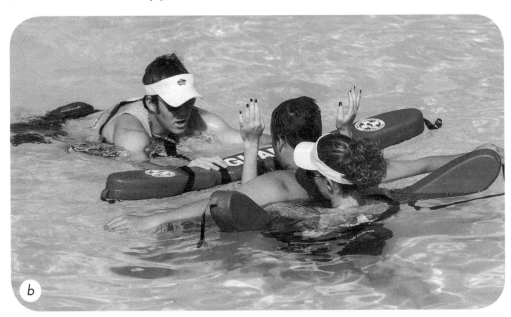

If you are performing the rear rescue, reach over the tube that is in front of the person and pull in tight. If you are performing the front rescue, push forward with extended arms *(c)*. When the person is secure, move to a takeout point.

c

Water Rescue Under the Surface

Rescues that must be performed while a person is submerged under the water can put you in a high-risk situation. Use the leg-wrap rescue to reach someone submerged underwater. This method gives you the ability to use the flotation capability of the tube to bring both you and the person to the surface without having to swim up.

Leg-Wrap Rescue

The benefits of this technique include the following:

- You do not make body-to-body contact with the drowning person.
- If the drowning person is struggling and grabs your legs, you can easily escape by pushing the person away using the strength of your legs and feet.
- Because you reach the person with your legs rather than your hands and arms, you don't have to submerge your body as far to make the rescue.
- Your hands are left free, which allows you to maintain control and contact with the rescue tube.

Position yourself behind the person *(a)*. Hold on to the rescue tube, take a breath of air, and submerge. Maintain your grasp on the rescue tube and extend your arms above your head to lower your body, feetfirst, toward the person.

a

Use your feet and lower legs to grab the person tightly under her or his arms (b). Rotate your feet to provide contact with the person's upper chest. If the person is struggling, apply pressure with your lower legs for more control.

Bend your knees and pull the rescue tube toward your chest. These movements will bring you and the person up to a position on the surface (c).

Reach over the rescue tube and perform a rear rescue (d).

A drowning person may be in deep water and submerged farther than your legs can reach while you hold on to the rescue tube body. In this situation you can use the strap to perform the extended leg-wrap or the superextended leg-wrap rescues.

Extended Leg-Wrap Rescue

If the person is too deep to be reached with a standard leg wrap, extend your reach by holding on to the tube strap, rather than the tube, when you perform the rescue.

Let go of the body of the rescue tube and lightly hold the rescue tube strap so that it will slide freely. Maintain a vertical body position with your legs together and your toes pointed. Keep your body as tight and streamlined as possible.

Turn your palms so that they face upward and lift your arms up over your head, pushing the water up toward the surface so that your body is propelled downward. This skill is known as a feetfirst surface dive. Maintain loose contact with the rescue tube strap as you lift your arms *(a)*.

If you need to descend deeper, reposition your hands at your sides to take another pull. To reposition, bend your elbows and pass your hands and arms in front of your body. Lowering your arms this way will help keep your body streamlined and won't break your momentum.

After you have performed a feetfirst surface dive, position yourself above and behind the person while maintaining contact with the rescue tube strap *(b)*. Place your feet and lower legs under the arms and around the person's upper torso and squeeze to maintain a grasp.

Extend your arm as far up the tube strap as you can while grasping the strap. Pull on the tube strap (hand over hand if needed) to bring yourself and the person toward the surface *(c)*. Let the flotation of the tube do the work; swimming to the surface with the person is not necessary.

c

As you reach the surface, place the tube across your chest. Bend your knees to bring the person up to the surface and into a position for a rear rescue *(d)*.

d

Superextended Leg-Wrap Rescue

If further extension is needed, the superextended leg-wrap rescue has been successfully used to reach persons submerged in 20 feet (6 meters) of water.

Remove the body strap from across your chest. Firmly grasp the end of the wide loop. Holding on to the strap, surface dive (feetfirst or headfirst) to a position just above and behind the person. If you have performed a headfirst surface dive, be sure to reverse yourself before you get within a few feet (a meter) of the person so that your legs are positioned downward *(a)*.

a

Grasp the person under the armpits and upper torso with your legs and feet *(b)*.

Pull up on the tube strap, hand over hand, to bring yourself and the person toward the surface *(c)*.

When you reach the surface, position the tube across your chest and then pull the person up into a rear-rescue position *(d)*.

Special-Situation Rescues

Occasionally, more than one person may need to be rescued at a time, or the person being rescued may be injured. You may lose control of your rescue tube, or a struggling person may grab you instead of the rescue tube for support. In these cases, you need to adapt to the circumstances. By understanding the objectives you need to accomplish—from both a water rescue and first aid standpoint—you can modify the skills you already know to make a successful rescue.

Rescuing Multiple Persons

If more than one person is in distress or drowning at the same time, you must determine whether attempting a multiperson rescue is safe. Remember that your primary objective is to maintain your safety by not making body-to-body contact. Your secondary objective is to provide flotation to the people you are rescuing so that everyone, including you, remains on the surface and breathes. A rescue tube can provide flotation for several people at once.

There is no step-by-step method for performing a multiperson rescue. You'll need to keep the objectives in mind and quickly decide on a course of action based on the circumstances.

Rescuing an Injured Person

There is no step-by-step method for rescuing an injured person because each situation is different. Your main objective is to place the injured person on the rescue tube so that he or she remains on the surface and breathes. Then you can progress to a takeout point so that you can provide first aid. Minimize movement of an injured area, such as a broken or dislocated arm, as you perform the rescue.

Rescuing a Person Having a Seizure in the Water

A patron who experiences a seizure while in the water may not have the body control to keep her or his head above water and breathe. The behaviors associated with seizures range from subtle changes in responsiveness to evident convulsions. A person having a convulsion may be jerking uncontrollably, with random arm and leg movements. A seizure usually lasts only a minute or so. Several minutes of recovery follows, during which the person may still be somewhat unresponsive.

When a seizure occurs in the water, the primary goal is to keep the person's head above water to reduce the chance of swallowing water, and so the person can breathe. You may want to place a rescue tube under the person, but you do not want to try to grab around a person having a seizure, such as you would in a rear rescue. Rather, hold the head in a position above the water first and then place the rescue tube under the person if possible or if needed.

If the seizing person can be safely extricated while the convulsions are occurring, consider doing so and continue with care on deck. You should also extricate immediately if you cannot keep the person's head above water. Otherwise, remove the person from the water after the seizure stops.

Emergency Escape

A person struggling in the water who grabs you instead of a rescue tube or other means of flotation has one objective in mind: to stay on the surface. If you realize that you are about to be grabbed, try to get a quick breath of air and position your head so that you will not be choked if someone grabs your neck. Use the phrase "suck, tuck, and duck" to remind you to suck in a breath of air, tuck your chin, and try to duck away from the person's grasp.

If a struggling person does grasp you around your head or neck, submerge under the water (*a*). Often, that action will cause the person to release you, because his or her objective is to remain on the surface.

If the person does not release you, place your hands on the person's upper arms.

Press firmly up and away while you duck out from the grasp (*b*). When you are free, quickly move backward out of reach. An alternative method is to place your hands on the person's hips and press up and away from there. Surface, reposition your rescue tube, and attempt the rescue again.

After the Rescue

Bringing a responsive person successfully to the safe point of exit is not the end of a rescue. You still have several important tasks to complete. After you have effectively managed an aquatic rescue and are at the pool wall or shoreline, the next step is to help the person exit the water. Then provide follow-up instructions and complete the paperwork necessary to document the rescue before releasing the person from the scene.

Remove

When you get to the safe point of exit, help the person you rescued exit the water. When possible, have the person climb out a ladder or walk out of shallow water. If a person must prepare to climb out of the pool at the side, be sure to help secure the person's grasp and stay close. Take care not to embarrass or call unnecessary attention to the person.

Another word for removal from the water when a person can't do it alone is extrication. Methods for removing a person with a suspected spinal injury from the water are explained in chapter 8, and methods for extricating an unresponsive drowning person are explained in chapter 11. Extrication methods useful in a waterpark or waterfront setting are explained in chapters 15 and 16, respectively.

Instruct, Release, and Report

Document water rescues in a rescue report using clear, concise language. Include follow-up instructions and obtain all the requested information so that the report is complete. Avoid stating your opinions of what occurred; stick to the facts. A sample rescue report is included in the web resource in the module for chapter 7.

When the rescue report has been completed, the person can be released from the scene if

- the person did not lose consciousness, even for a brief period;
- a serious medical condition or injury is not suspected;
- the person has been observed and has normal rate of breathing, circulation, and skin color; and
- the person is fully responsive (awake and alert) and not coughing or shivering.

Any person—adult or child—who has been in or under the water and has symptoms of difficulty breathing, excessive cough, or foam or froth in the mouth or isn't acting right immediately or within a few hours of being in the water had a nonfatal drowning and should seek care from a doctor. Symptoms usually appear immediately but may be delayed by a few hours or get progressively worse. Onset or worsening of symptoms usually occurs within the first 8 hours of submersion.

Your facility should have a release policy based on the circumstances. For example, a child should be released to the parent or caregiver. The conditions of release might include being required to wear a life jacket or being restricted to certain areas while at the facility. Before release, do the following:

- Provide safety instructions and discuss the incident so that the person understands what caused the need for the rescue and how to prevent it from happening again.
- Provide warning to any person who has been rescued from a submersion incident, even if the submersion was for a short time. Instruct the person to watch for excessive cough, difficulty breathing, or any other worrisome symptoms that develop within the first 8 hours after the incident and to seek medical care immediately if these develop.

Be sure to include any release instructions or conditions that you provide on the report form.

▶ VISIT THE WEB RESOURCE

You can reinforce your learning by visiting the web resource, where you can do the following in the interactive online learning activities based on chapter 7:

- View videos of rescue techniques.
- Complete sample rescue reports with factual and complete information.
- Test your knowledge and receive feedback.

CHAPTER SUMMARY

Key points	Best practices on the job
• A dangling rescue tube strap is a safety hazard.	• Keep your weight back and your body to the side when performing a land-based assist.
• A rescue tube provides a layer of safety for you and the person you are rescuing.	• Use a rescue tube for all water rescues.
• A rescue tube may come loose from your grip if not tight against the chest during a compact jump.	• Gather dangling rescue tube strap in your hand or tuck behind the tube.
• For longer distances, swimming with the tube behind you on approach may be faster.	• To avoid injury, turn your head to the side before making contact during a rear rescue.
• When contacted from behind, a person may instinctively throw back his or her head.	• Hold the rescue tube tightly across the front of your body with strap gathered while making a compact jump entry.
• A goal of a front rescue is to keep the person out of reach of your head and body.	• Keep driving forward with locked arms during a front rescue.
• During a two-guard rescue the front rescue occurs just as the lifeguard doing the rear rescue makes a target.	• Practice leg wrap rescues in a variety of depths and situations.
• For a leg wrap rescue, place your feet and lower legs under the arms and around the person's upper torso and squeeze to maintain a grasp.	• Maintain adequate fitness and strength levels to perform basic water rescues appropriate for your work environment.
• For a leg wrap rescue bring the rescue tube in place across your chest before bringing the person to the surface and placing in a rear rescue.	• Complete factual and complete rescue reports.
• A person having a seizure cannot remain on the surface to breathe without assistance.	• Keep the head of a person having a seizure above the water.
• If a struggling person grabs you, take a breath, submerge, press away, and duck out.	• Regularly participate in scenario-based audits of your ability to perform assists, rescues, and an escape.
	• Provide safety instructions and warning to watch for delayed symptoms after a drowning incident before releasing a person back to your facility.

Part IV

Emergency Care

Managing Suspected Spinal Injuries

CHAPTER OBJECTIVES

This chapter

- describes evidence-based approach to spinal injury management,
- identifies conditions that raise suspicion of spinal injury,
- describes skills for active and passive spinal motion restriction on land and in the water,
- identifies the need for coordinating site-specific protocols with EMS,
- provides objectives of extrication from the water, and
- provides backboarding information.

A severe spinal injury can create permanent paralysis and change a person's life in a matter of seconds. Because you have no way to diagnose the extent of an injury, the objective when you suspect a spinal injury is to minimize spinal motion in a way that does not cause pain or further complication, while maintaining the person's ability to breathe. You will do this until EMS arrives.

Evidence-Based Approach to Out-of-Hospital Spinal Injury Management

In the past, the fear of making a minor injury worse resulted in every suspected incident, however minor, being treated by immobilization on a backboard (also known as a long spineboard). The use of head immobilization devices (HIDs) and multiple body straps for immobilization in an aquatic setting usually guaranteed an EMS transport to a hospital for X-ray or additional tests with increased risk of radiation.

Medical science has failed to show any studies which prove benefit of immobilization for a person with a suspected spinal injury, but have identified many studies which show harm cause by immobilizing a person on a backboard (White et al. 2014; Kwan et al. 2001). Among other factors, immobilization on a backboard restricts breathing, can cause pressure sores, and can lead to increased testing upon arrival at a hospital. Similarly, the thought that we run the risk of turning a minor injury into a major injury if we don't carefully provide in-line stabilization has never been substantiated. Research suggests that damage to the cervical spine and spinal cord occurs with the impact of the initial injury, not subsequent movement (Hauswald 2013). Some studies even show that less spinal movement occurs when people extricate themselves as compared with immobilization on a backboard (Shafer and Naunheim 2009, Dixon et al. 2015).

As a result of this evidence, placing a person on a backboard has become controversial in EMS and out-of-hospital medical care. Many EMS systems are no longer backboarding patients as agencies move toward evidence-based medicine (EBM) in all elements of care, including out-of-hospital medical care (Morrissey 2013). In addition, multiple professional societies recommend limitation or discontinuance of spinal immobilization (National Association of EMS Physicians 2013, Quinn et al. 2014, American College of Emergency Physicians 2015). The decision whether or not to backboard patients speaks to the importance of coordinating the EAP at an aquatic facility with the local or transporting EMS agency or agencies (Dworkin 2001). If both organizations agree on the most appropriate management of a person with a suspected spinal injury, the transfer of care, interface between the agencies, and overall patient care will be more straightforward.

The position of Starfish Aquatic Institute, after reviewing the medical literature and in consultation with its medical directors, is that strapping a person on a backboard and placing head immobilization devices (HIDs) for the sole purpose of immobilizing the spine is not an evidence-based practice. The preferred protocol for StarGuard lifeguards uses passive or active spinal motion restriction rather than immobilization methods. These methods are described later in this chapter.

In some locations, there will not be agreement between the recommended Star-Guard protocols and local EMS agencies regarding the management of a person with a suspected spinal injury. Recognizing that local institutional practices and EMS interfaces may vary, content is provided later in this chapter for lifeguards who work in situations where their employer or responding EMS agencies continue the practice of using a backboard for immobilization, and subsequent transport to hospital.

Causes and Symptoms of Spinal Injury

Spinal injuries do not occur on land, or in the water, unless some sort of forceful trauma causes the injury.

Trauma events in an aquatic environment that might cause a spinal injury include the following:

- Falling from a height greater than the person's height
- Forcefully striking the head on the bottom
- Suffering a blow to the head, neck, or back as a result of a high-velocity collision with another person or hard-object surface

Maintain vigilance for injuries by actively scanning to observe the occurrence of trauma and recognizing symptoms.

Certain symptoms suggest the potential for injury. Call EMS if a person who has experienced trauma to the head, neck, or spine also has any of the following:

- **I**ntoxication
- **N**eck, head, or back pain
- **DI**stracting injury (serious trauma anywhere on the body)
- **A**ltered mental status (confusion, altered consciousness, slowed thinking, loss of balance, impaired vision)
- **N**umbness/weakness (inability to move a body part normally)

The list of symptoms can be easily remembered as the first letter of each results in the word INDIAN. Use of this mnemonic tool will bring a realistic approach to spinal injury management in aquatic settings, and reduce risk of causing further harm. Some EMS agencies use INDIAN or other similar mnemonic tools to determine which patients require additional care or transport to a hospital.

Spinal Motion Restriction Versus Immobilization

There are significant differences between a protocol for spinal injury management based on spinal motion restriction and a protocol based on immobilization (see table 8.1). With spinal motion restriction, backboards should be avoided if a person can control movements and comfortably remove himself or herself from the water. When used, backboards should be considered an extrication tool similar to a stretcher rather than an immobilization device. The backboard has handles so rescuers can effectively remove the person from the water.

TABLE 8.1 Spinal Motion Restriction Versus Immobilization Protocols

Spinal motion restriction (preferred)	Immobilization (if directed by local EMS)
Use INDIAN to identify symptoms and need to activate EMS. **For an alert person with neck pain as the only symptom:** 1. Allow the person to self-restrict movement based on comfort and limiting pain (passive spinal motion restriction). If in the water, allow the person to exit on own with assistance if needed. 2. Monitor until EMS arrives. **For a person with additional INDIAN symptoms:** 1. Provide active spinal motion restriction by holding the person's head, on land or in the water. 2. If in the water, place person on backboard for ease of removal. Apply chest strap as needed for safety. If there is concern the person cannot hold their own head still to limit pain during extrication, continue active spinal motion restriction. Apply backboard headpieces if there are not enough rescuers to apply active spinal motion restriction. 3. Remove strap or headpieces if used. Monitor until EMS arrives.	For any person with potential of injury: 1. Provide in-line stabilization. 2. Place person on a backboard for immobilization. Apply head immobilization device (HID) and multiple body straps to prevent movement and package for transport. 3. If in the water, extricate. 4. Monitor and leave packaged for transport until EMS arrives.

If a person in the water is unresponsive and not breathing normally, treat as a drowning.

Passive Spinal Motion Restriction for a Person With Neck Pain

Passive spinal motion restriction is simply instructing the person to limit movement on their own, such as telling the person, "Don't move in any way that causes pain."

A person who is conscious (awake and alert), with neck pain as the only symptom can be managed with passive spinal motion restriction.

1. Identify yourself to the person and ask for permission to provide care.
2. Tell the person to respond to your questions with verbal answers, rather than nodding or shaking the head. Tell the person to remain calm, taking care to not perform any movements that cause additional pain.

3. Assist and guide the person into a seated or faceup lying position in a safe, comfortable area, preferably in the shade, if the person is not already in such a position. For example, with assistance, the person can be guided to get out of the water using a ramp, steps, ladder, zero depth, or chair lift based on availability, comfort, and mobility. When the person is out of the water, guide to a chair in the shade or to a first aid area.

4. Activate the EAP and call EMS as indicated. Keep the person comfortable and monitor for any changes or worsening in condition until EMS arrives.

Assist the injured person out of the pool.

Active Spinal Motion Restriction for a Person With Additional Symptoms

A person with additional symptoms beyond neck pain is more likely to be injured and may need active spinal motion restriction. Active spinal motion restriction occurs when another person manually holds the injured person's head to limit movement. The methods vary based on whether the person is on land or in the water.

On Land

1. Identify yourself to the person and ask for permission to provide care. Activate the EAP and call EMS as indicated.

2. Tell the person to respond to your questions with verbal answers, rather than nodding or shaking the head.

3. If the person is seated or standing, place your hands on either side of the person's head and apply just enough even pressure to hold the head still *(a)*.

It is preferred to let a person leave the head and neck in any position that does not cause pain.

If a person is laying faceup, from a position behind the person's head, place your forearms on either side of the person's head with your hands on the shoulders *(b)*. This technique has been shown to provide more control of motion than methods involving the head but not the shoulders (Boissy et al. 2011).

4. Maintain normal body temperature and closely monitor until EMS arrives *(c)*.

In the Water

If the person is submerged or lying facedown in the water, and you did not observe or are not aware of a forceful trauma event, you should immediately enter the water and begin rescue breathing if needed, without delay for active spinal motion restriction.

If you did observe or are aware of a forceful trauma event, enter the water using an entry appropriate for the circumstances, taking care to avoid jumping on or near the person. Consider an ease-in entry if the person is close to you. If the person is facedown, move quickly, because the person cannot breathe until rolled over.

Provide active spinal motion restriction using any of the techniques described here. These methods are effective to help keep the person's airway above the surface of the water, and allow ease of movement to a safe point of take-out. If the person is facedown, use a method that includes rolling the person over. If the person is unresponsive and not breathing, immediately begin care for drowning.

Vise Grip

Position yourself near the person's chest *(a)*. In deep water, position your rescue tube low on your hips; in shallow water, the rescue tube may not be necessary.

Reach over the person and place your hands on his or her upper arms between the elbows and shoulders. Press the person's arms into the head to form a "vise" to minimize movement *(b)*. After you make contact and squeeze the arms to the head, do not let go or readjust your hand position.

Vise-Grip Rollover

Position yourself next to the person so that you both are facing the same direction *(a)*. In deep water, position your rescue tube low on your hips; in shallow water, the rescue tube may not be necessary.

Reach over the person and place your hands on his or her upper arms between the elbows and shoulders *(b)*. Press the person's arms into the head to form a vise to minimize movement. After you make contact and squeeze the arms to the head, do not let go or readjust your hand position.

Roll the person over slowly, keeping pressure on the arms *(c)*. Move forward only if you need momentum to execute the roll or if you need to move the person into a horizontal position. At this point you do not know whether the person's mouth is open or closed, and forward movement could cause the person to swallow water. If the person is unresponsive when rolled over, immediately begin rescue breathing and treat as a drowning.

Vise-Grip Rollover Reverse

Position yourself next to the person. With your arm closest to the person's head, reach under the person and grasp his or her outside arm between the elbow and shoulder *(a)*. Place your hand that is closest to the person on his or her arm between the elbow and the shoulder. Press the person's arms into the head to form a vise to minimize movement.

Roll the person over slowly away from you by pushing away with the hand closest to your body *(b)*.

Keep pressure on the person's arms as you move to a safe point of exit *(c)*.

Rollunder

Your goal is to provide equal pressure along both the front and the back of the person before you initiate the roll. Place one of your hands on the back of the person's head, with your arm down along the spine *(a)*.

At the same time you place your hand and arm along the front of the person, place the fingers of your other hand on the person's cheekbones, with your arm down along the person's chest. Maintain even pressure from the front and back, and avoid covering the person's mouth with your hand. To roll the person, submerge yourself and rise on the other side *(b)*.

The objective of the spinal rollover is to have one of your arms along the person's spine and your other arm along the person's chest *(c)*.

Ease-Up to Vise Grip

Use this technique if you observed a forceful injury and the person is submerged in deep water and cannot return to the surface unassisted. The first objective of the ease-up technique is to make just enough contact with the injured person to initiate a weightless rise to the surface. The second objective is to position a rescue tube so that as soon as the person is near the surface and within reach, you can initiate a vise grip in a smooth transition. The use of flotation eliminates the need to tread water at the surface and is easily performed by one rescuer.

Position yourself above and behind the person. Maintain contact with your rescue tube and extend your body, feetfirst, toward the person (a).

Secure the person with your legs just under her or his armpits. Make just enough contact to initiate a rise to the surface (b).

As the person begins to rise to the surface, release your legs and move away from the person. Position yourself to perform a vise grip or vise-grip rollover if the person is facedown (c).

Roll the person over, if necessary, to begin performing a rescue. Talk to the person to check his or her level of consciousness (d).

This technique can be used to prepare for extrication or backboarding if needed.

Change-Up

If your arm is under the person while you are providing active spinal motion restriction, you will need to reposition your arm so the backboard can be placed under the person.

While in the vise-grip position, apply pressure with your outer hand to squeeze the person to your chest. When the person is tight against your chest, release the grasp of your hand that is closer to your chest, reach over the person, and place this hand next to your other one *(a)*.

Keep squeezing the person's body to your chest and slide your arm that is under the person toward your body. Make contact with the person's upper arm and apply pressure *(b)*. When you are applying even pressure to the person's arms with both of your hands, move her or him away from your chest.

Use of a Backboard as an Extrication Tool

The objective is to remove the person from the water without causing pain, or further injury as a result of the person falling off the board. The number of rescuers available, and the means of possible exit will determine the method to use in a particular circumstance.

When four or more rescuers are available:

- Place the backboard underneath the person. Apply a chest strap if the person will be carried out or lifted to a deck that is above the water surface more than 1 foot (.3m).

- Position evenly around the board and grasp the handholds.
- One person maintains active spinal motion restriction.
- Carry the person out at the stairs or zero depth entry. If walk out is not possible, lift the board to the deck and slide it out.

When two or three rescuers are available:

- Place the backboard underneath the person.
- Apply a chest strap. Consider using additional straps for safety if a person will be lifted to a deck that is above the water surface more than 1 foot (.3m).
- Position one or two rescuers on the deck and the other in the water, grasping the handholds at the top and bottom of the board.
- Direct the person to remain still during extrication and not move in any way that causes pain. If the person is unable to do this, consider using an head immobilization device (HID).
- On count, the rescuer(s) at the top of the backboard slides it up and out of the pool using the runners, rather than lifting. The rescuer in the water pushes and provides support.

Use of a Backboard for Spinal Immobilization in the Water

If your local EMS protocol still uses immobilization, the objective is to maintain inline stabilization of the head throughout the process, and transfer control of the head in a systematic method. The body is strapped to the board to prevent movement. The specific techniques need to be modified for and practiced for use in shallow or deep water. If your employer or local protocol requires you to backboard people with suspected spinal injuries, you must receive additional training using the equipment at the facility where you work.

Two-Rescuer Backboarding

Following is an example of how using a backboard for immobilization can be accomplished with two rescuers. The specific procedure in place at the facility where you work may be different.

- The rescuer on deck brings the backboard and places it vertically in the water by grasping the handholds at the top of the backboard and sliding it vertically along the pool wall as deep as possible. Extending the elbows to push the top of the board outward will press the bottom of the board against the pool wall and keep it from moving.
- The rescuer in the water moves in slowly to the wall, and the person is lined up with the backboard. The rescuer on deck pushes the top of the board down to submerge the board slightly and pulls it back to allow it to rise up under the person. The goal is to place the person high enough so that the head is centered on the HID pad.
- The rescuer on the deck kneels down, stabilizes the board on the edge of the gutter or deck, and uses the shoulder press to provide active spinal motion restriction.
- The rescuer in the water first straps the person's chest and then applies the rest of the body straps, while the rescuer on deck maintains active spinal motion restriction.

- The rescuer in the water takes over control of the person's head by placing the fingers on the person's cheekbones and the forearm along the person's chest. The rescuer places the other arm under the backboard and presses upward for support.

- The rescuer on deck places both HID pieces at the same time and then applies the head strap. The rescuer in the water maintains active spinal motion restriction and monitors the person's condition until the HIDs are in place.

- The rescuer in the water checks the security and tightness of the body straps and adjusts them if necessary. On count, both rescuers slide the backboard up and out of the pool using the runners, rather than lifting. If needed, the rescuer in the water can climb out to help from on deck.

Team Backboarding for Immobilization

Team backboarding uses a backboard for immobilization when more than four rescuers are available. The specific procedure in place at the facility where you work may be different.

- The rescuer in the water signals for help to activate the EAP and provides active spinal motion restriction. Additional rescuers bring the backboard and place it in the water parallel to the injured person.

- The initial rescuer maintains active spinal motion restriction, while the additional rescuers lift the side of the backboard at an angle and then press the board down and under the person. The injured person's head should be on the HID mounting area. The rescuers position evenly around the backboard.

- One or more of the additional rescuers apply the body straps, starting with the chest and following with the rest of the body. The rescuer at the foot helps stabilize the board.

- When strapping is complete, a rescuer takes over active spinal motion restriction by placing the fingers on the person's cheekbones and the forearm along the person's chest. The rescuer places the other arm under the backboard and presses upward for support. The rescuer at the head of the board places both of the HID pieces at the same time and then applies the head strap.

- A rescuer checks the body straps for security and tightness and adjusts them if necessary. The rescuer at the head climbs out onto the deck and lifts the board above the pool edge. The other rescuers position themselves at the foot of the backboard and help slide the board onto the deck. Alternatively, the rescuers may carry the board with the person out of the pool.

VISIT THE WEB RESOURCE

You can reinforce your learning by visiting the web resource, where you can do the following in the interactive online learning activities based on chapter 8:

- ◆ Identify causes of spinal injury in an aquatic environment.
- ◆ Identify when to call EMS for a suspected spinal injury.
- ◆ View demonstrations of passive and active spinal motion restriction methods.
- ◆ Test your knowledge and receive feedback.

CHAPTER SUMMARY

Key points	Best practices on the job
• Recent literature reviews have failed to show any studies which prove benefit of immobilization for a person with a suspected spinal injury, but have identified many studies which show harm caused by immobilizing a person on a backboard. • Passive and active spinal motion restriction methods are preferred over immobilization. • It is important to know the protocol the local EMS prefers for a coordinated effort. • Passive spinal motion restriction is as simple as telling a person not to move in any way that causes pain. • Active spinal motion restriction involves another person holding the injured person's head still. • Use INDIAN to identify symptoms of injury and determine when to call EMS. • It is preferred to use a backboard as an extrication tool, much like a stretcher, rather than for immobilization. • If a person is unresponsive, maintaining an open airway, giving rescue breaths, and performing effective compressions, always takes priority over spinal motion restriction.	• Understand the causes and symptoms of possible spinal injury. • When appropriate, direct a person to self-restrict movement through passive spinal motion restriction. • Perform active spinal motion restriction for a person who cannot do it themselves. • When needed, use a backboard or other appropriate device to extricate a person with a suspected spinal injury from the water. • Know and practice the spinal injury management protocol for your facility.

Basic First Aid

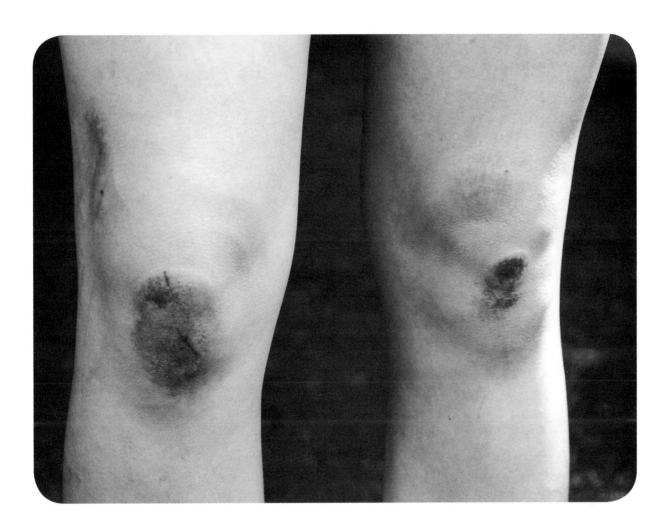

This chapter is reprinted and adapted, by permission, in part from American Safety and Health Institute with Human Kinetics, 2007, *Complete emergency care* (Champaign, IL: Human Kinetics). Updated information is licensed from the American Safety and Health Institute which is based on the latest international evidence-based science and treatment recommendations.

CHAPTER OBJECTIVES

This chapter

- reinforces the steps to recognize, assess, and prioritize first aid care, including how to triage multiple casualties and perform emergency moves when the scene is unsafe;
- identifies how to provide first aid care for injury; and
- explains how to provide care for sudden illness and altered mental status.

The more patrons who come through your gates every day, the more likely it is that some will become ill at your facility. Despite the best efforts to reduce risk, injuries may still occur.

Assessment and Scene Management

The first step in providing first aid care is to assess the situation and then alert others if you need help. You may also need to determine who is in need of immediate care if multiple people are involved (triage) and be prepared to move injured persons if the scene is unsafe.

PRIMARY ASSESSMENT*

Perform these steps quickly (a minute or less).

1. Assess the scene. If it is safe for you to approach, do so.
   - If the person is responsive, introduce yourself.
   - Let the person know that you are trained and there to help, and ask if it's OK to help.
2. Assess the person. Check for obvious life-threatening signs and symptoms. Ask the person or bystanders what happened.
3. Alert others, including emergency medical services (EMS), by activating your facility emergency action plan (EAP) if the person
   - is not breathing normally,
   - is unresponsive,
   - has severe bleeding,
   - is seriously injured,
   - has chest pain,
   - appears confused, or
   - cannot speak a simple sentence.

*Adapted, by permission, from American Safety and Health Institute with Human Kinetics, 2007, *Complete emergency care* (Champaign, IL: Human Kinetics), 19-64.

SECONDARY ASSESSMENT

If your first, or primary, assessment indicates no immediate life-threatening problems, conduct a secondary assessment.

Check for signs of injury to the person's head, neck, chest, abdomen, pelvis, and all four limbs through simple observation or by gentle touch.	If needed, remove or cut away clothing to get a better look at an affected body part. Compare one side of the body with the other. The acronym DOTS is helpful for remembering what to look for: • **D**eformities • **O**pen injuries or wounds • **T**enderness • **S**welling
Ask questions to gather information about the person's signs and symptoms and medical history.	Use the acronym SAMPLE to help you remember what to ask about: • **S**ymptoms: things the person is feeling such as pain, nausea, dizziness, or anything related to the situation • **A**llergies to medications, food, and environmental conditions • **M**edications that the ill or injured person is taking • **P**ast medical history that may be related to what is going on • **L**ast oral intake: what the person last ate or drank • **E**vents: what the person was doing just before symptoms began

Some people, especially young children, find it threatening when strangers want to touch their faces. If the person is anxious, start a physical assessment at the toes and work upward so that you can gain trust as you go. Speak face to face at eye level and be calm, friendly, respectful, and reassuring. If a child is more comfortable or calm with the parent, perform your assessment while the child is supported by the parent. In a critically ill or unresponsive child, you may need additional personnel to care for a distraught parent.

TRIAGE

Catastrophic events such as a waterslide or bleacher collapse, or natural disasters like a tornado or earthquake, chemical leak, or intentional acts involving explosions or weapons can cause multiple people to become injured or ill at the same time. In these mass casualty situations, you must use an organized approach to prioritize people by how urgently they need care. This process is called *triage*, a French word meaning "to sort," to provide the greatest good for the greatest number. Many methods of triage are used, so know which one your facility uses and practice it regularly. One method is described here.

First call out, "If you can walk, come to the sound of my voice."

Then move from person to person, quickly assessing their condition.

Sort those injured into four basic groups:

1. **Ambulatory** (able to walk). If people can walk, instruct them to remain at a safe location. People who are not ill, are uninjured, or have only minor injuries may be able to help provide first aid.
2. **Delayed**. The person does not have life-threatening injuries (e.g., a broken leg). Treatment may be delayed.
3. **Immediate**. The person has life-threatening injuries (e.g., profuse bleeding) that can be corrected or slowed down with minimal intervention. Rapid lifesaving treatment is urgent. These people will require evacuation first.
4. **Dead or expectant**. No signs of life, or death is expected because the nature of the injury cannot be corrected with the resources available.

Activate the EMS system early and convey the expected number of victims so that appropriate resources can be dispatched.

Use these steps as a guide for triage:

1. Assess for responsiveness. If the person is awake and responsive and no immediate life threats are present, such as profuse bleeding, consider the person delayed. *Move on to the next person. Begin with step 1.*

   If the person is unresponsive, tap or squeeze his or her shoulder and ask, "Are you OK?" If there is no response, move on to step 2.
2. Open the airway by tilting the head and lifting the chin. If the person takes a breath, place her or him on the side in the appropriate recovery position. This person is considered immediate. Move on to step 3.

   If the person does not take a breath, reposition the head to make sure that the airway is open. If the person still does not take a breath, consider him or her expectant. The time devoted to rescue breathing and chest compressions is not justified when multiple people need first aid. *Move on to the next person. Begin with step 1.*
3. Look for profuse bleeding. If present, take immediate action to stop it. If another first aid provider is available, ask her or him to maintain direct pressure on the wound. Consider this person immediate. *Move on to the next person. Begin with step 1.*

Remember that a person's condition can change, and, depending on available resources, you may need to reassess and triage all victims again. For example, a person with internal bleeding was considered ambulatory but is now unresponsive and considered immediate. Conversely, an initially unresponsive person may now be awake and alert, able to walk without difficulty, changing him or her from immediate to ambulatory. Triage based on life-threatening signs and symptoms, not how loudly a person is screaming or demanding help.

SIDE LYING RECOVERY POSITION

Place an unresponsive person who is breathing normally in the side lying recovery position.
Do not use the recovery position if the person has an injury to the neck, back, hip, or pelvis.

To place a person in the side lying recovery position:

- Assess for normal breathing *(a)*.

- Raise one of the person's arms *(b)*.

- Grasp the leg opposite the raised arm just above the knee and pull it up so the foot is flat on the ground *(c)*.

- Grasping the shoulder and hip, roll the person onto the side in a single motion, keeping the head, neck and shoulders from twisting *(d)*.

- Make sure the head ends up resting on the extended arm and the head, neck, and body are aligned. Roll far enough for the face to be angled towards the ground. Position the elbow and legs to help stabilize the head and body. Make sure there is no pressure on the chest that might restrict breathing *(e)*.

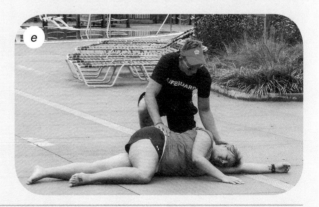

This position helps maintain an open airway, especially if the person vomits.

Frequently assess the breathing of anyone who has been placed in a recovery position, as condition can quickly become worse and require additional care.

EMERGENCY MOVES

Do not move or straighten an injured limb or move an injured person a distance unless it is necessary.	Move an injured person when • the scene becomes unsafe, • there is a chance of further injury (e.g., when the person is lying on a very hot or very cold surface), or • you cannot provide adequate care in the current location.
The fastest and easiest move is to use a drag.	Extremity drag: Grasp and pull on the person's ankles or forearms. Clothing drag: Pull on the person's shirt in the neck and shoulder area. Blanket drag: Roll the person onto a blanket and drag the blanket.

If you must move an injured extremity or injured person, take care to limit pain, reduce the chance for further injury, and facilitate quick and safe transportation to a health care facility.

When using a drag, pull in the direction of the long axis of the body. Never pull on a person's head or pull a person's body sideways.

When moving someone, use your legs, not your back, and keep the person's weight as close to your body as possible. Avoid twisting. Consider the person's weight and respect your physical limitations.

First Aid Care for Injury

Provide care based on the type of injury.

MANAGING SHOCK

Shock develops when poor blood flow creates a shortage of oxygen to body tissue. Any serious illness or injury has the potential to cause shock. If not treated early, shock can get worse and become life threatening. Early signs may be difficult to detect. Signs of shock may be the earliest indication of internal bleeding.

Signs and symptoms	First aid
A person may appear to be any or all of the following: • Uneasy • Restless • Worried • Confused Other more serious signs can develop gradually and progressively over time: • Responsiveness may diminish. • The skin may become pale, cool, and sweaty.	• A person in shock must get to a hospital as quickly as possible in order to survive. Early recognition, treatment, and activation of EMS are essential. Ensure an open and clear airway, confirm normal breathing, and control any external bleeding. • Then lay the person flat on the ground. It is ok to raise the feet about 12 inches if the person is uninjured and it does not cause pain or discomfort. • Maintain a normal body temperature. Insulate on top and underneath to prevent heat loss but be careful not to overheat. • Give nothing to eat or drink, even if the person asks for it. • Keep the person as comfortable and calm as possible and assess often until EMS arrives.

CONCUSSION

A significant blow or force to the head can result in internal injury to the brain. Most concussions are temporary and resolve naturally, but it is possible for one to progress into a life-threatening condition.

Signs and symptoms	First aid
Suspect a concussion if the person is unable to remember what happened just before or after the incident, or recall simple facts about it. Additional signs include: • Stunned or dazed • Headache • Nausea • Dizziness • Problems with balance or vision • Confusion • Loss of memory (before or after injury)	• Activate EMS or obtain access to another health care provider as soon as possible so that the person can be evaluated. • Do not allow the affected person to do anything that could pose a risk for additional injury (return to activity or sports, driving, use of machinery) until assessed and cleared by a health care provider.

CARE FOR WOUNDS

A wound is a break in the skin. All wounds need first aid, but EMS should be activated for major wounds or wounds that won't stop bleeding with firm direct pressure.

Type of injury: major wounds	First aid

Complete or partial loss of a body part	• Control any severe bleeding.
	• Treat for shock.
	• After the person is stable, locate the severed part if possible, because it may be able to be surgically reattached.
	   • Wrap the severed part in a sterile or clean cloth and place it in a tightly sealed plastic bag or waterproof container. Place the bag or container on ice.
	   • Do not soak the severed part in water, and do not put it directly on ice. Give it to EMS providers for transport with the person to the hospital.

Impaled object An impaled object is something that penetrates a body part and remains embedded.	• If necessary, remove clothing to confirm that the object has penetrated the skin. Look for any serious bleeding and control it with direct pressure. • Keep the person still. • Do not remove the impaled object. It can act like a plug and prevent serious blood loss, or it may be embedded into body parts or organs below the skin. • If needed, support the person's weight to relieve pressure on the object. Use padding to provide stability and comfort. • Treat for shock.
Open chest injury A puncture injury through the chest wall can disrupt the chest's ability to draw air into the lungs. Air movement can be indicated by foamy, bloody air bubbles. You may hear a sucking sound.	• Remove any clothing to expose the injury site. • Leave the open chest wound exposed. Do not apply any dressing or device. • If possible, allow the person to find and assume a comfortable position. • Reassure the person to keep her or him calm. Treat for shock. Regularly assess the injury until EMS arrives. • Treat for shock.
Open abdominal injury Injury to the abdomen may result in a condition known as evisceration, in which abdominal organs protrude through an open wound.	• The primary treatment is to protect the functioning organs from further injury. • Cover any organs with a thick, moist dressing. Do not try to push the organs back inside the body. • Do not apply direct pressure on the wound or exposed internal parts. • Treat for shock.

Type of injury: minor wounds	First aid
Breaks or openings in the skin • Abrasions (scrapes) • Lacerations (tear-like cuts) • Punctures • Incisions (caused by a clean sharp-edged object)	• If the wound is bleeding, apply direct pressure with a clean cloth or absorbent pad. • Wash with antibacterial soap and clean running tap water for about 5 minutes or until the wound is clean of foreign matter. • Apply triple antibiotic lotion or cream to speed healing and reduce infection. • Cover the area with an adhesive bandage or gauze pad.

CARE FOR WOUNDS

Type of injury: minor wounds	First aid
Splinter A splinter is a small piece of foreign material embedded into and just below the skin. Splinters need to be removed to keep the wound from becoming inflamed, leading to possible infection.	• Using a pair of tweezers, grab the protruding end of the splinter and pull it out along the direction it entered. • If the end is not protruding, use a small needle to loosen the splinter in the skin. Once you can grasp the splinter with tweezers, pull it out along the direction it entered. • If a splinter appears deeply embedded or you have been able to remove only a piece of it, the wound should be seen by a health care professional.

Encourage a person to have a wound evaluated by a health care professional when the wound has the following characteristics:

- Is deep or longer than half an inch, or about 1 centimeter (may need to be closed with stitches or skin glue)
- Is on the face, especially when close to the eye
- Involves injury to underlying structures such as ligaments or tendons
- Was caused by a dirty or rusty object
- Has dirt, stones, or gravel stuck in it
- Was caused by an animal or human bite
- Is extremely painful

CONTROL OF BLEEDING

Bleeding reduces the oxygen-carrying capacity of blood. If severe, it can quickly become life threatening. Remember to treat for shock whenever severe bleeding is present.

Type of injury	First aid
Severe bleeding from a wound	**Apply Direct Pressure** • Locate the point of bleeding. Rip or cut away the clothing if needed. • Place a clean absorbent pad directly over the wound. • Apply firm, direct pressure or instruct the person to do so. If a pad is not available, apply direct pressure with your gloved hand. 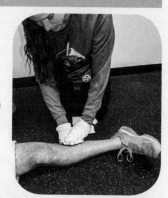 **Apply Pressure Bandage** • Wrap a roller *(a)* or elastic bandage *(b)* snugly over the pad. 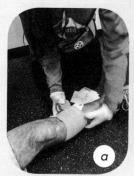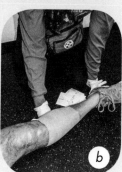 • Wrap with enough pressure to control bleeding but still allow a finger to be slipped under the bandage. • If bleeding continues or bandages become soaked, apply more pads or pressure bandages and maintain direct pressure. Do not remove the first pads or bandages.
Severe bleeding that cannot be controlled by direct pressure or if direct pressure cannot be applied effectively such as a mass casualty event, a person with large or multiple injuries, a dangerous environment, or for an inaccessible wound.	*If you are trained in the use of these options*, do the following: **Apply a Tourniquet** Commercially made tourniquets are ready to use and easier to apply than those made of improvised materials. A compressing band is snugly placed around a limb a few inches above the open injury. A solid handle, connected to the band, is used to tighten the band until bleeding stops. The handle is secured in place to maintain the constriction. Training in the application of a tourniquet is critical for its effective use. **Apply a Hemostatic Dressing** Manufactured hemostatic dressings are specially treated gauze that can be packed into a wound to help the blood clot and stop bleeding. These dressings are especially useful for body locations where direct pressure might not be effective (trunk, abdomen, groin) or when a tourniquet is not available or cannot control bleeding on its own.
Internal bleeding	A significant blow can cause bleeding inside the body that can be difficult to detect and impossible to stop without surgery. Signs of shock may be the earliest indication that internal bleeding is occurring. Other signs after abdominal trauma may include abdominal pain, nausea, and vomiting, bruising to the abdomen or sides. Early suspicion, based on the fact that a significant blow occurred to the body, and early activation of EMS are critical for effective treatment and, possibly, survival.

EYE AND FACE INJURIES

Type of injury	First aid
Toxic eye injury Any foreign substance that gets into the eye can cause a burning, red, bloodshot, or watery eye.	• Flush the affected eye with large amounts of tap water for at least 15 minutes. Use an eyewash station, drinking fountain, faucet, or garden hose running slowly. • If only one eye is injured, flush outward from the nose side of the affected eye to prevent contamination of the other eye. • When tap water is not immediately available, normal saline or another commercially available eye-irrigating solution can be used. • After flushing, if the person has pain or feels that something is in the eye, seek medical attention.
Chemical eye injury Corrosive chemicals splashed into an eye can quickly damage eye tissue and cause pain. Affected eyes will be red and watery.	• Identify the specific chemical that has injured an eye. • To get treatment recommendations, contact the local poison control center, a medical provider, or EMS. In the United States, the Poison Control Hotline is 800-222-1222.
Impaled object in the eye	• Activate EMS. • Stabilize the object and protect the eye from further injury. • Do not allow the person to rub the eye and do not try to remove the object. • For small objects, cover both eyes with loose gauze pads or a clean cloth. • Stabilize larger objects with a clean bulky cloth. Cover the uninjured eye with a loose gauze pad. Eyes move together. Covering both eyes prevents movement of the affected eye. • Having both eyes covered can be frightening. Calm, comfort, and describe what is happening to reduce anxiety.
Nosebleed A nosebleed usually involves one nostril.	• Have the person sit up straight with the head tilted forward. • Pinch the nose with the thumb and index finger for 10 minutes or have the person do this. • Have the person spit out any blood that collects in the mouth. • If the bleeding does not stop, seek immediate medical care. • *Do not* tilt the person's head back or have the person lie down. These actions may cause the blood to drip down the throat or into the stomach and cause vomiting. • *Do not* pack gauze in the nose. • Applying ice to the neck *is not* effective in controlling a nosebleed.
Dislocated or broken tooth	• If the lips, teeth, or gums are bleeding, have the person gently bite down on an absorbent pad. • An ice bag may help reduce pain and swelling. • Arrange for the person to be seen by a dentist as quickly as possible.
Knocked-out tooth	Make an immediate effort to get the person to a dentist. Early care (within an hour) gives the best chance for successfully reimplanting a tooth. Find the tooth and store it in a temporary solution of any of the following liquids, in order of priority: • Hank's Balanced Salt Solution (commercial product) • Bee propolis • Egg white • Coconut water • Ricetral (sodium chloride solution) • Whole milk If none of these solutions is immediately available, have the person spit, and place the tooth in the saliva. Handle the tooth only by the chewing surface (crown). Do not touch the root, the part of the tooth that embeds in the gum.

BONE, JOINT, AND MUSCLE INJURIES

The joints, muscles, and bones in the limbs are often exposed to external forces and injury.

Type of injury: soft tissue	First aid
Sprains Stretching or tearing injuries to ligaments that hold joints together **Strains** Stretching or tearing injuries to muscles or tendons **Muscle contusion** Bruising of a muscle	Distinguishing between the types of soft-tissue injuries can be difficult, so you should treat them all the same. • Apply cold to the area. A mixture of ice and water in a plastic bag or wrapped in a damp cloth works better than commercial gel packs. • Place a barrier, such as a thin towel, between the cold container and the skin. • Limit each application of cold to periods of less than 20 minutes.

Type of injury: bones	First aid
Fracture A break in the bone, which may or may not come through the skin **Dislocation** Separation of the bones	• Keep the limb in the position it was found. • Place your hands above and below the injury to stabilize the limb manually. • If bone is sticking out of the skin and bleeding is present, control it with direct pressure around the bone or injury site. • **If a painful, deformed, or swollen limb is blue or extremely pale, activate EMS or your emergency action plan immediately.** • If swelling is present, apply cold. (See soft-tissue injury.) • Apply a splint if you must move a person, EMS personnel are delayed or not available (e.g., during a natural disaster or a large-scale emergency), and you can do so without causing further injury or pain.

You can use a variety of materials to improvise a splint:

• Soft: towels, blankets, or pillows tied with bandaging materials or soft cloths
• Rigid: cardboard, wood, a folded magazine, a backpacker's sleeping pad

Follow these guidelines when you splint a limb:

• Immobilize the limb above and below the injury.
• Splint the limb in the position it was found.
• Pad the splints where they touch any bony part of the body to help prevent circulation problems.
• After splinting, check the limb frequently for swelling, paleness, or numbness. If present, loosen the splint.

BURNS

If a person is on fire, tell him or her to stop, drop, and roll.
If the person is in contact with electricity, shut off the power before providing care.

Type of burn	First aid
Minor burns symptoms • Pain • Redness • Swelling • Blisters	• Cool the burn area with cool or cold drinkable water as quickly as possible and continue cooling for at least 10 minutes. Do not apply ice. • Clean, cool, and cold (not frozen) dressings can be used to cool the burn if cool water is not available. • Cooling large thermal burns may cool the body overall, so take care to prevent hyperthermia, especially in children. • Leave blisters intact. After cooling, loosely cover the burn with a dry, sterile dressing. • Protect the burn from pressure or friction. • Avoid putting anything on the burn, including natural remedies.
Critical burns • Burns involving hands, face, eyes, ears, feet, and genitals • Electrical burns caused by contact with electrical wires, electrical currents, or lightning • Burns involving smoke inhalation, fractures, or other injury **Symptoms** • Skin may appear dry, leathery, white, blackened, or charred	• Activate EMS or obtain an immediate health care provider evaluation with any critical burn, especially if the burned person has blisters or broken skin, difficulty breathing, burns over a large surface area, or any general reason for concern. • Expose the burn. Cut and gently lift away any clothing covering the burn area. • If clothing is stuck to the burn, do not remove it. • Remove jewelry near the burn area if possible, because burns cause swelling. • Separate burned fingers or toes with dry, sterile nonadhesive dressings. • Lightly cover the burn area with a dry, sterile bandage or a clean sheet if the burn area is large. • If the burn was caused by electricity and the person is unresponsive, have someone get an AED if one is available. Perform CPR until an AED is ready. • If the burn was caused by electricity and the person is responsive, treat the burns you can see and seek medical assessment because the extent of the injury may not be apparent.
Chemical burns • Skin contact with wet, dry, or gaseous chemicals **Symptoms** • May cause an itching or burning sensation	• Brush off any dry chemical with a gloved hand. • Remove any contaminated clothing. • Flood the affected area with large amounts of water. Continue to flush with water for at least 15 minutes. • Cover any visible burns loosely with a dry, clean pad and seek further medical attention. • If a chemical gas has been breathed in, treat it as an inhaled poison.

First Aid Care for Illness and Altered Mental Status

A person who suddenly becomes ill usually has associated signs and symptoms. A sign is something you can observe. A symptom is something that the person complains about.

Altered mental status is a change in personality, behavior, or alertness that can range from mild anxiety to inability to speak and communicate to complete unconsciousness. It is a serious warning sign in both adults and children. The period of altered mental status may be brief or prolonged.

IDENTIFYING A POSSIBLE STROKE

A *stroke*, or brain attack, happens when the blood supply to part of the brain is suddenly interrupted or when a blood vessel in the brain bursts, spilling blood into the spaces surrounding the brain, causing brain cells to die.

Rapid diagnosis and treatment in the hospital is critical to limit the amount of brain damage and reduce long-term disabilities.

Signs and symptoms	First aid
• *Sudden* numbness or weakness of the face, arm, or leg, especially on one side of the body • *Sudden* confusion, trouble speaking, or trouble understanding • *Sudden* trouble seeing in one or both eyes • *Sudden* trouble walking, dizziness, loss of balance, or loss of coordination • *Sudden* severe headache • Ministroke (transient ischemic attack, or TIA): same symptoms as a stroke, but it lasts for only a few minutes and may lead to stroke *Note:* A person having a stroke might be mistaken for being drunk.	Use the FAST method to determine whether someone could be suffering from a stroke. **Face:** Ask the person to smile. Does it look uneven? **Arms:** Ask the person to raise both arms. Does one drift down? **Speech:** Ask the person to speak a simple sentence. Do the words sound strange? **Time:** If yes, immediately call EMS. • Do not give the person anything to eat or drink. • Calm, comfort, and reassure the person until EMS arrives. • Monitor closely for heart attack or sudden cardiac arrest.

IDENTIFYING A POSSIBLE HEART ATTACK

During a heart attack, blood flowing through the heart becomes blocked. A heart attack is different from sudden cardiac arrest (when the heart suddenly stops because of abnormal electrical activity in the heart) and has different symptoms and treatment.

Signs and symptoms	First aid
A heart attack can have a wide range of signs and symptoms, from slight to severe. • Chest pain or a dull discomfort behind the breastbone that may or may not spread to the arms, back, neck, jaw, or stomach • Shortness of breath • Nausea, dizziness, light-headedness • Heavy sweating • Fear of impending doom (feeling that something extremely bad is going to happen but not sure what) • Uncertainty and embarrassment • Denial (victim often refuses to accept or believe she or he may be having a heart attack, which can delay treatment and increase the risk of death) The absence of chest pain, especially in women, people with diabetes, and the elderly, does not mean that the victim is not having a heart attack. Women often describe indigestion rather than chest pain. Other unusual symptoms of heart attack include headache, ringing in the ears, dizziness, hiccups, and belching.	• Activate EMS immediately. If an automated external defibrillator (AED) is available, have someone get it. • Allow the person to find the most comfortable position in which to breathe. Loosen tight clothing. Calm, comfort, and reassure the person. • If available, encourage the person to chew one noncoated adult or two low-dose aspirin, unless the person is allergic or has recently had surgery or suffered a stroke, or you are uncomfortable with administration of aspirin. • Ask the person or any bystanders about prior problems or medications being taken. Assist the person in taking nitroglycerine if it is available and prescribed.

HYPOGLYCEMIA

Hypoglycemia occurs when blood sugar becomes very low. It is a common condition, especially in people with diabetes. Early treatment of mild hypoglycemia is important to keep it from progressing and becoming severe (diabetic emergency) and life threatening.

Signs and symptoms	First aid
<ul><li>Pale or sweaty</li><li>Altered mental status</li><li>Anxiety or trembling</li><li>Pounding heart</li><li>May appear drunk</li><li>Hungry or weak</li><li>Fainting</li></ul>	Do the following if the person is known to have diabetes and is responsive (awake, able to swallow),<ul><li>Attempt to raise the person's blood sugar level as quickly as possible by giving glucose tablets, or if they are not available, dietary sugars such as Mentos, Skittles, jelly beans, or orange juice.</li><li>Recognize that improvement will be gradual and give additional glucose tablets or dietary sugar and call EMS if the person does not improve and behave normally within 10 to 15 minutes.</li></ul>If the person is unresponsive or unable to swallow,<ul><li>do not give anything by mouth and</li><li>call EMS immediately.</li></ul>

SEIZURES

Most seizures happen without warning, last only a short time, and stop without any special treatment. People known to have frequent seizures do not usually need to go to the hospital.

Signs and symptoms	First aid
A simple seizure means no loss of consciousness.<ul><li>Staring spells</li><li>Confusion</li><li>Wandering aimlessly</li><li>Strange behavior</li></ul>A complex seizure means loss of consciousness.<ul><li>The person suddenly becomes stiff and falls to the ground.</li><li>Twitching or shaking of the body occurs (convulsions).</li><li>The person recovers quickly but may be confused.</li></ul>	Simple<ul><li>Do not restrain the person.</li><li>Guide the person away from dangerous situations.</li><li>Comfort, calm, and stay with the person until the seizure is over.</li></ul>Complex<ul><li>Stay calm and note the time.</li><li>To avoid injury move objects away from the person that he or she may strike.</li><li>Do not restrain the person.</li><li>Allow the seizure to take its course.</li><li>Do not put anything in the person's mouth, including your finger. The person has no danger of swallowing the tongue.</li><li>When the seizure is over, place the person in the recovery position.</li><li>Provide privacy to minimize embarrassment.</li></ul>

BREATHING DIFFICULTY OR SHORTNESS OF BREATH

Breathing difficulty or shortness of breath can be life threatening. It is common in persons with asthma but can also be a symptom of other serious medical emergencies.

Signs and symptoms	First aid
Symptoms can be very mild to life threatening. • Sudden onset of wheezing • Shortness of breath • Constant coughing • Chest tightness • Extreme difficulty breathing, with the chest and neck pulled in • Stooped body posture • Bluish color to lips and face	• Allow the person to find the most comfortable position in which to breathe. • Loosen any tight clothing. • If the person has prescribed medicine for asthma (using a nebulizer or metered-dose inhaler) and is unable to administer it, provide assistance. • Alert EMS if the person does not improve **five minutes** after the initial treatment with medication. A bluish-purple tissue color, especially in the lips or fingers, is a serious sign, indicating a developing lack of oxygen. Do not wait to see if the person's condition will improve. Activate EMS immediately, and if an AED is available, have someone get it.

SEVERE ALLERGIC REACTION (ANAPHYLAXIS)

Anaphylaxis is a sudden, life-threatening severe allergic reaction. It is usually caused by an insect sting or bite, or a specific food or product that the person is allergic to, such as peanuts or shellfish. Swelling of the lips, eyelids, throat, and tongue can block the airway, which can be fatal without prompt treatment.

Anyone with a history of anaphylaxis should keep an epinephrine auto-injector, or EpiPen, on hand at all times. The pen contains epinephrine, a substance that temporarily reverses the allergic reaction. The device is designed to work through clothing.

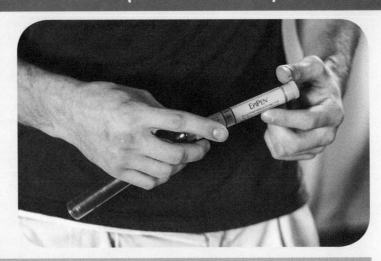

Signs and symptoms	First aid

Rapid onset of the following:
- Hives or itching
- Swelling of lips, eyelids, throat, and tongue
- Extreme difficulty breathing
- Coughing or wheezing
- Sensation of heart pounding
- Hives or itching
- Abdominal pain or cramping
- Altered mental status
- Blueness of skin, lips, nail beds
- Complete airway obstruction

- If the person carries an epinephrine auto-injector prescribed by a physician, help him or her use it. If the person is unable to use it, you should administer it, depending on the laws or regulation in your location. **Waiting for EMS may significantly increase the risk of death.**
- Activate EMS.
- If the person does not respond and EMS arrival will exceed 5 to 10 minutes, administer a second dose.

To administer an EpiPen, do the following:

1. Remove the EpiPen from the storage container. Do not use if the solution is discolored or a red flag appears in the clear window. Do not put your thumb, fingers, or hand over the tip.

   Form a fist around the injector unit and have the needle tip pointing downward *(a)*.

2. With your other hand, pull off the safety release cap *(b)*. Do not pull off the safety release cap until you are ready to administer the medication.

SEVERE ALLERGIC REACTION (ANAPHYLAXIS)

Signs and symptoms	First aid

3. Hold the needle tip near the person's outer thigh *(c)*.

4. Swing and jab the unit firmly against the outer thigh until it clicks so that the unit is at a 90-degree angle to the thigh.

5. Hold the auto-injector firmly against the thigh for approximately 10 seconds *(d)*. (The injection is now complete. The window on the auto-injector will show red.)

6. Pull the injector straight out *(e)*. The needle will retract underneath the safety cap. Massage the injection site for about 15 seconds.

7. Carefully place the used auto-injector, needle end first (without bending the needle), into the storage tube of the carrying case. Ask EMS providers for help in proper disposal.

SEVERE ABDOMINAL PAIN

Severe abdominal pain can be a warning sign of serious illness, especially if it appears suddenly or is a new experience for the person.

Symptoms	First aid
Rapid onset of any of the following: • Severe pain • Rigid abdomen • Abdomen tender to touch Nausea and vomiting may be present along with pain.	• Activate EMS. • Allow the person to find a position of comfort to relieve the pain. • Do not give the person anything to eat or drink.

EMERGENCIES DURING PREGNANCY

Illnesses and problems can occur during pregnancy that have symptoms of severe abdominal pain and can put both mother and child in danger. Activate EMS. If significant vaginal bleeding is occurring, have the woman press a sanitary pad or towel to the area. Have the woman assume the position that makes her most comfortable. If a side-lying position is preferred, place the woman on her left side in the recovery position.

POISONING AND OPIOID OVERDOSE

To determine whether a substance is a poison, call the Poison Control Hotline at 800-222-1222 (in the United States) to talk to a poison expert. When possible, know the name of the product or toxic substance, the circumstances, and time of exposure.

Type of substance	First aid
Swallowed poisons Poisons that can enter the body through the mouth include the following: • Household cleaning products • Cosmetics • Pesticides, paints, solvents • Contaminated foods • Poisonous plants or plant parts	• Talk to a poison expert or activate EMS if the person exhibits sleepiness, seizures, difficulty breathing, or vomiting. • Do not give anything by mouth or try to induce vomiting. • If possible, obtain the bottle, container, or a sample of the poisoning substance to take to the hospital emergency department.
Skin contact poisons Poisons that can enter the body through contact include the following: • Corrosives (alkalis, acids, hydrocarbons) • Poisonous plants (poison ivy, oak, sumac)	• Quickly remove contaminated clothing. • Quickly and lightly brush off any dry chemical or substance that is on the skin. Use a cloth or gloved hand. • Rinse skin with large amounts of water. • Take care that you don't contaminate yourself. • Talk to a poison expert or activate EMS if the person exhibits sleepiness, seizures, difficulty breathing, or vomiting.
Inhaled poisons Poisons that may be in the air and enter the body while breathing include the following: • Chlorine gas • Natural gas • Carbon monoxide • Harmful dusts, fogs, fumes, mists, gases, smokes, sprays, or chemical vapors	• Get the person to fresh air right away. • Monitor for signs of difficulty breathing or other symptoms and treat accordingly. • Talk to a poison expert or activate EMS if the person exhibits sleepiness, seizures, difficulty breathing, or vomiting.
Opioid overdose In high doses, opioids such as morphine, heroin, tramadol, oxycodone, and methadone can cause respiratory depression and death. Opioid overdose is a public health crisis. Symptoms include the following: • Altered mental status—unable to talk or respond • Slow, shallow breathing or no breathing • Slow, erratic, or no pulse • Pale, clammy face • Choking sounds or snore-like gurgling sounds	• Activate EMS immediately and begin CPR if needed. • If available and you are trained, administer naloxone. Naloxone is an antidote to opioid overdose and can completely reverse its effects if administered in time. Naloxone administered by bystanders, particularly by family members and friends of those known to be addicted, is a potentially life-saving treatment.

BITES AND STINGS

Bites and stings can occur from a wide variety of insects, reptiles, other animals, and even humans. Most are not serious and cause only minor reaction such as swelling, redness, pain, and itching. Some bites and stings are more serious and create severe reactions, especially for people who are very young or old, have existing medical issues, or are allergic.

Type of bite or sting	First aid
All snakebites • Single or double fang marks • Intense, burning pain and localized swelling • Possible bleeding	• Have the person sit passively, and activate EMS. • Control bleeding, if present. • Cover the bite with an adhesive bandage or gauze pad. • Keep the injured part immobilized below heart level. • Do not cut through snakebite wounds or apply suctioning, ice, or tourniquets. These actions are of no proved value and may be dangerous.
Coral snakebite A bite from a coral snake may have delayed symptoms and whole-body effects such as nausea, vomiting, sweating, weakness, altered mental status, difficulty breathing, and rapid heart rate.	Apply a pressure bandage around the entire length of the bitten extremity to slow the spread of the venom. The pressure bandage should be snug but not so tight that you cannot slip a finger under it.
Venomous spider bite Minor reaction: Small puncture marks and possible bleeding. Over time, tenderness, swelling, pain, itching, redness, and heat at the site can develop. Severe reaction: Whole-body effects can occur, including cramping pain and muscular rigidity in the abdomen or shoulders, back, and chest; fever; chills; rash; anxiety; weakness; nausea or vomiting; difficulty breathing.	• Keep the person warm, reassured, and quiet. • Seek medical attention. • Activate EMS for a severe reaction.
Insect sting Minor reaction: Bite site painful, red, swollen, itchy Severe reaction: Potentially fatal, whole-body affect that may include hives (raised itchy bumps on skin), swelling of mouth or throat or both, shortness of breath or difficulty breathing, nausea or vomiting, chest pain or palpitations, anxiety or weakness, fainting	Minor reaction: • If the stinger is present in the skin, remove it by scraping with a fingernail or edge of a rigid piece of plastic such as a credit card. • Wash the sting site with clean running tap water for several minutes. • Cover the area with an adhesive bandage or gauze pad. • Apply ice to reduce pain and swelling. Place a thin towel or cloth between the cold source and the skin and limit application to 20 minutes or less. • Consider using over-the-counter anti-itch medications such as calamine lotion or Benadryl. Severe reaction: • Activate EMS. • If the person carries a prescribed epinephrine auto-injector, help her or him use it, or if she or he is unable, you should administer it (see the table Severe Allergic Reaction [Anaphylaxis]).

BITES AND STINGS

Type of bite or sting	First aid
Tick bite The primary concern with a tick that has attached itself to the skin is the transmission of disease.	To remove a tick, do the following: • Grasp it close to the skin with tweezers or use your fingers protected by gloves. Pull straight up with a steady, slow motion. • If portions of the tick remain embedded in the skin or symptoms of a severe reaction develop, seek medical attention. • Do not use heat, alcohol, or ointments to remove a tick.
Marine animal sting Minor reaction: pain at the sting site; raised, red itchy rash Severe reaction: difficulty breathing, heart palpitations, weakness, fainting	• Carefully wipe off stingers or tentacles using forceps or by scraping them off with the edge of a rigid piece of plastic such as a credit card. • As soon as possible, wash the sting site with vinegar for at least 30 seconds. • Shower or place the site in hot water (as hot as the person can tolerate) for at least 20 minutes or until the pain subsides. • If a wound results from a stingray barb, carefully clean out the wound site. • If spines from a sea urchin are embedded, carefully remove them with tweezers or use your fingers protected by gloves. • If a severe reaction occurs, activate EMS.
Human or animal bites • Pain • Bleeding • Wounds • Possible tissue amputation	• Control bleeding if present. • Wash the site with clean running water for about 5 minutes. • Cover the area with an adhesive bandage or gauze pad. • Apply ice to the area to reduce pain, bleeding, and swelling. • For a severe bite, activate EMS. • Save any tissue parts that were bitten off. Treat them as you would an amputation.

EXPOSURE TO HEAT (HYPERTHERMIA) AND DEHYDRATION

Exposure to hot and humid conditions can lead to dehydration, heat exhaustion, and heatstroke. These serious conditions require immediate attention. Do not underestimate the seriousness, especially if the person is a child or elderly.

Signs and symptoms	First aid
Exertional dehydration	• In the absence of shock, confusion, or inability to swallow, give the person a carbohydrate-electrolyte beverage (e.g., sports drink) or coconut water to drink. If these beverages are not available, give water. • Treat for heat exhaustion if additional symptoms are present.
Heat exhaustion Early signs and symptoms • Heavy sweating • Thirst • Minor muscle twitches that lead to painful cramping Later signs and symptoms • Pale, cool, and moist skin • Headache • Nausea and vomiting • Weakness, dizziness • Feels faint or collapses	• Move the person to a cooler place. • Loosen or remove excess clothing. • Have the person lie down and raise the legs 6 to 12 inches (14 to 30 cm). • Spray water or apply cool, wet cloths to the person's head and torso. Use a fan if available to speed evaporation. • Give the person a cool sports drink to replace lost fluids, salts, and minerals. If not available, give water. • If the person does not improve within a few minutes or seems to get worse, activate EMS.
Heatstroke Many or all of the symptoms of heat exhaustion, along with the following: • Altered and decreasing mental status (confusion, hallucinations, bizarre behavior, seizure, unresponsiveness) • Possible hot, red, dry skin	• Activate EMS. • Move the person to a cooler place but do not delay aggressive body cooling to do so. • Spray or pour water on the person and fan him or her. • Apply ice pack to the person's neck, groin, and armpits or cover the person with a wet sheet. • Place the person in the side-lying recovery position. • Provide continuous cooling until EMS arrives. • Do not give the person anything by mouth if she or he is vomiting or unresponsive.

EXPOSURE TO COLD (HYPOTHERMIA)

Cold, wet temperatures or being in cold water can result in a lowering of the internal body temperature. Hypothermia can be life threatening.

Signs and symptoms	First aid
Early signs and symptoms • Pale, cold skin • Uncontrollable shivering • Difficulty speaking • Loss of coordination • Altered mental state Later signs and symptoms • No shivering • Slow (or absent) breathing or heartbeat	• Get the person to a warmer place. • Remove wet or constricting clothes and replace them with dry clothes and blankets. • Cover the person's head and neck to help retain body heat. • Place the person near a heat source and place containers of warm, but not hot, water in contact with the skin. • Do not massage limbs, give anything to eat or drink, or allow the person to expend energy. • Activate EMS if symptoms do not improve or worsen or the person is unresponsive.

 # VISIT THE WEB RESOURCE

You can reinforce your learning by visiting the web resource, where you can do the following in the interactive online learning activities based on chapter 9:

◆ Conduct a virtual primary and secondary assessment.

◆ View videos of how to place a person in a recovery position.

◆ Evaluate scenarios and decide the best treatment.

◆ Check your knowledge and receive feedback.

CHAPTER SUMMARY

Key points	Best practices on the job
• All blood and other bodily fluids should be treated as if they are contaminated. • Survey the scene before approaching. If it is not safe, get out! • SAMPLE helps gather information about signs and symptoms. • DOTS helps gather information about injury. • Triage may be necessary in the event of mass casualty. • Direct pressure is the first choice for control of severe bleeding; use of a tourniquet or hemostatic dressings are other options. • Do not move an injured person or straighten a limb unless necessary. • A person in shock must get to a hospital as quickly as possible. • Do not cover an open chest wound. • Call Poison Control Hotline for a person with chemicals in the eye. • A person with a nosebleed should sit straight up with head tilted forward. • Make an immediate effort to get a person with a knocked out tooth to the dentist. • Place your hands above and below the injury to stabilize a fracture. • A person with a suspected concussion must be evaluated by a doctor or healthcare provider. • Cool a burn area with cool or cold water for at least 10 minutes. • Place an unresponsive person who is breathing in the recovery position. • Use the FAST method to determine if a person may be suffering from a stroke. • A heart attack is different than sudden cardiac arrest (SCA). • Hypoglycemia occurs when a person's blood sugar is very low; Mentos, Skittles, or other dietary sugar can help. • Do not restrain a person having a seizure. • Breathing difficulty can be life-threatening. • Anaphylaxis is a severe allergic reaction that can be stopped by using an EpiPen. • Severe abdominal pain can be a warning sign of serious illness. • Opioid overdose should be treated with a Naloxone antidote. • Some bites and stings can cause serious reactions. • Exposure to hot and humid conditions can cause dehydration, hyperthermia, and heat stroke. • Exposure to cold can cause hypothermia and frostbite.	• Use personal protective equipment when administering first aid and follow infection-control procedures. • Introduce yourself and ask permission to provide care if a person is conscious. • Conduct a primary and secondary assessment to determine what care is needed. • Recognize and provide basic and appropriate care for injury. • Recognize and provide basic appropriate care for sudden illness or altered mental states. • Understand when to activate EMS. • Regularly practice basic first aid skills for a variety of scenarios.

Basic
Life Support

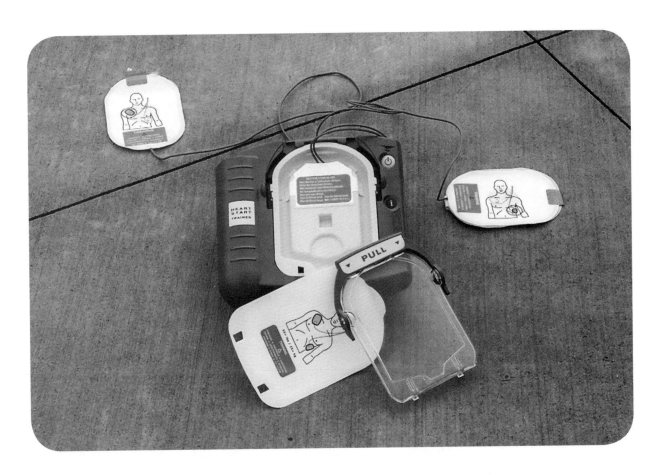

This chapter is reprinted and adapted, by permission, in part from American Safety and Health Institute with Human Kinetics, 2007, *Complete emergency care* (Champaign, IL: Human Kinetics). Updated information is licensed from the American Safety and Health Institute which is based on the latest international evidence-based science and treatment recommendations.

CHAPTER OBJECTIVES

This chapter

- describes Sudden Cardiac Arrest (SCA) and secondary cardiac arrest;
- provides information at the professional rescuer level about rescue breathing, cardiopulmonary resuscitation (CPR), and automated external defibrillation (AED), which together are known as basic life support (BLS);
- identifies how to provide rescue breathing for a person who has a pulse but is not breathing;
- explains how to provide high-performance CPR and how to use an AED until EMS arrives;
- considers special conditions for CPR; and
- describes how to aid adults, children, and infants who are choking.

Cardiopulmonary resuscitation (CPR) allows a responder to restore limited oxygen to the brain through a combination of chest compressions and rescue breaths to delay brain cell death until the person's breathing and heartbeat are restored, if possible.

Sudden Cardiac Arrest (SCA)

The most urgent and frequent need for CPR occurs if an adult suddenly collapses or is unresponsive and without normal breathing or an obvious pulse. In these circumstances, sudden cardiac arrest is the likely cause. SCA occurs when the heart's electrical system malfunctions and the heart abruptly stops working without warning. SCA is different from a heart attack, which is caused by a blockage in the heart that prevents blood flow.

SCA is one of the leading causes of death among adults in North America. When SCA occurs, most persons have an abnormal heart rhythm known as ventricular fibrillation, or v-fib. The normal electrical impulses in the heart unexpectedly become disrupted and disorganized. The normally coordinated contraction of the heart muscle is lost and replaced by a chaotic, quivering condition. Blood flow to the brain and vital organs abruptly stops. The lack of blood flow and oxygen supply to the brain causes the person to lose consciousness and collapse. Abnormal gasping can occur. Breathing may stop completely. Without early recognition and care, the person will not survive.

CPR is the immediate treatment for a suspected sudden cardiac arrest. However, CPR alone is not enough, because the heart must be shocked to return to a normal rhythm.

The most effective way to end fibrillation is defibrillation, using a defibrillator and electrode pads applied to the chest. An automated external defibrillator, or AED, is a small, portable, computerized device that is simple for anyone to operate. A controlled electrical shock is sent through the heart to stop ventricular fibrillation, allowing the heart's normal electrical activity to return and restore blood flow. Successful defibrillation is highly dependent on how quickly it occurs.

The **sudden cardiac arrest chain of survival** is often used to describe the best approach for treating sudden cardiac arrest. Each link in the chain is essential for a person to survive. If a single link is weak or missing, the chances for survival are greatly reduced. The greatest chance for survival exists when all the links are strong:

1. Early recognition of cardiac arrest and activation of EMS
2. Immediate CPR with high-quality chest compressions
3. Rapid defibrillation, or electrical shock, to the heart
4. Effective basic and advanced EMS care and transport
5. Effective post-cardiac arrest care at a hospital

SCA usually occurs in active, outwardly healthy adults or teens with no known heart disease or other health problems. SCA occurs less frequently in children. The most common causes of SCA in a child is a hard blow to the chest, which causes a disruption of the heart's regular rhythm.

Secondary Cardiac Arrest

Unlike sudden cardiac arrest in which the heart is the primary problem, cardiac arrest can also be the end result of a loss of airway or breathing. Without oxygen, the heart slows and eventually stops. This is known as secondary cardiac arrest. Problems that can result in secondary cardiac arrest include

- drowning;
- choking;
- drug overdose, especially opioids and heroin;
- hazardous breathing conditions in confined space; and
- underlying medical conditions.

In these instances, immediate CPR, with an emphasis on effective rescue breaths, may be the only chance to restore signs of life.

Children are more likely to experience a secondary cardiac arrest rather than SCA. This is an important consideration in how you approach a child or infant you think may have arrested. CPR procedures differ slightly for adults, children, and infants. Although no single factor can distinguish an infant from a child and a child from an adult, to simplify training, CPR guidelines use the age ranges in the following list:

- An adult is anyone eight years old or above.
- A child is one year old to eight years old.
- An infant is less than one year old.

Determining age can be difficult, and exactness is not necessary.

The chain of survival for children includes the following links:

1. Prevention of the typical causes for airway and breathing emergencies
2. Early CPR, with an emphasis on effective rescue breaths to reverse the effects of a weakened heart, and, if needed, defibrillation with an AED
3. Prompt activation of EMS to quickly get professional care

4. Rapid pediatric advanced life support procedures and medications used by paramedics, nurses, or doctors to help sustain the chance for recovery and survival

5. Integrated post-cardiac arrest care to increase the likelihood for long-term survival

Assessment

The first steps in treating a person who has collapsed or is unresponsive is to conduct a primary assessment to see whether the person needs rescue breathing or CPR. The assessment is simply a quick check for normal breathing and an obvious pulse and should take no longer than 10-15 seconds.

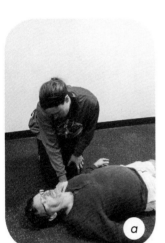

- Before anything else, pause and assess the scene for hazards. If the situation is dangerous to you, do not approach. If safe to do so, tap or squeeze the person's shoulder. Ask loudly, "Are you OK? *(a)*" If the person does not respond, signal or yell for help.

- With the person faceup on a firm, flat surface, look quickly at the face and chest for normal breathing and check for an obvious pulse. Normal breathing is effortless, quiet, and regular. Do not be fooled by gasping actions. Weak and irregular breathing, gasping, snorting, or gurgling is not considered normal.

- To check for an obvious pulse slide your fingers into the groove between the bump at the front of the neck and the muscle next to it *(b)*. If pulse is not obvious within 10 seconds, assume it is absent and immediately begin care *(c)*.

For an infant, check for responsiveness by tapping the bottom of the foot *(d)* and check the brachial pulse in the upper arm *(e)*.

- If normal breathing is found, place an uninjured person in the side recovery position. A person who is breathing normally will have a pulse.

- If the person is not breathing, or only gasping, and does not have an obvious pulse, send someone to call EMS and to get an AED while you begin CPR. *If you are alone with an adult*, place in a recovery position, call EMS, and get an AED yourself. *When alone with a child or infant*, provide 2 minutes of care first.

- If the person is not breathing, or only gasping, and has an obvious pulse, perform rescue breathing only.

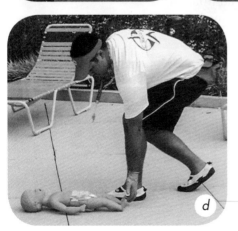

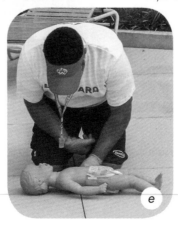

Chest Compressions

External compressions of the chest increases pressure inside the chest and directly compresses the heart, forcing blood to move from the chest to the lungs, brain, and the rest of the body. Creating and maintaining this pressure not only keeps vital organs alive but also increases the chances that defibrillation will be successful.

After chest compressions are started, it takes time to build up enough pressure to make blood flow. When chest compressions are stopped, the pressure and blood flow drop quickly. Thus, frequent interruption of chest compressions may contribute to poor survival rates. For that reason, minimize interruptions in chest compressions during CPR.

Adult or Child

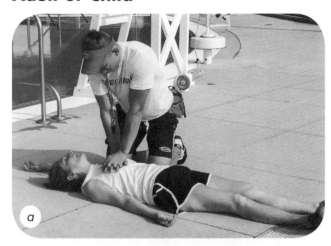

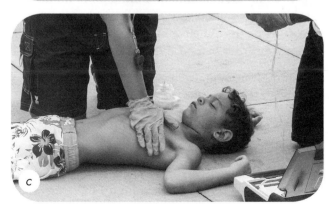

- Position the person faceup on a flat, firm surface. Kneel close to the side of the person. You may find it helpful to raise the person's arm overhead to allow your knees to get in close to the body *(a)*.
- Place the heel of one hand on the center of the chest, on the lower half of the breastbone. Place the heel of your other hand on top of the first. You can interlace your fingers to keep them off the chest. For a child, you may use one or two hands *(b)*.
- Bring your body up and over the chest so your shoulders are directly above your hands. Straighten your arms and lock your elbows.
- Bending at the waist, use your body weight to push straight down to a depth of at least 2 inches (5 cm), but not much more. For a child, compress at least 1/3 the full depth of the chest *(c)*.
- Lift your hands enough to release the pressure on the chest and allow it to recoil fully to its normal position. Do not lean on the person's chest.
- Without interruption, immediately move into the next compression. Continue compressions at a rate between 100 to 120 times per minute.

Quality matters! The better you compress, the greater the influence on survival. Focus on high-quality techniques. Avoid leaning on the person's chest between compressions.

Infant

- Position the infant faceup on a flat, firm surface. Place two fingertips on the breastbone just below the nipple line *(a)*.
- Compress at least one-third the diameter of the chest, or about 1 1/2 inches (4 cm). Lift your fingers and allow the chest to recoil fully to its normal position. Without pausing, continue into the down stroke of the next compression. Without interruption, continue compressing at a rate between 100 to 120 times per minute. Keep up the force and speed of compressions, but be sure to allow the chest to fully recoil to its normal position between compressions.
- When two or more rescuers are present, compress the breastbone using two thumbs, with your fingers encircling the chest. This position allows for more effective compressions. The other rescuer will be providing rescue breaths *(b)*.

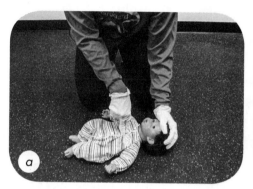

Opening the Airway and Rescue Breathing

Rescue breaths are artificial breaths given to someone who is not breathing normally. They are given by blowing air into the mouth to inflate the lungs. The airway is the only passageway between the mouth and lungs. It must be open so that air can freely enter and leave the lungs.

Someone who is unresponsive can lose muscle tone. If flat on his or her back, the base of the tongue can relax and block the airway. The tongue is attached to the lower jaw. Lifting the jaw forward while keeping the mouth open pulls the tongue away from the back of the throat and opens the airway. Regardless of the method used to open the airway, these are important considerations.

The risk of contracting a disease while giving CPR or during CPR training is extremely low, but as a trained provider you should use a protective barrier device such as a CPR mask when giving rescue breaths to help you avoid exposure. You can open the airway from beside the person or from behind the person's head.

- If you are alone, the head-tilt, chin-lift from the side will usually be best so you don't have to interrupt care to move position for compressions.
- If you are with other rescuers, a triple airway maneuver from a position behind the head is a convenient and effective approach, especially if you will be using a bag-valve mask or AED.
- Establishing an airway for an unresponsive person is a higher priority than protecting a suspected injury to the spine. Tilt the head and lift the chin when necessary to open the airway.

- If you remove your hands from the head, the airway will close again. You will need to open the airway each time you give rescue breaths.

The steps for opening the airway and giving rescue breaths should take no longer than about 10 seconds.

With a CPR Mask

1. Place the Mask

Inspect the mask to make sure that the one-way valve is in place. Place the mask flat on the person's face by placing the top of mask over the bridge of the nose, if using a triangle shaped mask, or with the opening over the person's mouth if using a "blob" style mask. The person's mouth should be slightly open. Use your thumbs and forefingers to provide uniform pressure around the mask. Practice regularly with your equipment before an emergency, as mask styles and hand placement to create a good seal vary. With some masks it may be more effective to open the airway first, then place the mask and make a seal.

2. Open Airway

From the side, tilt the head and lift the chin. Place your hand on the person's forehead. Place the fingers of your other hand under the bony part of the chin. Apply firm, backward pressure on the forehead while lifting the chin and thrusting the jaw upward to lift the face up into the mask to create a tight seal. Use the thumb of your hand lifting the chin to control the bottom of the mask. Maintain the head tilt with your hand on the forehead. Avoid pressing into the soft tissue of the chin with your fingers, which can obstruct the airway. Use your thumbs and fingers as necessary to maintain an airtight seal of the mask on the face.

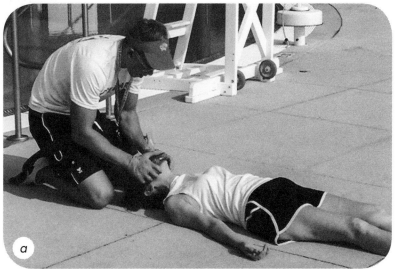

In an infant, tilt the head and lift the chin only slightly to open and maintain an airway.

From behind the head, use the triple airway maneuver *(b)*. Place one hand on each side of the person's head and use your thumbs and heels of your hands to hold the mask in place. Then place your index fingers under the angles of the person's lower jaw, just below the ear. **Lift and tilt** the person's head back. Press up with your index fingers to **thrust the jaw forward**. Use your thumbs to **open the mouth** and press the person's face up into the mask. Reposition your fingers to make a good seal if needed.

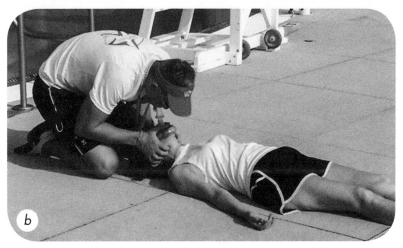

3. Give Breaths

Take a normal breath and blow through the valve opening *(c)*. Your exhaled air still contains enough oxygen to keep someone alive. Each breath should be about one second and make the chest visibly rise, but no more. Remove your mouth and let the person exhale completely. In CPR two rescue breaths are given at a time. Take a fresh breath before delivering another rescue breath.

For an infant give a puff of air *(d)*.

With a Bag-Valve Mask (BVM)

A bag-valve mask device (also known as a bag-mask device) allows rescuers to provide rescue breaths without having to blow into a person's mouth, offering the best barrier protection.

1. Prepare Bag-Valve Mask

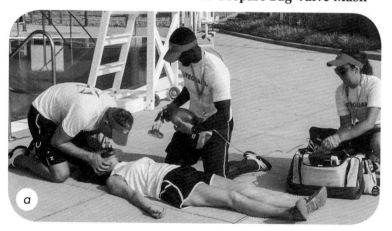

To provide high-quality rescue breaths, two rescuers should use the bag-valve mask. Provide rescue breaths with a CPR mask until the bag-valve mask is ready *(a)*. Inspect the bag-valve mask to make sure that it is ready for use. Bag-valve mask rescue breaths for children or infants are done in the same manner as for an adult. The size of the device should be appropriate for the age and size of the person. If using supplemental oxygen, connect to the bag-valve mask and allow the reservoir bag to fill completely. Flow rate should be at least 10 liters per minute.

2. Place the Mask and Open the Airway

Position yourself above the person's head. While a second provider holds the bag with both hands, place the mask flat on the person's face *(b)*. Place your palms and thumbs on both sides of the mask. Hook your fingers under the angles of the jaw, just below the ears. Open the airway from behind using the triple airway maneuver.

3. Deliver Breaths

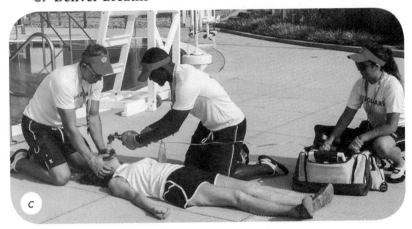

Have a second person squeeze the bag to deliver a breath and then release to let the bag fill with air before squeezing again to provide a second breath *(c)*. Each breath should be one second in length. Create a visible rise of the chest, but no more.

With a Face Shield

Face shields minimize direct contact with a person but are not the first choice for those who respond at the professional rescuer level. In some instances, however, a face shield may be the only barrier available.

1. Place the breathing port of the shield over or into the person's mouth. Spread the rest of the shield flat over the person's face. Tilt the person's head and lift the chin to establish an open airway.

2. Pinch the person's nostrils closed either under or over the shield.

3. Take a normal breath. Open your mouth wide and press your mouth on the shield over the person's mouth to create an airtight seal.

4. Blow through the shield to deliver a breath. Each breath should be one second in length and have enough air to make the chest visibly rise, but no more than that.

5. Remove your mouth and let the air exhale from the person's lungs after each breath. Take a fresh breath before delivering rescue breaths.

The same technique can be used to provide mouth-to-mouth rescue breaths if you elect not to use a barrier device. Switch to a CPR mask or bag-valve mask device as soon as possible.

Mouth-to-Nose Rescue Breathing

When you have difficulty with mouth-to-mouth rescue breathing, you may want to use mouth-to-nose rescue breathing. To give mouth-to-nose rescue breathing, tilt the person's head back with one hand and use the other hand to close the person's mouth. Seal your lips around the person's nose and give slow breaths that make the chest rise. If the person is an infant, place your mouth over the infant's mouth and nose. Because an infant has a small face, covering both is the best way to make a seal.

Rescue Breathing for a Person With a Pulse

When a person is unresponsive, not breathing, or only gasping, but has a pulse that you can clearly feel, you need to provide rescue breaths without doing compressions.

- For adults, give one breath every 5 to 6 seconds, or about 10 to 12 breaths per minute. Deliver each breath over 1 second and make the chest visibly rise, but no more. Feel for a pulse about every 2 minutes for no more than 10 seconds. If a pulse is absent or you are unsure, begin CPR, starting with compressions.

- For children and infants, give one breath every 3 to 5 seconds, or about 12 to 20 breaths per minute. Each breath should make the chest visibly rise. Reassess the pulse every couple of minutes for no more than 10 seconds. If a pulse is absent or you are unsure, begin CPR, starting with compressions.

If a child or infant has a pale or blue tissue color that does not improve with rescue breathing or has a heart rate under 60 beats per minute, perform CPR.

Defibrillation Using an AED

Automated external defibrillators (AEDs) are designed to be simple to operate. Voice prompts will guide you in using the device. The same basic steps for operation apply to all brands of AEDs. If someone is unresponsive and not breathing, perform CPR until an AED is ready to analyze the heart rhythm.

Procedures for AED Use

When the AED arrives at the scene, perform these steps:

1. Turn on the AED, which starts voice instructions and readies the device for use. Opening the lid will turn on the power with some AEDs. With others, you need to press a power button.

2. Adhere the defibrillation pads to the person's bare chest. Pads are placed in specific locations to direct the electrical shock through the heart. Most pads are preconnected to the device, but some require you to plug in a connector. Make sure to choose the correct pads (adult or child). Do not use the child pads or system for an adult. Remove the self-adhesive backing and place the pads firmly to the person's bare chest. Place the pads while the person giving CPR continues with compressions to minimize interruption.

3. Allow the AED to analyze the heart rhythm. An AED automatically starts analyzing after the pads are in place. A voice instruction will state that the

analysis is in progress. Movement can interrupt the analysis. Be sure that no one touches the person while the AED is analyzing the heart rhythm and that the person is still. If defibrillation is required, a voice instruction will indicate when the AED is charged and ready.

4. Safely deliver a shock if directed to by the AED. To prevent accidental shock, keep others clear. Give a verbal warning and look to make sure that no one, including you, is in contact with the person before delivering the shock. On most AEDs you press a button to deliver a shock.

Immediately after a shock is delivered, resume CPR, starting with chest compressions. Voice instructions and additional analysis by the AED will guide you through further care.

Considerations for AED Use

Whenever possible, position the AED near the head and next to the rescuer who will be operating it.

Before attaching the AED, quickly check for the following situations:

- **Chest hair**. If the person's chest is covered with hair, electrode pads may not make effective contact with the skin. If this is a problem, quickly shave the chest in the area of the pads and attach another set of electrodes.

- **Water**. Move the person out of water before attaching the AED. Water or sweat on the person's chest may prevent the pads from adhering well, reducing the potential for a successful shock. If the person's chest is wet, sweaty, or dirty, quickly clean and dry it before attaching the AED.

- **Medication patches**. Remove medication patches using a gloved hand and wipe the skin area clean before attaching the AED electrode pads. Medication patches left in place may block the shock and can cause small burns to the skin.

- **Implanted medical devices**. Pacemakers and other medical devices implanted in the chest can interfere with the use of an AED. A noticeable lump and surgical scar will be visible. Place the electrode pads at least 1 inch (2.5 cm) away from an implanted device.

- **Oxygen**. Do not use oxygen when delivering shocks with an AED. Persons and their bedding have been set on fire during defibrillation. Remove the mask and place it at least 3 feet (1 m) from the person or shut off the oxygen flow when delivering shocks.

- **Metal or wet surfaces**. These materials pose no shock hazard to either you or the person, but make sure that the pads do not directly touch any metal surface and that the person is not in freestanding water. Cell phones do not interfere with the AED. Always follow the manufacturer's recommended safety precautions.

AED Use on Children and Infants

Cardiac arrests involving children are primarily caused by the initial loss of the airway or breathing. Well-performed CPR with effective rescue breaths may be the only treatment required for successful resuscitation. But conditions can occur for which defibrillation of a child or infant is warranted.

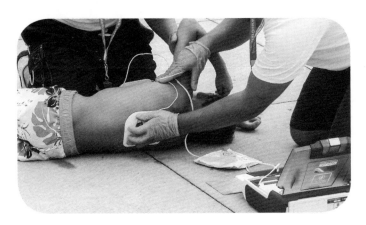

Placement of child AED pads differs from placement of adult AED pads.

If an AED designed for a child or infant is not available, use a standard machine. Most AEDs have specially designed pads, cables, or other mechanisms available that reduce the defibrillation energy to a level more appropriate for a smaller body size. Some AED pads may require the rescuer to place one pad on the child's chest and one on the back. Always look at the diagrams on the pads and place them as shown. You may need to use different cables or insert a key or turn a switch to deliver a lower amount of electricity for a child. An AED is used on an infant in the same manner as it is used on a child.

Troubleshooting an AED

If an AED detects a problem with the device during use, a voice or visual prompt, screen message, or lit icon will be displayed to guide you through corrective actions. Stay calm and do what the AED tells you to do. Here are some examples:

- If a message regarding the pads occurs, the pads are not completely adhered to the skin or the connection to the AED is poor. Press the pads firmly, especially in the center, to make sure that they are adhering well. Make sure that the pads' cable connector is firmly connected to the AED. If the chest is wet, remove the pads and wipe the chest dry. Apply a new set of pads. If pads do not stick because of chest hair, pull the pads off and quickly shave the hair. Apply a new set of pads.

- If a message indicating motion occurs, make sure that the cables are not being moved around. Stop all sources of movement, such as chest compressions or rescue breaths.

- If a message regarding the battery is displayed, the battery power is probably low. Energy may be sufficient for only a limited number of shocks. If the AED fails to operate, the depleted battery should be removed and replaced.

AED Maintenance and Quality Assurance

AEDs perform regular self-tests to make sure they are ready for use. An AED that fails a self-test will alert you with an audible or visual prompt. Contact authorized service personnel immediately.

Inspect AEDs at least monthly. If the AED has a visual status indicator, check it to make that the device is operational. Examine the expiration dates on pad packages and spare batteries, and inspect the AED for obvious damage. Make sure that the battery and a replacement battery (or batteries) are operational and ready to use.

Store AEDs with the necessary equipment to respond to a cardiac arrest. The equipment should include the following, at a minimum:

- Personal protective equipment (CPR shield or mask and disposable gloves)
- Utility scissors (to cut clothing and expose chest)
- A disposable razor (to shave a hairy chest)
- Disposable towels (to dry the chest)
- A plastic biohazard bag (to dispose of used supplies)

High-Performance CPR

CPR is a skill, and, like any physical skill, the quality of it can vary greatly, depending on things such as experience, practice, and physical ability. The quality of CPR matters. Higher quality CPR performance is directly related to an improved chance of survival.

High-performance CPR begins with high-quality CPR skills:

- During compressions, compress the adult chest at least 2 inches.
- Compress at a rate of between 100 and 120 compressions per minute.
- Avoid leaning on the chest and allow it to fully recoil between compressions.
- Avoid excessive volume when providing rescue breaths.

The ability to perform "perfect" CPR skills is difficult for anyone. The best approach is to narrow the gap as much as possible between skill guidelines and actual ability. The only way to develop and maintain high-quality CPR skills is through ongoing practice. Brief, yet frequent, skill practice sessions can be an effective way to accomplish this.

Using a CPR feedback device, like the LOOP Learning System, during practice, also helps. A feedback device provides real-time feedback on the rate, depth, and timing of compressions. Users are able to make immediate adjustments to existing skills and develop a better "feel" for the improved performance.

High-quality skills are only part of high-performance CPR. Preparing how to manage a cardiac arrest is also important. Realistic, scenario-based drills are an excellent way to prepare. Practice using a team approach. Orchestrating the actions, much like a pit crew in a car race, will improve efficiency and, most importantly, minimize interruptions.

Lifeguards in training use the LOOP Learning System during CPR practice.

Understand the common roles in resuscitation. The plan can be adjusted to work with as many people who would typically become available to respond.

- **The initial responder** identifies cardiac arrest, activates the EAP and immediately begins CPR, providing both compressions and breaths. As other responders become available, multiple response tasks can be done at the same time.
- **The EMS activator** will make sure EMS or an emergency action plan has been activated, an AED is being brought to the location, and that ongoing communication with EMS continues.
- **The responder behind the head** maintains an open airway and mask seal and provides rescue breaths.
- **The responder next to the person** provides compressions.
- **The AED operator** attaches and operates an AED. When an AED arrives it is immediately attached without interrupting CPR. The AED operator makes sure other team members are not in contact with the person being treated during AED analysis and when delivering a defibrillation shock.
- **A team leader** takes a more general perspective to troubleshoot and improve overall team performance.
- **An identified CPR provider-in-waiting** allows for a quick and smooth change every few minutes of the rescuer(s) providing compressions and rescue breaths, as a normal part of the approach, as high quality CPR is tiring.

Depending upon the staffing level at your facility, other responders may be assigned roles to bring and integrate adjunct equipment such as a bag-valve mask, provide crowd control, direct EMS to the scene, or other tasks specific to your EAP.

Interruptions during CPR, especially to compressions, significantly decreases CPR quality. Team members need to be comfortable with any role. In many cases, team members may have to assume multiple roles.

A realistic approach to practice is to continue without interruptions and allow mistakes to happen. After a drill is completed, a debriefing session lets team members reflect on how to improve things. The ability to integrate these improvements into an additional scenario can further improve long-term performance.

High-performance CPR is a combination of high-quality CPR skills and an efficient team-based approach to resuscitation. Developing and maintaining the ability to deliver both of these through ongoing commitment and practice allows for the most effective approach to prepare for treating a cardiac arrest. Your employer may consider a high-performance CPR approach. Your willingness and commitment to participate will be essential to its success.

ADULT AND CHILD CPR AND AED

Assess

If safe to do so, tap or squeeze the person's shoulder. Ask loudly, "Are you OK?" Look quickly at the face and chest for normal breathing and check for an obvious carotid pulse in the neck. In the absence of normal breathing and obvious pulse, have someone alert EMS and get an AED. If alone with an adult, do this yourself. If alone with a child, provide 2 minutes of care before doing this yourself.

Give 30 Compressions

Remember that quality matters. Push hard, at least 2 inches (5 cm), but not much more.

Push fast, at a rate of at least 100 compressions per minute, but not more than 120. Do not lean on the chest between compressions to allow the chest to fully recoil.

Give Two Rescue Breaths

Establish an airway. Make the chest visibly rise over one second with each breath, but no more. Take a fresh breath before delivering rescue breaths. Do this quickly, in less than 10 seconds.

Repeat Cycles of 30 Compressions and Two Breaths

Don't stop! Continue until the person shows signs of life, an AED is ready to analyze heart rhythm, another rescuer or EMS takes over, or you become too tired to continue.

With Multiple Rescuers

One rescuer performs compressions, and the other rescuer performs rescue breaths. Quickly switch or change the person doing compressions every 2 minutes.

With a child, perform cycles of 15 compressions followed by 2 breaths.

Others integrate adjunct equipment such as a bag-valve mask or AED as it arrives to the scene and provide other tasks according to the emergency action plan.

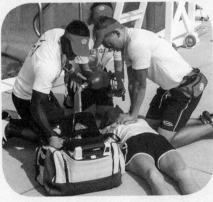

(continued)

ADULT AND CHILD CPR AND AED (CONTINUED)

When Available, Attach AED	Turn on power to start voice instructions. Bare the person's chest and wipe dry if needed. Place the AED pads (while CPR compressions and breaths continue) and listen for voice instructions. 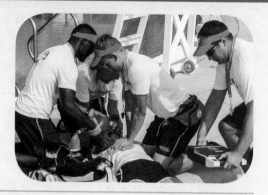
If Indicated, Deliver Shock	Allow the AED to analyze the heart. Stop all movement, including CPR. If shock is advised, make sure no one is touching the person and press the shock button to deliver shock.
Resume CPR	Immediately after delivering shock, or if a shock is not advised, resume CPR, starting with chest compressions. Follow any additional voice instructions from the AED. Continue with minimal interruption. If the person responds, stop CPR and place the person in the recovery position. Leave the AED on and attached in case cardiac arrest returns.

CPR Considerations During Pregnancy

When a woman who is in the later stages of pregnancy is lying on her back, the weight of the baby in the uterus can restrict blood flow. This restriction can make CPR compressions less effective. To improve blood flow during compressions, another rescuer can use a technique known as left uterine displacement (LUD) to gently move the baby. If you are on the woman's left side, reach over the belly, place both hands (with fingers down) at the edge of the bulge, and manually pull the baby toward the woman's left side. If you are on the woman's right side, place one hand (turned sideways) along the bottom of the bulge and push the baby toward the woman's left side.

INFANT CPR AND AED

Assess

If safe to do so, tap the bottom of the infant's foot and shout loudly. Look quickly at the face and chest for normal breathing and check for obvious brachial pulse in the infant's upper arm. In the absence of normal breathing and obvious pulse (or less than 60 beats per minute, with pale or blue tissue color), have someone alert EMS and get an AED. If alone, stay with the infant and provide 2 minutes of care before doing this yourself.

Give 30 Compressions

Place two fingertips on the breastbone just below the nipple line. Push hard, straight down at least one-third the diameter of the chest, or about 2 inches (5 cm).

Push fast, at a rate of at least 100 compressions per minute, but not more than 120. Do not lean on the chest between compressions so that the chest can fully recoil.

Give Two Rescue Breaths

Tilt the head and lift the chin slightly to establish an airway. Give puffs (not full breaths) to make the chest visibly rise over one second with each breath, but no more. Take a fresh breath before delivering rescue breaths. Take no longer than 10 seconds to give breaths.

Repeat Cycles of 30 Compressions and Two Breaths

Don't stop! Continue until the infant clearly shows signs of life, an AED is ready to analyze the heart rhythm, another rescuer or EMS takes over, or you become too tired to continue.

With Multiple Rescuers

One rescuer performs compressions by compressing the breastbone using two thumbs and hands encircling the chest; the other delivers rescue breaths at a rate of 15:2 (15 compressions followed by two breaths).

Use an AED if Available

Use infant pads if available. Otherwise, follow the AED pad placement for a child.

ADULT OR CHILD CHOKING—SEVERE BLOCKAGE

Assess

Ask, "Are you choking?" If the person nods yes or is unable to speak or cough, act quickly! If a bystander is nearby, have her or him activate EMS.

Position Yourself

Stand or kneel (for a child) behind the person. Reach around and locate the navel with your finger. Make a fist with the other hand and place it thumb-side down against the abdomen, just above your finger and below the person's ribs. Grasp your fist with your other hand.

Give Thrusts

Quickly thrust inward and upward into the abdomen. Repeat. Give each thrust with the intent of expelling the object. Continue until the person can breathe normally.

If Person Becomes Unresponsive

Carefully lower the person to the ground, positioning the person faceup on a firm, flat surface. If not already done, activate EMS. If you are alone with a child, provide at least 2 minutes of CPR before activating EMS.

ADULT OR CHILD CHOKING—SEVERE BLOCKAGE

Perform Compressions

Begin CPR, starting with compressions.

Look in the Mouth

Look for an object after each set of compressions. Remove any visible object.

Attempt a Rescue Breath

Open the airway and try to make the chest rise with a rescue breath. Continue the cycle until the person shows obvious signs of life or another provider or the next level of care takes over.

INFANT CHOKING—SEVERE BLOCKAGE

Assess

Look at the infant's face. If the infant is silent, unable to cry, or has blue lips, nails, or skin, act quickly! If a bystander is nearby, have him or her activate EMS.

Give Five Back Blows

Straddle the infant facedown over your forearm, with the head lower than the chest. Support the infant's head by holding the jaw. Using the heel of the other hand, give five back blows between the shoulder blades.

Turn the Infant Over

Sandwich the infant between your forearms and turn her or him onto the back. The legs and arms are straddling your other arm.

Give Chest Thrusts

Place two fingers on the breastbone just below the nipple line and give five chest thrusts. Repeat back blows and chest thrusts until the infant can breathe normally. Give back blows and chest thrusts with the intent of expelling the object.

If the Infant Becomes Unresponsive

Place the infant on a firm, flat surface.
If you are alone, provide at least 2 minutes of CPR before activating EMS.

Perform CPR

Begin CPR, starting with compressions. Look in the mouth for an object after each set of compressions before giving rescue breaths. Remove any visible object. Continue CPR until the infant shows obvious signs of life or another provider or the next level of care takes over.

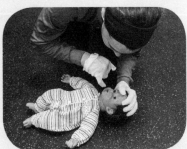

VISIT THE WEB RESOURCE

You can reinforce your learning by visiting the web resource, where you can do the following in the interactive online learning activities based on chapter 10:

- ◆ Practice timing for high-quality CPR compressions.
- ◆ Watch videos of CPR demonstrations.
- ◆ Test your knowledge and receive feedback.

CHAPTER SUMMARY

Key points	Best practices on the job
• Sudden cardiac arrest occurs when the heart's electrical system malfunctions and the heart abruptly stops beating. • Sudden cardiac arrest is different than a heart attack, which occurs when blood flow is blocked to the heart. • CPR alone is not enough to treat sudden cardiac arrest; the heart must be shocked back into rhythm with an AED. • Gasping, snorting, or gurgling sounds are not normal breathing. • Quality of CPR matters! Quick response matters! • Keeping the airway open is crucial for delivery of effective rescue breaths. • Avoid excess volume during rescue breaths. • High performance CPR is a combination of high-quality CPR skills and efficient team based approach to resuscitation.	• If a person is unresponsive, quickly check for normal breathing and obvious pulse (for no more than 10 seconds). • Push fast during compressions at a rate between 100-120 times per minute. • Push hard during compressions; at least 2 inches (5 cm) but not much more. For a child or infant compress at least 1/3 the full depth of the chest. • Do not lean on the chest during compressions to allow the chest to recoil. • Give two rescue breaths that make the chest visibly rise in 10 seconds or less. Deliver compressions at a ratio of 30:2. With multiple rescuers, use a ratio of 15:2 for a child or infant. • Minimize interruptions. • Develop high quality CPR skills using a feedback device during training. • Develop and maintain high performance CPR through regular team-based scenario training.

Rescue Breathing and CPR for Unresponsive Drowning Persons

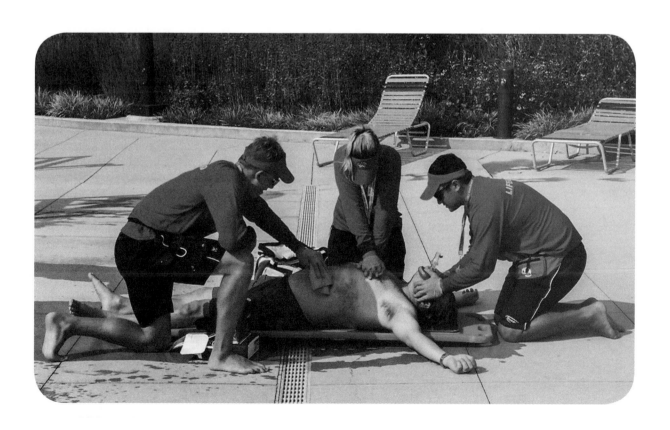

CHAPTER OBJECTIVES

This chapter

- examines special considerations when caring for drowning persons,
- describes how to modify rescue skills for an unresponsive drowning person,
- explains the importance of rescue breathing and how to perform it in the water,
- describes how to extricate an unresponsive person from the water,
- explains how to work as a high performance team and integrate adjunct equipment,
- discusses the use of emergency oxygen and transfer of care to EMS, and
- explains what to do and what to expect after a drowning incident.

Your goal in managing an unresponsive, nonbreathing drowning person is simple: Obtain an open airway as quickly as possible and begin rescue breathing. This chapter explains how to adapt your skills to provide the best care for a drowning person and establish a framework for response.

Special Considerations for Drowning

International CPR guidelines recognize drowning as a special situation because the primary cause of death by drowning is lack of oxygen to the brain (Szpilman et al. 2012, Travers et al. 2015, Monsieurs et al. 2015, Australian Resuscitation Council 2015, American Heart Association 2015, International Liaison Committee on Resuscitation 2010, Vanden Hoek 2010). This condition is known as hypoxia. Besides being the cause of unresponsiveness, immersion in water creates other considerations that can affect emergency care procedures:

- **Drowning does not stop until rescue breaths are given**. Because of the hypoxic nature of drowning, the recommended treatment sequence is airway (A), breathing (B), and compressions (C) to circulate blood throughout the body.
- **Five initial rescue breaths should be given** (Szpilman et al. 2012, Monsieurs et al. 2015, Australian Resuscitation Council 2015). Breaths should be given without delay upon initial contact with the person—even in the water.
- **Vomiting is highly likely**. The person may have swallowed large quantities of water, often causing a swollen stomach. Almost 90 percent of drowning patients vomit at some point during CPR (Manolios and Mackie 1988, Farr et al. 2015). Vomit can effectively be removed by turning the head to the side and performing a finger sweep with a gloved hand. A suction device may be helpful in removing large amounts of vomit from the airway, but it should be used only if necessary

and if it can be integrated within a team response so that the vomit is removed quickly with minimal delay in care.

- **Foam and mucus are likely to come out of the mouth and nose, and it cannot be totally removed in the prehospital setting** (Szpilman et al. 2012, Bierens et al. 2016). This foam is often mistaken for vomit, but it is something completely different. Foam is frothy and may be white or tinged with blood or completely bloody. You will need to be prepared to maintain an airway and continue ventilations through the foam so that care is not delayed. The foam may continue to be produced for some time, and it cannot be totally removed, so suction devices and turning of the head are unnecessary in this situation.

- **The person may make gasping or snoring noises**. Although these noises may sound like attempts to breathe, they are caused by changes occurring in the body. Unless the person is responsive and breathing normally, continue providing rescue breathing or chest compressions as needed.

- **If you are not 100 percent sure that you are feeling the person's pulse during a pulse check, start chest compressions**. Checking the pulse of an unresponsive person is difficult (Monsieurs et al. 2015, Brennan and Braslow 1998, Chamberlain et al. 2002, Eberle et al. 1996, Lapostolle et al. 2004, Liberman et al. 1999, Moule 2000, Nyman and Sihvonen 2000, Perkins et al. 2005, Ruppert et al. 1999, Tibballs and Russell 2009), so imagine the challenge when you are wet and winded after executing the rescue. Though there is a minimal chance of causing harm by doing chest compressions on someone with a pulse, the benefit of starting compressions immediately far outweighs the risks. Starting chest compressions on someone with a heartbeat is better than withholding them from someone that needs them.

- **Unless significant amounts of bodily fluids are present, do not delay rescue breathing to put on gloves**. Your hands will be wet, and putting on protective gloves may be difficult and time consuming. Rescuers who come to assist should put on gloves and be prepared to deal with any bodily fluids (Mejicano and Maki 1998, Bierens and Berden 1996).

- **Regardless of the method you use to extricate, move the person completely out of the water and away from the water's edge in case an AED will be applied**. You also want to give yourself and other responders room to perform CPR, so a move to about 6 feet (2 m) away from the water is ideal when possible.

- **You will need to dry the person's chest to apply the AED pads.** The pads won't stick or work properly if the chest is wet.

- **Family presence during resuscitation is a reasonable and potentially desirable option**. Studies show that family members may want to be present during a resuscitation attempt (American Heart Association 2015). Families report a sense of closure seeing that the guards and EMS personnel did everything they could during a resuscitation event. An experienced staff member should be assigned to the family to answer questions, explain procedures, and offer comfort. Consideration should be given to provide them with chairs and keep them at a safe distance so that they do not interfere with the resuscitation.

- **Bystanders may attempt to become involved**. Your facility should have a policy in place regarding bystander involvement, and you should practice how to deal with this situation before it occurs. In many instances, giving a bystander a role in helping you provide care can be a valuable resource, but a bystander should not be allowed to take over the scene. This includes bystanders who identify that they are doctors, nurses, or paramedics.

- **The scene will be noisy, and you may not be able to hear an AED**. If you use an AED, consider having a designated rescuer or bystander listen closely to the AED prompts and call out the commands.

- **If you use emergency oxygen, keep the cylinder in the bag or case**. The rescue scene area may be slippery, and many people may be moving about. Keeping the cylinder in the case will prevent it from being knocked over and create a potentially dangerous situation.

- **Follow-up care is required—even for a drowned person who completely recovers at the scene** (Szpilman and Soares 2004, Chin et al. 1980, Lopez-Fernandez et al. 2012, Milne and Cohen 2006, Papa et al. 2005, Pearn 1980, Pratt and Haynes 1986, Rivers et al. 1970, Noonan et al. 1996, Saule 1975, Gregorakos et al. 2009). Anyone who has received some form of resuscitation for drowning needs to have follow-up evaluation and care in a hospital, regardless of the person's condition after the event.

- **Team-focused CPR can reduce stress, improve performance, and contribute to an increased chance of patient survival** (American Heart Association 2015). Practice of the unresponsive drowning protocol should be frequent.

Unresponsive Drowning Protocol

This protocol puts together the components necessary to provide effective and early rescue breathing, and high-quality, team-based CPR for a drowning person. The protocol begins with a single rescuer, and the protocol is adjusted as the EAP is activated and other rescuers and equipment become available (see table 11.1).

Table 11.1   Unresponsive Drowning Protocol

Begin rescue breathing in the water starting with 5 initial breaths, then 1 breath every 5 seconds until extrication.	

Upon extrication open the airway and quickly check for normal breathing and obvious pulse for no more than 10 seconds.	• If the person is not breathing but has an obvious pulse:
	  • Give 5 effective rescue breaths that make the chest rise. Breathe through foam.
	  • Continue giving rescue breaths at a rate of 1 breath every 5 seconds.
	  • Check for pulse every 2 minutes.
	• If no pulse (or not sure):
	  • Give 5 effective rescue breaths that make the chest rise. Breathe through foam. It is ok to start with compressions if effective rescue breathing was started in the water.
	  • Give 30 compressions.
	  • Give 2 breaths.
	  • Alternate 30 compressions and 2 breaths until an AED is applied and ready to analyze.

High-quality CPR skills are emphasized throughout.	

Rescue of an Unresponsive Drowning Person

When you rescue a person who is facedown on the surface or submerged, you will not know the level of responsiveness until the person's face is lifted out of the water. A responsive person will cough, sputter, move, and begin to regain normal breathing. An unresponsive person will be limp and not move or breathe in response to your moving her or him.

Because the person has been without oxygen, the first objective is to get oxygen into the body as quickly as possible. Opening the airway and rescue breaths may be enough to revive the person and cause breathing to resume on its own, which is known as return of spontaneous breathing (ROSB).

Equipment

The rescuer entering the water should have a rescue tube and CPR mask. The mask should be capable of making a reasonable seal in the water, and the one-way valve should be made of plastic or a nonabsorbent material (not paper or fiber). The mask should be easily accessible (e.g., either kept in a pack around the waist or attached to the rescue tube).

Additional rescuers bring other equipment that may be available, such as the backboard for extrication, AED, emergency oxygen, BVM, gloves, and suction device. Emergency equipment should be kept together in a defined location and in some type of case or bag that can be quickly brought to the scene. As much as possible, equipment should be preassembled and ready for use.

Open Airway Position in the Water

When you place an unresponsive drowning person on a rescue tube using a rear rescue, you are in an excellent position to provide immediate rescue breathing. The person's head will fall back into an open-airway position. You can begin rescue breathing and still be able to swim and progress toward a safe point of exit.

To avoid being injured by the person's head as you place him or her on the rescue tube, consider using the head-cradle technique to adapt the rear rescue and provide head control *(a)*.

In a rear-rescue position, use your hands to cradle the head *(b)*.

As you pull back, bring the person's arms over the tube *(c)*.

Move to a position behind the person's head. Quickly check for normal breathing. If the person is not breathing normally, signal to activate your emergency action plan (EAP) for an unresponsive drowning person and begin rescue breathing.

Providing rescue breathing as soon as possible, while you're still in the water, can be crucial to a successful rescue outcome (Szpilman et al. 2012, Szpilman 1997, Szpilman and Soares 2004), especially when you are not sure how long the person has been submerged and without oxygen. Let's look at how to perform this technique in more detail.

Rescue Breathing in the Water

Rescue breathing can be performed effectively when a person is placed in an open airway position on a rescue tube, and you have a CPR mask capable of making a good seal in the water. Your position, combined with the flotation of the rescue tube, will allow you to control the airway and provide breaths as you are making progress toward a safe point of exit from the water.

Mouth to Mask

The mask used for in-water rescue breathing should have a one-way valve made of plastic or a nonabsorbent material (not paper or fiber). The mask should be easily accessible (e.g., either kept in a pack around your waist or attached to your rescue tube).

1. Obtain your mask and shake out any water.

2. From a position behind the drowning person's head, place the mask over the person's nose and mouth. If you have a "blob" style mask, be sure that the opening is over the person's mouth.

3. Make a good seal by tilting the head and lifting the chin up and jaw forward. Pull the head and face to the mask instead of just pushing the mask harder onto the face.

4. Lean forward while pulling the person's head slightly down and toward you to bring your mouth to the mask valve.

5. Take a normal breath and place your mouth on the mask valve. Breathe out for about 1 second with enough force to make the chest rise, but no more.

6. Give 5 initial breaths. Allow the chest to fall after each breath before beginning the next one.

7. Continue giving breaths at a rate of 1 breath every 5 seconds. Your position behind the head will allow you to control the airway and provide breaths as you are making progress toward a safe point of exit by swimming or walking on the bottom.

Mouth to Mouth

Mouth to mask should always be the preferred means of providing rescue breathing in the water. At times, however, a mask may not be available. Research indicates that providing mouth-to-mouth breathing in the water may be just as effective as providing mouth-to-mask breathing and poses almost no additional risk of serious disease transmission (Mejicano and Maki 1998, Bierens and Berden 1996). There is a risk for minor disease transmission, such as common colds. You should consider the risks and benefits of providing immediate care when a mask is not available.

1. Position yourself beside the person.
2. Open the airway by tilting the head and lifting the chin up and jaw forward. Placing your arm between the victim's arm and the rescue tube may provide additional support.
3. Pinch the person's nose shut.
4. Take a normal breath and make a seal over the person's mouth with your mouth.
5. Breathe out for about 1 second with enough force to make the chest rise, but no more.
6. Give 5 initial breaths. Allow the chest to fall after each breath before beginning the next one.
7. Continue giving breaths at a rate of 1 breath every 5 seconds, while making progress to a safe take out point by swimming while holding the person's head and maintaining an open airway, or walking on the bottom.

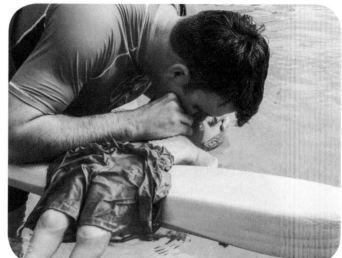

To get a good seal on a small child, you may need to cover the child's entire nose and mouth with your mouth.

Sudden Cardiac Arrest (SCA) in the Water

We know that there is a difference in the causes and treatment of drowning and cardiac causes of cardiac arrest. Both cause unresponsiveness, but in drowning, the person is unresponsive because of lack of air (hypoxia). In sudden cardiac arrest, the person is most likely unresponsive because of an electrical malfunction of the heart.

If you witness a previously active adult suddenly collapse in the water, you should assume that they have had a sudden cardiac arrest or other medical problem and extricate immediately without delay for rescue breathing. However, if you did not witness the collapse, you must still treat any unresponsive event that happens in the water as a drowning.

Extrication

To extricate means "to remove." Your objective when removing a drowning person from the water is to do so as quickly as possible using an appropriate method for the circumstances that minimizes the risk of injury to either the person or rescuers. The following factors may affect the type of removal method you choose:

- Size of the deck and gutter. Extrication is much easier if the water and deck are at nearly the same level.
- Equipment and people available to assist.
- Size of the drowned person. You may not need a backboard to lift a small person out of the water.

Practice various methods of extrication at your facility using the equipment available. This practice will help you determine which techniques are effective in meeting the objectives for extrication.

Backboard Pullout

A backboard, found at most aquatic facilities, is an ideal tool to use for quick extrication. It will need to be brought quickly to the safe point of exit by another person who can help. When removing a large or heavy person from the water, you may need additional people.

The backboard acts as a fulcrum on the edge of the pool and minimizes risk of injury to rescuers or the unresponsive person. The initial rescuer continues rescue breathing in the water until the extrication board is ready (a).

Place the backboard vertically in the water. For more stability, push the top of the board out so the bottom of the board is against the wall (b).

The rescuer in the water lifts the unresponsive person's arm up to the rescuer on deck *(c)*.

The rescuer on deck holds the person's arm (just above the wrist) with one hand and the top of the board with the other *(d)*. Begin to allow the board to float up under the person's back by pushing the top of the board down and pulling it toward the wall.

The rescuer in the water quickly pulls the rescue tube out from under the person so it is not trapped between the person and the board as the board rises.

The rescuer in the water can quickly move to the end of the board to help push the board up or can climb out to help pull the board out.

The rescuers communicate to coordinate the removal effort. One rescuer should give a prompt, for example, "On my count, ready, one, two, three."

The rescuer or rescuers at the top of the backboard tilt it back and down, and then slide and pull the board up and out of the water and onto the deck *(e)*. The rescuer or rescuers in the water help push. If the backboard has very short runners on the bottom (or no runners), be careful when placing the backboard on the decks so that fingers or hands of the rescuers don't get pinched underneath.

Pull the board and person all of the way out of the water and to a place where there is enough room to perform CPR.

Backboard Walkout

A backboard walkout extrication can be useful where the water is shallow and there are wide stairs or a zero-depth area. This extrication requires four rescuers or more if the unresponsive person is large or very heavy. Follow these steps to perform a backboard walkout:

1. Submerge the backboard and slide it under the unresponsive person.
2. Position rescuers evenly around the board, with at least two on each side. The rescuers grasp the handholds.
3. Move toward the exit area while floating the board and person until near the exit or until the water is less than waist deep.
4. Keep firm grasp of the handholds and support the board while walking out of the zero-depth area or up the stairs.

Lift Out

A lift-out extrication can be useful where the water is shallow, the unresponsive person is a child, and the deck is close to the water surface. In this instance, lifting a child out may be the fastest choice for extrication. Cradle the child firmly with support under the neck and hips, and lift out onto the deck. Avoid pulling the child up over the edge and take care to keep the head from hitting the edge or deck.

Use of Adjunct Equipment

Adjunct means something that is supplementary rather than an essential part. In drowning resuscitation the essential component is the person delivering rescue breaths, and if needed, CPR. Other equipment may be helpful, but should not take away from or interfere with your ability to perform CPR with high-quality skills and minimal interruptions.

AED

When a person's heart has stopped due to lack of oxygen during drowning, the heart will most likely not have a "shockable" rhythm. If available, an AED should be utilized, but be prepared that it may indicate "no shock advised," especially until the underlying hypoxia improves.

Emergency Oxygen

Because of the hypoxic nature of drowning and the interval between the event and arrival of EMS, emergency use of supplemental oxygen can be lifesaving. The International Life Saving Federation (ILS) and other national and international training agencies support its use (Szpilman et al. 2012, Travers et al. 2015, Monsieurs et al. 2015, Australian Resuscitation Council 2015, American Heart Association 2015, International Liaison Committee on Resuscitation 2010, Vanden Hoek 2010).

Given the potential benefit, properly trained lifeguards should give emergency oxygen when it is available. This text provides information about emergency oxygen (see the appendix), which should be supplemented with hands-on practice with the equipment at your aquatic facility to constitute appropriate training. In most countries, regulations on the use of emergency oxygen are defined. As with any protocol, regulations from the authority having jurisdiction in your location will apply.

The decision to have and use emergency oxygen should be based on its feasibility at a particular location or in a specific situation. If emergency oxygen is available and you are trained to use it, include it as part of your unresponsive drowning protocol.

Bag-Valve Mask

A bag-valve mask (BVM) can be helpful to deliver rescue breaths when at least two rescuers are present. One rescuer maintains an open airway and the seal of the mask against the face, the other rescuer squeezes the bag to deliver a breath.

Manual Suction Device

Note again that drowning persons may have copious amounts of foam present. You should not attempt to suction foam. Suctioning should be performed only on vomit and water that is obstructing the airway. If a manual suction device is brought to the scene, have another rescuer prepare the device and place it in the ready position. Ideally, the suctioning device and the rescuer responsible for suctioning are located on one side of the patient, and the other equipment, such as oxygen or AED, is on the other side. This setup prevents vomit or other fluids from getting on the other equipment.

- Prepare the device. Depending on the manufacturer, you may need to remove a protective tip or size and attach a catheter tube.
- Turn the person's head to the side.
- Place the suction end of the device in the victim's mouth, along the side of the cheek and toward the throat.
- Squeeze the handle or trigger to pull the fluids and secretions into the device. Suction for up to 15 seconds, but no more, if needed to clear the airway. Resume CPR.
- Dispose of the collection container according to your facility's policy for potentially infected bodily fluids. Insert a new container so that the device is ready for the next event.

High-Performance "Pit Crew" Response

During a drowning emergency, working as a team is important. After extrication, care for a drowning person continues on land. Remember that the drowning process does not stop until effective rescue breaths are given.

The amount of people available to respond may vary according to different staffing levels throughout the day. You will need to practice the protocol at your facility with the least amount of responders, as well as the most, to see how the flow changes as more rescuers become available and equipment arrives at the scene. The position descriptions and diagrams provided here are examples only, and may need to be modified to meet site-specific needs and circumstances. The goal is to develop and practice the best possible team response based on the number of people and equipment available.

- Position ABC – **A**ssessment, **a**irway management, effective rescue **b**reathing, high-quality **c**ompressions if needed. This position is used when a rescuer is performing all components of CPR until others arrive, or while equipment is being prepared or applied by another rescuer.

- Position AB – **A**irway management and effective rescue **b**reathing.
- Position C – High-quality **c**ompressions.
- Position D – **D**evices. Prepare and apply adjunct equipment as available. There may be more than one position D if multiple devices such as an AED and emergency oxygen and a BVM are available.
- Position S – **S**cene management. Based on the circumstances, coordinate care, provide crowd control, or replace rescuers as needed to avoid fatigue.

As rescuers arrive on scene, each person assumes a position and performs the functions for that position.

Initial Rescuer

In most cases the initial rescuer is the person making a water rescue and starting rescue breathing in the water while waiting for extrication *(a)*. However, first contact with the unresponsive drowning person may be after he or she has been removed from the pool by bystanders. You may have to provide care by yourself until other rescuers arrive, and rescue breathing may not have been given in the water. In this situation do the following *(b)*:

- Quickly check for normal breathing and an obvious pulse for no more than 10 seconds.
- If you feel an obvious pulse but the person is not breathing, position yourself behind the head (position AB). Open the airway using the triple airway maneuver and provide 5 initial rescue breaths. Continue giving 1 breath every 5 seconds. Check for normal breathing and pulse every 2 minutes.
- If you do not feel an obvious pulse, position yourself at the side of the person (position ABC). Open the airway using a head tilt – chin lift. Provide 5 initial rescue breaths, followed by 30 compressions. Continue to provide CPR by alternating 30 compressions and 2 breaths until others arrive.

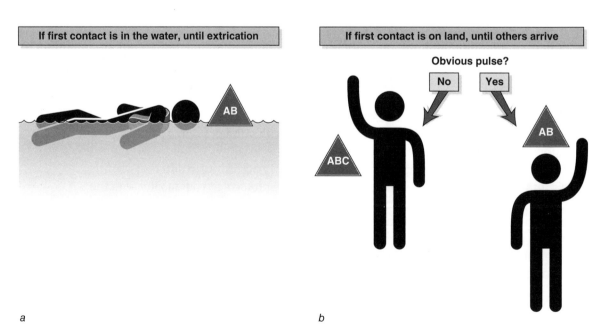

a *b*

With Two Rescuers

While the initial rescuer is providing care, the second rescuer brings available equipment. If extrication is needed the rescuers work together and then the rescuer closest to the head performs a quick check for normal breathing and an obvious pulse. If an AED is available, the rescuer in position ABC provides rescue breathing and CPR while the other rescuer turns on and operates the AED. If an AED is not available, the second rescuer assumes position AB, and also integrates the BVM or emergency oxygen if available and if it can be accomplished with minimal interruption to CPR. Rescuers alternate giving compressions about every two minutes to avoid fatigue and maintain high-quality compressions.

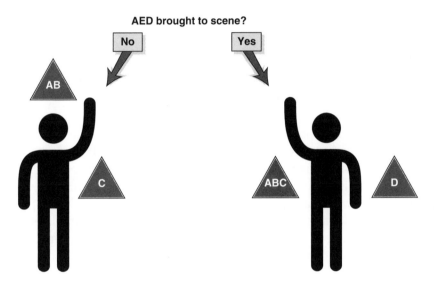

With Three or More Rescuers

As additional rescuers or equipment arrives, the tasks can be further divided among the rescue team for a coordinated effort.

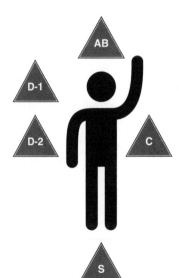

- Position D-1 prepares the BVM and emergency oxygen, hands the mask to the rescuer in AB, and then squeezes the bag to deliver breaths as needed.

- Position D-2 turns on and operates the AED. Position D-2 can also alternate compressions every 2 minutes with position C so there is minimal interruption.

- Positon S evaluates the scene and coordinates care, provides crowd control, rotates in for position C, or completes other tasks as circumstances and the facility EAP indicate.

Transferring Care to EMS

As part of the facility emergency action plan (EAP), a staff person should be assigned to direct EMS to the rescue scene. When they arrive, they will likely tell you to continue your resuscitation efforts for a few more minutes as they set up equipment and prepare to take over care. During this transition, follow the directives that the emergency medical personnel give you and be prepared to answer questions about the drowning patient's condition, length of time unresponsive, and other symptoms or circumstances.

Your facility EAP should also have someone assigned to obtain helpful information such as the name of the EMS responding unit and name of the hospital to which the person is being transported. If the situation permits, an assigned person should obtain replacement equipment from the EMS vehicle if they are taking your equipment, such as backboard or AED pads.

Be aware that EMS may not transport the person to a hospital right away or may not transport the person at all. EMS may provide prehospital care on-site under medical direction rather than in the back of a moving ambulance. In the event of a drowning or SCA fatality, the person may be declared dead on site and left at your facility until a coroner or other authorities arrive.

Coping With Emotional Distress After the Incident

The hours after an unresponsive drowning incident will be challenging, especially emotionally. Because you are a witness to the event, you will be asked to write a description of what happened. You will likely be questioned by the police to determine whether the drowning can be ruled an accident, or whether homicide, suicide, or other criminal behavior played a role. You may not know the condition of the person or have any way of finding out. Incident reports will need to be completed, the treatment area and equipment cleaned, and other responsibilities taken care of. You need to take care of yourself and your coworkers both physically and emotionally after the incident. Follow the guidance provided by your employer about how to handle such things as requests from media or others for interviews or information.

In the days, weeks, or months after the incident, you may be questioned again by insurance company representatives, attorneys, and others. Reports may appear in the media that may disturb you, especially if the reports contain inaccurate information or do not tell the whole story. You need to be prepared for the symptoms that stress can cause, even long after the event.

Everyone involved during or after a drowning incident will suffer some level of emotional distress—you, your coworkers, the victim, the victim's family, and even bystanders. Factors that may make such incidents more distressing include the following:

- A fatal outcome
- An incident involved multiple people, a child, or a close friend or relative

Symptoms of a traumatic stress reaction include a pounding heartbeat and fast breathing, which may begin during or within minutes of the traumatic event. Feeling guilty for not having done more, worrying about the safety of loved ones, having nightmares, and repeatedly thinking about the event may follow the incident.

Stress reactions are a normal human response to a traumatic event and are usually temporary. With the help of family and friends, most people gradually feel better as time passes. If you think you need extra help coping after a traumatic event, call your doctor or ask friends whether they can recommend a mental health professional. If you have any thoughts of hurting yourself or others, notify someone or call 911 immediately. Your workplace may have an employee assistance program available to help you. The following are strategies to help you cope:

- As soon as possible after the incident, relieve the stress by getting physically active. Go for a swim or a run or do another workout activity.

- Get back to your regular patterns of work, school, and social events. The familiarity of day-to-day activities will provide stability in your life.

- Take advantage of the debriefing sessions that your facility may schedule to deal with critical-incident stress. These sessions are usually conducted for your benefit within a few days of the incident. Mental health care professionals trained to help emergency care workers deal with stress after a traumatic event will facilitate these group discussions.

- When you start to feel overwhelmed, talk to friends or relatives close to you who will be supportive without being judgmental.

VISIT THE WEB RESOURCE

You can reinforce your learning by visiting the web resource, where you can do the following in the interactive online learning activities based on chapter 11:

- ◆ Identify roles and positions for a "pit crew" high-performance team response.
- ◆ Analyze unresponsive drowning scenarios.
- ◆ Test your knowledge and receive feedback.

CHAPTER SUMMARY

Key points	Best practices on the job
• Drowning occurs because a person has been without oxygen. • Drowning does not stop until the first breath goes in. • Foam coming out of the nose and mouth is likely. • Breathe through foam – don't delay care by attempting to remove it. • Give 5 initial rescue breaths – begin in the water if possible. • A CPR mask for use in the water should not have a paper or fiber filter. • Use of equipment should not delay or interrupt care. • A "pit crew" team response is best for high-performance management of drowning • A drowning event is likely to trigger a traumatic stress reaction in all involved.	• Have a CPR mask and rescue tube readily available. • Practice rescue breathing in the water. • Maintain high-quality CPR skills with frequent practice. • Practice high-performance drowning protocol in team-based scenarios to be able to fill into any position.

Part V

Workplace Environment

Facilitating Workplace Safety

CHAPTER OBJECTIVES

This chapter

- identifies workplace hazards,
- describes how to conduct a workplace site safety survey,
- explains the concept of three points of contact, and
- explores safety and health considerations important to lifeguards.

Tripping over tools, equipment, or a patron's belongings and falling on wet or slippery surfaces are common causes of injuries. Lifeguards also frequently injure their ankles, knees, or backs after slipping, falling, or jumping from the guard chair. Injuries caused by jumping into shallow water and lifting or twisting during training drills or rescues occur more often than they should. Rounding out the list are injuries that occur when a lifeguard comes in contact with machinery, equipment, or chemicals. Factors that often contribute to injuries include being in a hurry, talking with coworkers or patrons, slipping on wet or slick surfaces or equipment, carrying equipment, failing to use appropriate personal protective equipment, or failing to maintain three points of contact with ladders on guard chairs.

Although your focus as a lifeguard is on the safety of patrons, your personal safety in and around an aquatic environment is important as well. Many of your work-related tasks seem to carry little or no risk for injury. But even the simplest of activities can cause injury when performed improperly or when prudent precautions are not taken. You should know how to manage some of the workplace safety risks of your profession:

- Sun exposure
- Slips, trips, and falls
- Lifting, twisting, reaching, and bending during rescues
- Using tools or equipment
- Prolonged standing or sitting
- Site-specific concerns such as chemicals, confined spaces, weather, or illness

Minimizing the Risk of Workplace Injury

Your participation in minimizing the risk of injury is essential for a safe and healthful workplace. Take the time to conduct a 30-second workplace site safety survey before beginning a job task to reflect on the potential job safety hazards or concerns that relate to the specific work site or task.

30-Second Site Safety Survey*

*Park District Risk Management Agency 2011

1. Pause before you approach: Are there any obvious potential safety hazards? Generally, your first impression will be correct.

2. Observe your surroundings: Is there something about the location, depth of water, or surface that could create a hazard or injury?

3. Ask yourself about traffic: Will the amount of pedestrian traffic cause a safety hazard or concern?

4. Protect yourself: Should you be wearing personal protective equipment? Are you wearing the appropriate footwear to perform the job safely? What are safe lifting techniques? Do you have your sunscreen, sunglasses, and umbrella? Do you have drinking water to keep hydrated?

5. Consider the unknown: What unique aspects of the site could cause a safety concern? Will the equipment, materials, or job task introduce safety concerns?

Workplace Hazards

In addition to performing the 30-second site safety survey for specific job tasks, you should reflect on other considerations throughout your workday, including equipment and machinery hazards; slip, trip, and fall hazards; lifting hazards; and site-specific hazards.

Equipment and Machinery Hazards

- Do I have the right equipment for the job?
- Is the equipment in good repair and operating correctly?
- Do I have the proper personal protective equipment?

Slip, Trip, and Fall Hazards

- Are there potential tripping hazards?
- Is the ground or surface slippery or wet?
- Will I need to step over or around equipment?
- Should I use three points of contact?
- Do I have the proper footwear?

Lifting Hazards

- What are the proper body mechanics or lifting plan for the job?
- Do I need to get help?

Site-Specific and Chemical Hazards

- Are there job-specific hazards to consider?
- Do chemicals, electricity, or severe weather pose a hazard?
- Do I know the guidelines for chemicals and hazardous materials? If you must handle chemicals or hazardous materials, you have a legal right to know about any risks associated with chemical products, and a Safety Data Sheet (SDS) provides this information. Follow the established guidelines and precautions as detailed in the SDS your employer will provide you. In addition, your employer should provide training for safe handling of these chemicals and hazardous materials and maintain correct labels and warning signs. Pool chemicals can lead to injury when mixed together or when appropriate personal protective equipment is not used during handling (CDC 2016). The CDC had published safety recommendations based on review of reports of pool chemical associated injuries (see figure 12.1).

Figure 12.1   Know safe handling precautions for handling chemicals and hazardous materials.

- In the event of a toxic spill, of either a known or an unknown chemical, clear the area immediately. Do not attempt to clean up a spill or enter a confined space without specific training and protective gear. If hazardous chemicals are used or stored at your facility, emergency action plans (EAPs) should be in place to handle a chemical spill.
- Do not attempt to clean up a chemical spill or enter a confined space without specific training and protective gear.

Practical Guidelines for Workplace Safety

- Know and practice the emergency action plans at your facility for fires and emergency evacuations, know and practice procedures for performing rescues or first aid duties, and be familiar with alarm system requirements.
- Walk, don't run, on the pool deck—even during emergencies. You cannot provide care to someone else if you are injured on the way to the scene. Train yourself to walk quickly with purpose rather than run (see figure 12.2).
- Keep floors cleared of obstructions and keep guardrails and covers to pits or vats in place.
- When possible, avoid closing or opening your facility when you are alone. If you are alone, consider carrying a cell phone or a personal defense device such as pepper spray and have your whistle ready in case you need to signal for help.
- Follow all the rules and policies of your facility at all times, even when you are using the facility for after-hours training or staff events.
- If you work outdoors, carry insect repellant.
- Obtain practical (hands-on) instruction for equipment you will be authorized to use such as a pool vacuum, lawn tools, or motor-powered watercraft.

Figure 12.2   Walk quickly with a purpose on the pool deck rather than run.

- Notify your supervisor immediately or call your local emergency number (e.g., 9-1-1) if a patron physically threatens you or if violent behavior breaks out or appears likely at your facility.

Three Points of Contact*

*Park District Risk Management Agency 2011

Injuries occur because entering and exiting pools, or mounting and dismounting lifeguard chairs, include the potentially hazardous activities of reaching, twisting, pulling, and climbing. The three-points-of-contact method will help you reduce or eliminate many of the injuries associated with these on-the-job activities (see figure 12.3). The one exception to using the three-points-of-contact method is when you are performing a compact jump while training or performing a rescue.

To perform three points of contact, do the following:

- Wear appropriate water shoes when possible and feasible, to avoid slipping.

- Get a firm grip on the ladder or chair and maintain three points of contact. Two hands and one foot or two feet and one hand should be on the equipment at all times.

- Break three points of contact only when you reach the ground or lifeguard chair platform.

- Mount and dismount facing the ladder or chair.

Don't climb with the rescue tube in your free hand. Either set the tube down on the deck or lifeguard chair when

Figure 12.3   Three points of contact.

climbing out of the pool and climbing or descending the lifeguard chair. After you are firmly standing on the pool deck or seated in the guard chair, strap the rescue tube in position. You may also have another guard hand you the tube. Never jump from the lifeguard chair or platform down to the deck.

Using Safe Lifting Techniques

Injuries occur because moving people or equipment includes the potentially hazardous activities of lifting, reaching, and pulling. Use these techniques when performing extrication or any type of lifting:

Figure 12.4 When moving or lifting heavy items, keep your back straight and lift or lower using your legs.

1. Clear a path before lifting. Know what may be behind you if you will be moving.
2. Have a firm hold. Keep the object close to your body for stability.
3. Have a solid base of support. Keep your feet about shoulder-width apart. When moving, take small steps.
4. Raise and lower by bending your knees and lifting with your legs. Keep your back straight (see figure 12.4).

Using safe lifting techniques will help you reduce or eliminate many of the injuries associated with strain on the back.

Health Considerations

Besides managing safety risks in the workplace, lifeguards need to be aware of health considerations such as skin damage, skin cancer, eye injuries, foot care, and illnesses.

Skin Cancer Awareness

If you lifeguard outdoors, you will be exposed to the elements, including sunlight. The sun emits ultraviolet radiation, which is the primary cause of skin cancer. Chronic exposure to the ultraviolet rays of the sun can also cause skin damage, premature aging, and eye damage. If you work outdoors, you are at risk. The good news is that skin cancer is preventable, but before we talk about protection and screening, here are some sobering facts (Skin Cancer Foundation 2011):

- Between two and three million skin cancers occur globally each year.
- In the United States, one person dies every hour from skin cancer, primarily melanoma.
- Melanoma is the most common form of cancer for young adults 25 to 29 years old and the second most common form of cancer for young people 15 to 24 years old.
- More than 90 percent of all skin cancers are caused by sun exposure, yet fewer than 33 percent of adults, adolescents, and children routinely use sun protection.
- One blistering sunburn in childhood or adolescence more than doubles a person's chances of developing melanoma later in life.
- The effects of skin aging caused by ultraviolet radiation can be seen as early as in a person's 20s.
- Putting proven cancer prevention and early detection techniques into action could eliminate thousands of cases and deaths each year.

The sun emits many wavelengths of light, but UVA and UVB are those that can have the most effects on your skin through overexposure. UVA rays penetrate through glass and clouds and penetrate the skin to its deep layers. UVA is responsible for tanning and contributes to two types of skin cancer. UVB rays penetrate only the superficial layers of skin and are responsible for the reddening and blistering of sunburns. UVB rays are most prominent in the heat of the day from 10 a.m. to 4 p.m. and can be reflected. This property of UVB rays makes them dangerous around water, snow, and ice.

The global solar UV index has been developed to indicate the strength of the solar UV radiation on a scale from 1 (low) to 11-plus (extremely high) (World Health Organization 2002). The ozone layer, which shields the earth from UV radiation, can be affected by depletion and seasonal weather changes. Weather services around the world predict the UV index for the next day and issue the UV index forecast. If the level of solar UV radiation is predicted to be unusually high, you should take appropriate sun-protective precautions and avoid overexposure.

Your lifeguarding job should not be an excuse to get a suntan. You must take personal responsibility to protect yourself, and the best way to accomplish this is to use skin protection products and to cover up.

- *Always* use sunscreen and lip coat rated at SPF 30 or higher. Apply sunscreen at least 30 minutes before exposure. Reapply every two or three hours or more often if you have been sweating or swimming. Lifeguard staff should use a sunscreen log for documenting application.

- In addition to using sunscreen, use sunshade. Have at least one physical barrier, such as a hat, shirt, or umbrella, between you and the sun. Wide-brim hats and tightly woven clothing designed for sun protection are best (see figure 12.5).

- Examine your skin regularly and seek a physician's opinion if you have suspicious-looking moles or dark areas on your skin. You should have a skin cancer check performed by a physician yearly.

Figure 12.5 Lifeguards must follow sun protection best practices.

Facts About Sunscreen in the United States

- To clarify confusing labeling, the FDA released new guidelines and regulations for sunscreen (FDA 2012). A sunscreen may be labeled *broad spectrum* if it provides protection against ultraviolet A (UVA) and ultraviolet B (UVB) radiation.

- Only broad-spectrum sunscreens with a sun protection factor (SPF) of 15 or higher can state that they protect against skin cancer if used as directed with other sun protection measures.

- Sunscreens with an SPF of 2 to 14 will be required to have a warning stating that the product has not been shown to help prevent skin cancer or early skin aging.

- The terms *sunblock*, *sweatproof*, and *waterproof* are no longer allowed on sunscreen labels.

- A sunscreen may claim to be **water resistant**, but the product must specify whether it offers 40 minutes or 80 minutes of protection while swimming or sweating, based on standard testing. Sunscreens that are not water resistant must include an instruction for consumers to use a water-resistant sunscreen if swimming or sweating.

- Sunscreens cannot claim to provide sun protection for **more than two hours** without reapplication.

- The FDA reiterated that sunscreen alone is not enough and that it should be used in conjunction with a complete **sun protection** regimen, including seeking shade and wearing long pants, long-sleeved shirts, hats, and sunglasses.

Eye Care

Your eyes are one of your most important lifeguarding tools. Most of your time is spent scanning for visual indications of problems. Adequate eyesight is critical for your success. Follow these tips to protect your vision:

- Shield your eyes from the effects of the sun, wind, water, and dust by wearing sunglasses that are both ultraviolet protective and physically protective.
- Wear sunglasses with lenses that filter 100 percent of UV rays. Glasses with side protection that do not obscure your peripheral vision are best.
- Have your eyes tested at least once a year to screen for vision problems.
- If you wear glasses or contact lenses to correct your vision, wear them at all times when you are on duty. If you wear contact lenses, close your eyes briefly when you enter the water to avoid losing your lenses. If you know you will be swimming with lenses in or may have to get in the water during a rescue, consider wearing disposable lenses so that if they do come out, you can easily replace them.
- Keep your lenses clean and replace them as needed. Chlorine and other pool contaminants may remain on a contact lens and cause eye inflammation.
- Wear sunglasses that are both ultraviolet protective and physically protective.

Foot Care

Appropriate footwear can help protect you from injury due to slips and falls, exposure to bodily fluids, and burns from hot deck surfaces. Footwear should not interfere with your ability to make a rescue, and it should be able to drain water and dry quickly to avoid bacteria build up. It is also important that footwear have a nonskid sole, fit snugly, and do not "flop" if you need to walk quickly during an emergency. Shoes designed for water wear are ideal (see figure 12.6).

Figure 12.6 Wear appropriate footwear to avoid injury, illness, and burns.

Illness

The following methods will reduce work-related illnesses:

- Minimize your risk of dehydration, heat exhaustion, or heatstroke by drinking lots of water. Keep a water bottle on the stand and make sure you have protection from the sun.
- Obtain a hepatitis B vaccination if you have not been immunized.
- Use personal protective equipment (PPE) and follow universal precautions when in contact with blood, bodily fluids, or other potentially infected material.
- Do not swallow recreational water.
- Always use your personal protective equipment when cleaning up bodily substances.
- Dry wet swimwear frequently to avoid skin chafing and urinary tract infections.
- If you work at an indoor aquatic venue, especially those with waterfalls or sprays, you may become exposed to chlorine-resistant bacteria in small water particles that have become airborne. Lifeguards who work long shifts in this type of environment appear to be at higher risk. Seek medical attention if you develop chronic respiratory symptoms such as a cough or difficulty breathing.
- Stay hydrated.

▶ VISIT THE WEB RESOURCE

You can reinforce your learning by visiting the web resource, where you can do the following in the interactive online learning activities based on chapter 12:

◆ Evaluate workplace scenarios and make decisions about ways to minimize risk.

◆ Watch a video about chemical safety.

◆ Test your knowledge and receive feedback.

CHAPTER SUMMARY

Key points	Best practices on the job
• Do not attempt to clean up a chemical spill or enter a confined space without specific training and protective gear. • Climbing up or down from a lifeguard station or tower can be dangerous. • Workplace slips and falls are a common cause of injury. • When moving or lifting heavy items, keep your back straight and lift or lower using your legs. • Sun exposure can cause skin cancer. • Ultraviolet light can damage the eyes. • Bare feet around an aquatic facility are at risk of injury, burns, or exposure to bodily fluids, fungus, chemicals, and other hazards. • High temperature and humidity can cause dehydration.	• Drink water frequently and have it on the stand if possible to avoid dehydration. • Use three points of contact when climbing up or down a lifeguard chair. • Walk with a purpose, don't run. • Receive specialized training before handling chemicals or dangerous equipment. • Use safe lifting techniques. • Always use sunscreen and lip coat rated at SPF 30 or higher. Apply sunscreen at least 30 minutes before exposure. • Wear a physical barrier for sun protection such as a shirt or hat, or be completely shaded by an umbrella. • Wear sunglasses that are both ultraviolet protective and physically protective. • Wear appropriate footwear to avoid injury, illness, and burns.

Meeting Workplace Expectations

CHAPTER OBJECTIVES

This chapter

- explains the components of professionalism and the way in which these traits relate to your performance as a lifeguard;
- explains the need for ongoing and site-specific training;
- reinforces the need for responsibility, accountability, and good judgment;
- identifies what to expect from your employer; and
- identifies what your employer will expect from you.

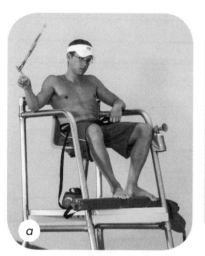

Professionalism is one of the most important components of the StarGuard course because it carries through to everything you do. Even something as simple as the way you sit in the lifeguard stand can affect the professional image you project. Note the differences in figure 13.1 between a professional posture and an unprofessional posture.

Professionalism can be expressed in many ways; the most common is the opinion others have of you based on the way you act, talk, dress, or perform your duties. This chapter explores how to maintain a high level of professionalism in your workplace.

How your guests, coworkers, and employer perceive you can have a significant effect on your success as a lifeguard. Your positive actions define you as a professional. Your unprofessional actions can place patrons at risk.

Figure 13.1 *(a,b)* Exhibiting unprofessional behavior while on lifeguard duty; *(c,d)* exhibiting professional behavior while on lifeguard duty.

Projecting a Professional Image

To perform your job at a high level, you must instill confidence in the patrons you serve. Because they may know nothing about you, the only way they can evaluate your ability is through what they see. If you slouch in the lifeguard stand looking bored and twirling your whistle, they will assume you are bored and don't care about the safety of those in your care. If you seem more interested in goofing around with your coworkers or kids at the pool than in doing your job, this image will affect the opinion others have of both you and the facility you represent. Your actions speak louder than your words. You can project two kinds of behaviors: (1) those that enhance your image and (2) those that demean your image.

Professional Behaviors

Your positive actions define you as a professional. Your unprofessional actions can place patrons at risk. You can do several things every day to build up your professional image, including the following:

- Wear a clean, neat uniform that distinguishes you from the crowd.
- Maintain excellent posture. When sitting you should have your feet flat, your shoulders forward, and the rescue tube across your lap with the strap gathered.
- Keep focused and follow StarGuard best practices.
- Behave as you expect others to behave.
- Speak to others as you wish to be spoken to.

Unprofessional Behaviors

Some behaviors are not appropriate for lifeguards, harm your professional image, and may place patrons at risk. Make a conscious effort to eliminate any of these behaviors while **on the stand or in view of patrons**:

- Slouching
- Whistle twirling
- Looking bored (e.g., frequently looking at watch)
- Sitting with legs crossed or leaning your head on your hand or hands
- Socializing
- Talking on the phone
- Texting
- Reading, smoking, chewing gum, grooming, or eating
- Talking in a belittling manner, gossiping, or using profanity
- Participating in pranks or encouraging unsafe patron behavior
- Appearing to be unfocused or tired
- Using the rescue tube as a backrest or footrest
- Playing with rescue equipment
- Diving or cannonballing from the lifeguard stand
- Wearing sloppy or inappropriate clothing or personal attire

Professionalism, however, goes beyond your actions. It involves your commitment to performing at a high level. This commitment requires ongoing training to maintain your skills and fitness at rescue-ready levels, the ability to take responsibility for your performance, and good judgment.

Preservice, In-Service, and Fitness Training

It is imperative that all lifeguards hired are currently able to perform effectively in the workplace. As a result, your employer will need to assess your ability, before allowing you to be on lifeguard duty (MAHC 2015). This assessment will typically be conducted during pre-service training, during which you will also practice skills on the equipment available at your facility and learn the emergency action plans.

In-service training is an important part of your professional development. Depending on the requirements of your facility, you can expect to spend several hours per month in site-specific training sessions. Topics should be geared toward maintaining your rescue and basic life support skills, using the rescue equipment at your facility, practicing surveillance skills, and reviewing other information related to your responsibilities. In-service training conducted where you work enhances your development in the following ways:

- Continuing to assess that you can perform and helping you gain confidence (which will be evident not only to your employer but also to you)
- Strengthening teamwork with your coworkers

Ongoing in-service training is an important workplace expectation.

- Identifying areas of concern and developing more effective EAPs
- Building endurance and stamina, especially in regard to physical conditioning
- Reinforcing your knowledge of workplace safety standards

Physical conditioning to maintain rescue-ready fitness levels is also important. Your fitness training schedule should be appropriate for the physical response and rescue demands of the lifeguarding position you hold at your workplace. In most instances, at a minimum you must maintain the physical ability to perform effective CPR compressions, descend to the deepest area you are assigned, and swim to the farthest point in the area you are assigned.

Accountability

Expect to be involved in an evaluation system such as a lifeguard audit or review that measures your ability to perform your prevention, surveillance, response and rescue, emergency care, and professional skills. Whether this evaluation is conducted by your supervisors or others, it will provide you with an accurate picture of how well you focus on the important objectives of your job.

The first part of a lifeguard review, which is usually conducted without your knowing that you are being watched, documents your level of professionalism, the prevention strategies you are using, and the level of surveillance you are providing. The second part usually consists of an aquatic rescue and emergency care scenario to evaluate your ability to manage an emergency. The objectives of an audit or review are as follows:

- Document your ability and the operational procedures in place to support you
- Identify any areas that need improvement so that remediation and education can be conducted
- Recognize and award you for outstanding performance

For those facilities that use the StarReview system, awards and recognition are given to the lifeguards who are part of the review, and an overall facility award is given based on operational and management evaluation. Awards are based on earning a rating of three, four, or five stars. Lifeguards and facilities that earn awards are set apart by actions, appearance, attitude, and workplace culture. This distinction validates consistent planning, training, and risk management practices that exceed standards.

Reviews (audits) are valuable competency assessment and motivational tools.

Judgment Skills

When you are on the job, you will often face choices that determine how you act. Your ability to use sound judgment to make decisions will mean the difference between being valued at your workplace or not, and it may mean the difference between saving a life or not. What types of decisions might you have to make? What would you decide if the following thoughts were going through your head?

- *I wonder if that is a shadow on the bottom or if I'm just seeing things. Should I go check it out or wait to see if it moves or goes away?*
- *The water is a bit cloudy, and I can't see the bottom. Should I close the pool even though I know people will be upset?*
- *Should I put on sunscreen or get a tan?*
- *My replacement didn't show up on time, and I have to be somewhere. Should I leave?*
- *My friends want me to go with them to a baseball game. Should I call in sick even though I know the pool will be short a lifeguard?*
- *I partied late last night, got hardly any sleep, and feel terrible. Should I let my supervisor know and reassign my duties, or should I go on the stand and fake being alert?*
- *It will be slow at the pool today, and I know my supervisor won't be around. Should I call some friends to come hang out with me while I work?*

These are just a few of the types of decisions you will make every day. Depending on the choice you make, the long-term consequences could be devastating. Your decisions should be based on the principles that value life, including yours, above all else. The decisions you make outside the workplace can also have serious consequences. You might think that what you do on your own time doesn't matter, but the effects of substances such as alcohol or drugs or the consequences of lack of sleep can carry over into your working hours even though the activity occurred on your personal time.

What to Expect From Your Employer

The StarGuard course provides the information you need to understand the objectives of lifeguarding, teaches you the required physical skills, and suggests best practices as methods to help you perform. Each aquatic facility is different, however, and uses different types of rescue equipment and procedures. Therefore, you need to make sure that your employer provides you the necessary equipment and supplemental training and support to do your job. At a minimum, your employer should provide the following:

- Personal protective equipment, such as gloves and a barrier mask
- Rescue tube
- Umbrella or shade for outdoor venues
- Drinking water

- Lifeguard identification, such as a uniform
- Communication or signal device
- Telephone to call EMS
- First aid supplies
- A break from scanning at least every hour
- Ability to change position so that you can stay alert and can scan the bottom
- Orientation to and practice of the facility's emergency action plan (EAP)
- Training in how to safely handle chemicals and hazardous materials if you are responsible for using them
- Orientation to and practice with the rescue equipment present at your facility
- Orientation to facility operating procedures
- Ongoing in-service training
- Ongoing performance assessment
- Coverage under a liability insurance policy or immunity from liability

If your employer does not provide this support, you may be in a position in which it is impossible for you to perform at minimum standards.

What Your Employer Will Expect From You

A big part of being professional is being a good employee. You may just be entering the workforce, and this may be your first job. You need to know what will be expected so that you don't make mistakes that could jeopardize your job or ruin opportunities in the future. Just as you need support from your employer to do your job, your employer needs support from you to operate a safe facility. Your employer should require you to do the following:

- Provide proof of certification or authorization for lifeguard, CPR, first aid, and other required emergency care courses.
- Provide proof, through skills assessment, that you can perform rescue skills, including testing to see whether you can descend to the deepest area of the pool to which you will be assigned.
- Uphold employment agreements, whether written or verbal. If you are hired with the understanding that you will work certain dates, such as through the summer, you must honor this agreement.
- If you cannot work an assigned shift, find an approved substitute or follow the procedure set up at your facility. Calling in at the last minute or not showing up for a shift compromises the safety of everyone at the facility.
- Participate in a drug-testing program. Depending on the regulations in your location, this program may include preemployment screening, random testing, or postincident testing.
- Exhibit a high level of professionalism and follow StarGuard best practices.

▶ VISIT THE WEB RESOURCE

You can reinforce your learning by visiting the web resource, where you can do the following in the interactive online learning activities based on chapter 13:

- ◆ Identify behaviors that can contribute to or take away from a lifeguard's professional image.
- ◆ Evaluate scenarios to improve your judgment and decision-making skills.
- ◆ Test your knowledge and receive feedback.

CHAPTER SUMMARY

Key points	Best practices on the job
• Your positive actions define you as a professional. • Your unprofessional actions can place patrons at risk. • Your employer is responsible for providing you with the site-specific ongoing training and the equipment necessary to do your job. • You are responsible for following best practices on the job.	• Arrive on time and always find a substitute if you can't work. • Project a positive attitude. • Wear a clean, appropriate uniform. • Regularly attend inservice training. • Maintain fitness and skills at rescue-ready levels. • Uphold employment agreements—especially remaining until the end of the season. • Be committed to improvement and accountability. • Serve as a role model and leader to your peers. • Participate in regular audits and performance evaluations. • Do not twirl your whistle; use your rescue tube as a footrest or backrest; slouch or use other relaxed posture; appear bored, unfocused, tired, or not engaged with the zone; socialize, text, read, or eat while on the lifeguard stand or in view of guests; use poor judgment in your actions; or come to work high or hung over. • Demonstrate that you understand the importance of your job, are motivated, and accept responsibility. • Undergo ongoing training and skills assessment (provided by your employer) related to the site-specific needs at the facility where you will work.

Considering Site- and Situation-Specific Circumstances

CHAPTER OBJECTIVES

This chapter

- identifies considerations for single-lifeguard facilities;
- provides strategies for lifeguarding people with disabilities and describes the challenges of lifeguarding during parties or special events;
- examines considerations when lifeguarding swim team practice or during swim instruction classes;
- examines considerations when lifeguarding swim meets, open-water swims, or triathlons;
- identifies the risks involved in lifeguarding outside the workplace; and
- provides information about training options for lifeguarding in wilderness and open-water settings.

The basic concepts and skills of lifeguarding apply to any aquatic environment: Everyone is at risk of drowning, and your job is to perform preventive interventions, look for distress and drowning, and respond in an emergency. But aquatic environments—and how patrons use them—vary, and to be effective, you may need to consider additional strategies. As explained in chapter 2, the management of the facility where you work, or those who hire you for special events, will set the policies and operating procedures that guide your day-to-day actions. The goal of this chapter is to provide an overview and awareness of site- and situation-specific considerations. The suggestions may or may not be feasible or relevant in your situation, and the information does not cover all possible circumstances. Chapter 15 provides additional site-specific information for the waterpark environment, and chapter 16 provides information for nonsurf waterfronts. The most common site-specific consideration involves a situation in which a single lifeguard is on duty.

Single-Lifeguard Facilities

Having more than one lifeguard on duty has many advantages and is the preferred situation, but this setup is often not feasible, particularly for small, infrequently used venues. Economic or logistic limitations may mean choosing between having one lifeguard or none. If you work at a single-guard facility, you need to be aware of how to adapt the StarGuard Risk Management Model to your circumstances.

Prevention Considerations

Most single-guard facilities are not open to the general public, meaning that those who attend do so through a residence, membership, or guest relationship. This relationship allows patrons to be informed in advance of policies, rules, and their responsibility in preventing illness, injury, or drowning at the facility. The facility should have a written safety plan to address the specific risks as well as support staff who would be present to assist in an emergency or provide support by monitoring performance of the lifeguard on duty.

When you are by yourself, your primary responsibility and attention will need to be on patron surveillance. You'll need to perform other responsibilities such as cleaning, administrative tasks, and customer service at times when you are not responsible for scanning so that those tasks don't intrude on your ability to provide constant and dedicated surveillance. You must manage these duties in a way that does not interfere with your ability to enforce rules, and see the entire pool—including the ability to scan the bottom frequently.

Surveillance Considerations

When you are the only lifeguard, the entire water area is your zone, 100 percent of the time. Your scanning strategies and responsibilities do not change, but because no one can rotate in for you, you must consider the following:

- How will you work in breaks from surveillance? You may have periods when no patrons are at the facility, followed by periods of high use. Or your facility may have patrons in the water for your entire hours-long shift, and you will need to have a procedure for keeping patrons out of the water while you are on break or performing other tasks. During long shifts you need to take a break to keep your vigilance level adequate so that you can provide effective patron surveillance. One method is to clear the water for 10 minutes every hour so that you can break from surveillance, perform prevention or maintenance tasks, and care for yourself. Everyone should clear the water—including adults, who are at risk of having a medical emergency while swimming that would require your immediate attention. Other staff may need to be at poolside to ensure that patrons stay out of the water unless there is a means of appropriately securing the area against entry until you are back in a position to provide surveillance. Heat, humidity, and patron count may warrant more frequent breaks.

- Most single-guard facilities require that patrons check in or provide proof of membership or use privileges. How can you manage this process so that it does not interfere with your ability to provide surveillance?

- Is the lifeguard station located in a position where you can see the entire zone, including the access point into the facility? You need to be able to see when patrons arrive and when they leave.

- Lifeguards at single-guard facilities have more personal interaction with the patrons and are often expected to be social and accommodating. What strategies will you employ to deal with patrons who request attention that takes away from your ability to provide surveillance?

The safety plan at your facility should address and provide you with site-specific guidance for these considerations.

Response and Rescue Considerations

When you are the only lifeguard, being able to alert others that you need help is critically important. You will need to know the system at your facility for summoning others and for contacting EMS. The most effective communication system is an alert button so that you can quickly activate the emergency response of coworkers, such as front desk personnel, who have been instructed on how to help you and who know the facility's emergency action plan. The alert button is wired directly to a place where someone is always present to hear it. The button should be close to you, ideally on your person, so that you don't have to travel to the button before assisting a distressed or drowning victim, thereby losing valuable time.

A secondary method is to use whistle or air horn signals. You should practice to be sure that those who will respond can hear the signals, in a variety of noise conditions. In cases when you cannot alert coworkers that you need help, you will have to rely on bystanders. Tell bystanders what you need them to do. Use clear and concise directions.

Some ways to use support personnel or bystanders include the following:

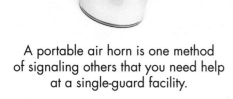

A portable air horn is one method of signaling others that you need help at a single-guard facility.

- Calling EMS. Be sure the calling instructions and facility address are clearly identified near the phone.
- Meeting EMS to direct them to the scene.
- Clearing the pool and crowd control.
- Bringing equipment.
- Helping you extricate the victim.
- Helping you perform CPR compressions.
- Helping you perform rescue breaths if the person is trained to do so.
- Locating family members if they are not present.
- Calling for the assistance of others within your facility's chain of response.

Emergency Care Considerations

During an emergency, bystanders can be used to help you provide CPR if they are willing. Research has shown that bystanders can perform effective chest compressions with minimal instruction. While you manage the airway and provide rescue breaths between sets of compressions, direct the bystander to

- place the heels of her or his hands on the center of the victim's chest and
- keeping her or his arms straight, push hard at a rate of 100 to 120 times per minute, letting the chest recoil after each push.

If needed, you can monitor the count and let the bystander know to stop after 30 compressions so that you can provide 2 rescue breaths. As needed, provide feedback to the person giving compressions about the rate.

Workplace Considerations

The single-lifeguard workplace can be extremely challenging. Performing well at multiguard facilities is easy when something is always going on and supervisors are constantly monitoring your performance. But when you are alone, you need to have a high level of personal responsibility and accountability to maintain best practices and a high level of vigilance. A true measure of your professionalism is what you do when no one is watching. You should always follow best practices that are appropriate for the situation and avoid behaviors that take away from your professional image. When patrons are present there is no place for socializing, texting, talking on your phone, reading, sleeping, or other behaviors that would not be allowed if you were being directly supervised all the time.

At a single-guard facility you need to have a high level of personal responsibility and accountability to maintain best practices and a high level of vigilance.

Lifeguarding People With Disabilities

Most people know someone with a disability or may even have one themselves. A disability occurs when a health condition or disorder results in an inability to perform typical functions, such as walking, learning, working, eating, grooming, and sometimes social interactions. A disability can be caused by conditions at birth, genetic reasons, trauma, or illness later in life.

Individuals who come to your facility may have disabling conditions that cause them to function differently. A person with a disability might visit an aquatic facility alone or accompanied by family members or a caregiver. As medical science continues to advance, you can expect more and more people with disabilities to be active in the community. Your professional responsibility should be to help people with disabilities enjoy the aquatic recreation environment with dignity (Lepore et al. 2007). Because a person with a disability may function differently from a person without a disability, you may have to communicate with him or her in a different manner, provide accessibility or other accommodations, and consider additional safety issues.

It is important to realize that many disabilities are nonvisual, meaning you can't tell by looking at a person that a disability is present. This understanding is especially important for a person with autism or other cognitive disability.

Your responsibility is to help swimmers with disabilities
safely enjoy the water with dignity.

Communication

Do not make assumptions about the abilities of a person with a disability. When you talk with a person with a disability, the following guidelines will help you communicate effectively:

- Use person-first language, such as "person with a disability" instead of "disabled person."
- Don't raise your voice; speak in a normal tone.
- When assisting people with disabilities, first ask whether they want help, and if so, ask how they would like to be helped. Ask the person directly rather than speak to the caregiver about the person.
- Make certain that assistive features of the facility, such as pool lifts, are clean and in working order.
- Talk to the patron the same way you would want someone to talk to a member of your family or to you.

Accessibility and Accommodation

Every pool in the United States must be equipped by law with a lift device to assist people with disabilities with entering and exiting the water. Be familiar with the type of lift at your facility and how to use it.

It is also important for you to know your facility's procedure to follow if a guest with a disability needs to have a policy adapted to accommodate his or her ability to use features. For example, some facilities provide a special needs access pass to guests with disabilities to reduce the wait time in long lines or other accommodations.

Safety

When enforcing safety regulations, keep in mind that the rules are meant to keep all patrons safe, including people with disabilities. You can be flexible about rules for a patron with a disability, however, as long as being flexible doesn't create a safety hazard. To keep all pool patrons safe, follow these guidelines:

- If a patron with a disability breaks a pool rule, warn him or her and explain the rule just as you would to any other swimmer.
- Watch a person with a disability when she or he is in the water, just as you would any other swimmer while you are scanning. It isn't necessary to know in advance that a person with a disability is in your zone—your scanning, targeting and assessing the situation remain in effect for all swimmers (Grosse 2014). Some of the person's normal movements may look like distress but are not. Watch for changes in the disabled person's movement patterns. If you notice something different or unusual, target the person, assess the situation, and decide whether you need to take action.
- Some people with disabilities will be accompanied by assistive animals, such as dogs, cats, or even monkeys. These well-trained assistants are allowed on the pool deck but not in the water in most circumstances.

Let's now look at some strategies to consider when lifeguarding at events such as parties or during programs and competitions.

Lifeguarding Special Events and Programs

Chapter 2 identifies the high-risk nature of birthday parties, camps, and other group outings at an aquatic facility. These same risks can be present at events that your facility hosts, such as inflatable play structures use and "dive-in" movies, concerts, and staff events, whether held during or after hours.

Inflatable Structures

Portable and inflatable water play and water adventure courses are becoming increasingly popular and are found in both pool and open water environments. The configurations and features vary, and so will the safety operating procedures that should be in place. You will need to follow manufacturer's guidelines for safe installation. When evaluating the policy and procedure for your operation, use the StarGuard risk management model to assess the way to reduce risk.

Follow the policy and procedures set forth by your facility for safety when using an inflatable play structure.

Prevention questions to consider:

- How will access be controlled?
- Will there be a swimming ability or age requirement?
- Will lifejackets be required? How will these be sized and distributed?
- What is the maximum number of users allowed at a time on the structure?
- What rules will be in place and how will users be made aware of the rules?

Surveillance questions to consider:

- Where should the lifeguard(s) be positioned to be able to scan the area on top and below every area of the structure with no blind spots?

Response and rescue questions to consider:

- Has an emergency action plan (EAP) been developed and practiced for responding to an emergency when the structure is in place?
- Do rescue methods need to be adapted?

Emergency care questions to consider:

- If an injury occurs on the structure will first aid be provided there, or will the person be moved off the structure and out of the water?

Workplace environment questions to consider:

- What behaviors are expected of staff to present a professional approach to managing operation and safety on the structure?
- Are staff allowed to use the structure? If so, do they understand the need to follow the rules like everyone else, and have a lifeguard providing surveillance when in use?

For special events where guests float on the surface on equipment, requiring everyone to wear a life jacket is one strategy to aid with surveillance during the event.

Movies, Concerts, and After-Hours Parties

Special events bring a higher level of excitement to an aquatic facility. Consider these situations:

- If events are held after dark, consider ways you will have to adapt your surveillance strategies. If patrons are watching movies from within the water, one method is to require that everyone float on the surface on a tube or raft—no swimming—so that when you scan you are looking for empty floats as a sign to target and assess. Note that the presence of the floats could obscure your view of the bottom, making it difficult to scan. Other strategies include requiring that everyone wear a life jacket and having a pair of scuba divers providing surveillance from under the water.

- If music or movies are loud, you may need to adapt your emergency communication signals so that they can be heard over the noise. Alternatively, you could develop a system of visual signals if feasible.

- If alcohol is served at special events, remember that patrons who are drinking are at higher risk of drowning and making poor decisions about their ability in the water.

- The same level of surveillance needs to be provided when staff are using the facility. Staff should follow the same rules and expectations required of patrons.

Swim Classes and Swim Team Practice

The role of the instructor or coach is to teach and focus on his or her students. Safety practices should be a part of any program, but your role is to provide dedicated surveillance of the entire zone. Consider these situations:

- Young children who are nonswimmers or weak swimmers can quickly and silently slip off the edge and immediately submerge to the bottom. Pay particular attention to the areas along the wall during your scan. If parents are allowed on deck during programs, other siblings often accompany them. The adults may get distracted, allowing children to wander off—often toward the pool.

- Participants in water fitness or therapy classes may lose their footing, tip into a floating position on or just under the surface, and be unable to right themselves to breathe. This situation is even more likely if the person is wearing flotation or resistance devices on the ankles or lower body.

- If scuba training is conducted in your facility, coordinate with the instructor to determine communication signals and your role in rescuing a submerged diver. Dive instructors are trained in the techniques to use in a scuba emergency, but a situation may occur in which the instructor is the person in need of care.

Swim lessons can be a high risk situation and should have a dedicated lifeguard providing surveillance.

- If military training is conducted at your facility, coordinate with the commanding officer to determine communication signals and your role in rescuing a submerged soldier. Military training often involves activities that would not normally be allowed, and clear understanding by all involved about expectations, assumption of risk, and the EAP is important.

- Lifeguarding a team of highly skilled swimmers, divers, water polo players, or synchronized swimmers may seem unnecessary. But instances of death and drowning during practice occur more often than you may think. Skilled athletes are not immune to medical emergencies such as seizures, heart attacks, asthma, dehydration, or sudden underwater blackout that occur suddenly and silently in the water. Collision injuries with the bottom or other swimmers can also occur.

Swim Meets

Most aquatic sport competitions are held under the sanction of a governing organization that sets safety guidelines and rules. Sanctioned competitive swim meets usually have a person designated as a safety marshal who will help enforce rules, such as feetfirst entries during warm-up and designated lanes for supervised practice of dives off the starting platforms. Communicate with the safety marshal ahead of time to make certain that everyone understands the EAP for the event and to ensure that it does not conflict with the EAP for the facility.

Medical emergencies that occur in the water are a risk
during team practices or competitions.

Open-Water Swims and Triathlons

Consider these challenges of open-water swims and triathlons:

- Swimmers can get kicked or pushed under by crowd crush during a mass start.
- A person who experiences a medical emergency while in the middle of the pack will be hard to spot and get to.
- The course may be spread over a long distance, so visual communication between spotters may be hard to see and whistles may be hard to hear, especially if it is windy.
- Swimming against waves, currents, or tides may cause swimmers to expend more energy than expected or to become seasick.
- With the growing popularity of triathlons, more novice and inexperienced athletes are participating. Do not assume that all participants in a triathlon are strong swimmers.
- Water temperature can play a factor in whether or not a race should be held. Guidelines vary depending upon the sanctioning body. The most common international guidelines set a temperature not lower than 64.4° Fahrenheit (18° C) and not higher than 87.8° Fahrenheit (31° C).
- In an open-water swim, the final decision of whether or not to conduct the race may rest on your assessment of the safety of the conditions.

The tragic and untimely deaths of swimmers in competitive environments have resulted in a push for improved safety protocols, precautions, and procedures in open-water swimming events (Pound et al. 2011).

If you are assigned to lifeguard at one of these events, you will likely be a part of a rescue team that includes spotters in kayaks or on other watercraft, along with support personnel such as EMS, rescue divers, and event managers such as the race director, safety officer, and race referee. You should receive race-specific orientation and training before the event that provides information about

- course layout and expected conditions,
- the type of start,
- communication signals,
- the safety and surveillance plan,
- the EAP for responsive and unresponsive victim incidents, and
- the evacuation plan.

Prerace training and orientation should include practice scenarios with the rescue team.

Each type of aquatic activity or setting has unique challenges to be considered.

Lifeguarding Outside the Workplace

You may be asked by friends, family, or acquaintances to lifeguard outside your workplace, such as for special events or parties at private homes. Often in these situations the hosts do not expect you to enforce rules because they don't want to spoil the fun and may not understand the risks. Rescue equipment may not be available, and you may not be familiar with emergency procedures for that location.

Absolutely do not drink alcohol and avoid distractions like food and games with guests. If you need to take a restroom or food break from scanning, appoint a sober, responsible person to watch the water. Give the person your whistle, rescue tube, or some other token as a reminder that she or he is watching the water. There are numerous case reports of children drowning at crowded backyard parties because everyone thought that someone else was watching the pool.

Unless you are representing and being paid by your employer in an after-hours situations, you will not be covered by liability insurance unless you have your own policy. In these situations, make sure that the host clearly defines what is expected of you. You should get those expectations and a release from liability in writing. Define expectations and get a release from liability in writing before lifeguarding outside the workplace.

Lifeguarding in Wilderness or Open Water Settings

Many organized groups visit remote places and find themselves swimming in rivers, creeks, springs, and lakes. Lifeguarding in wilderness environments requires strategies and adaptations different from traditional lifeguard training. The Wilderness StarGuard

Wilderness StarGuard provides specialized training for remote environments.

program is a specialty certification offered to wilderness-based youth programs and camps, backcountry guide services, paddling schools, and other outdoor leadership organizations, delivered through a partnership with Landmark Learning.

Open-water settings, particularly beaches with surf, tides, and currents, require an additional lifeguard skill set than what is covered in the basic StarGuard course. In particular, site-specific protocols for rescue equipment (boats, Jet Skis, paddle boards, kayaks), communication, search and recovery, dangerous aquatic conditions and hazardous areas, working within a public safety response team, intervention procedure, and conditioning for long-distance swims and runs must be included, along with practice and field training in open-water rescues. For more information about open water and surf lifeguard training, contact the Starfish Aquatics Institute.

▶ VISIT THE WEB RESOURCE

You can reinforce your learning by visiting the web resource, where you can do the following in the interactive online learning activities based on chapter 14:

◆ Evaluate scenarios that could occur at an aquatic facility and build decision-making skills.

◆ Test your knowledge and receive feedback.

CHAPTER SUMMARY

Key points	Best practices on the job
• At a single guard facility you need to have a high level of personal responsibility and accountability to maintain best practices and a high level of vigilance.	• Know how to adapt your skills and strategies to meet the needs of a specific activity, situation, or site (e.g., an inflatable play structure, swim meet, triathlon, open-water swim).
• Your responsibility is to help swimmers with disabilities safely enjoy the water with dignity.	• Follow the operating policies and procedure in place at your workplace and understand how to interact effectively with people with disabilities.
• Each type of aquatic activity or setting has unique challenges to be considered.	• When making adaptations for site and situation specific circumstances, understand the objectives of your training and the ultimate goal of your actions.
• Beaches with surf, tides and currents require an additional lifeguard skill set which includes fitness conditioning and field training.	• Define expectations and get a release from liability in writing before lifeguarding outside the workplace.
• Lifeguarding outside the workplace exposes you to legal risks.	

15

Lifeguarding at Waterparks and Similar Venues

CHAPTER OBJECTIVES

This chapter

- identifies features of a waterpark;
- identifies additional prevention, surveillance, response, rescue, and emergency care strategies for the waterpark setting; and
- reinforces workplace safety and performance expectations for the waterpark setting.

If you will work at a waterpark or a facility with play features such as slides or moving water, you must complete the waterpark training module in addition to the basic StarGuard course. The waterpark module may be taught at the same time as your StarGuard course or presented as a separate training session. Each section of this chapter covers a StarGuard Risk Management Model component as it applies to lifeguarding in waterparks. *Note:* The material presented in this chapter supplements the other chapters in this text.

Waterpark Features

The unique features at waterparks or at aquatic facilities with attractions like those at a waterpark require additional prevention, surveillance, and response strategies. Let's look at the most common attractions and features you will find at a waterpark.

Waterslides

Waterslides have a dispatch area, a flume, and a terminus, or end. The dispatch area is where riders gather and enter the flume. The flume is the riding channels of a waterslide that accommodates riders using or not using mats, tubes, rafts, and other transport vehicles as they slide along a path lubricated by a water flow. The terminus is where the slide action ends. The terminus may be in a landing, or catch, pool or in a runout section of the flume. A landing pool is a designated section located at the exit of one or more waterslide flumes. This body of water is intended and designed to receive a user emerging from the flume for the purpose of ending the slide action and providing a means of exit to a deck or walkway area.

Waterslides are of several types:

- **Body slides and tube slides.** These fiberglass flumes might be open (with high, curved walls) or enclosed to form a tube through which the rider slides. The classification of slide is determined by whether a guest rides with or without an inflatable tube. Some slides have a combination of open and closed areas. The end of the flume is about even with the water surface, and the flow of the water pushes riders into a catch pool about 3 to 4 feet (.9 to 1.2 m) deep. Wider flumes are designed to hold an inner tube on which the rider sits. Tubes might be single for one rider or double for two riders at a time. Another type of body slide is called a drop or shotgun slide because instead of pushing the rider into a catch pool at water level, the slide ends several feet (about a meter) above the surface, and the rider drops the distance from the slide to the water. Catch pools for drop slides are deeper.

- **Drop slides.** Drop slides release guests into the water from a height above the water rather than deliver them to the water entry point.

- **Speed slides.** Speed slides are narrow, steep, straight slides that start from a high tower. They are body slides, but they don't push the rider into a catch pool. Instead, when the slide reaches the ground, the rider is pushed down a long flume until the movement stops. The flume run-out area usually contains just a few inches (several centimeters) of water.

- **Children's slides.** Children's slides are not high and are usually attached to a play structure, although some are stand-alone attractions. These slides usually send a rider into a few inches (several centimeters) of water at the bottom of the slide. Some are similar in construction to a playground slide and are mounted on the pool deck or within the basin of a pool. These slides allow riders to slide from an elevated height into the water.

- **Multilane or mat slides.** Multilane slides are similar to speed slides but are usually not as tall and several riders can participate at once. Multilane slides are often designed to be used with a foam mat for the rider to sit or lie on.

- **Family raft slides.** Raft rides are usually a combination of wide, closed, and open flumes that can accommodate a raft holding several people. These slides push the raft into a catch pool, usually 3 to 4 feet (.9 to 1.2 m) deep, at the end of the ride. Blaster raft rides are similar to family raft rides but have rollercoaster-like features that allow the raft to go both uphill and downhill throughout the ride.

- **Serpentine slides.** Serpentine slides are waterslides with twisted flume segments.

- **Specialty slides.** Attractions that combine features of several types of slides or have unique elements of thrill are continually being introduced into the waterpark environment. Examples include flumes that enter into a vortex with a drop into water below and shotgun drop slides in which the rider stands on a platform that falls away to drop the rider into a vertical flume.

Wave Pools

A wave pool creates an experience similar to the water action of an open-water surf environment. A wave pool is usually fan shaped, with a wide zero-depth "beachfront" entry area where the water meets the "shore" and a narrow, deeper area where the waves are generated and pushed out to the zero depth. Swimmers are usually not allowed access along the back wall of the wave pool where the waves are created.

Flowing Currents

A flowing-current attraction is commonly known as a lazy river ride. A lazy river is a long, narrow, shallow pool of water moving in one direction. Guests usually float on inner tubes as they are pushed by the slow-moving current, although some attractions allow guests without tubes to be in the water as well. A lazy river usually has several points along the route where guests can enter or exit the water. A wave river or torrent river uses wave action to move riders faster along the route.

Play Structures

Play structures are usually located in shallow water and have multiple levels that include waterslides, interactive water features, and tipping beakers.

Specialty Rides and Attractions

Other popular waterpark attractions include surf pools dedicated to the sport of surfing and not general play, stand-alone rides that generate a flow of water to create a surfing experience, climbing walls, and in-water areas for basketball or volleyball. New types of attractions are always being designed and introduced to the waterpark industry, and that trend is likely to continue.

Facilities Similar to Waterparks

A waterpark is not the only place where you might find waterslides, interactive water features, and other water attractions. A spray ground or spray park or splash pad consists of a variety of water-play elements without any standing water. Because there is no standing water, lifeguards may not be required. Activity pools (also known as leisure pools) are designed primarily for play activity and combine a variety of design features such as lap swimming lanes, a small lazy river, a zero-depth entry, waterslides, and possibly other water elements such as pad walks in one venue, rather than having the features spread out as in a larger waterpark. This type of facility is becoming common in both indoor and outdoor community recreation and resort settings. Waterslides are often added to older swimming pools as part of a renovation. You will use the same waterpark strategies and considerations for lifeguarding these attractions, adapted for the specific location.

This type of leisure pool has many of the features of a waterpark.

Prevention Strategy at Waterparks

The waterpark industry has an overall excellent track record of providing safe recreation. The most effective way to reduce the risk of injury to guests enjoying waterpark attractions is to enforce the rules for proper usage consistently and regularly inspect the attraction.

Safety and Use Instructions

Each area or attraction should have safety and use instructions clearly posted for guests. These instructions should answer the following questions for each attraction:

- Must guests be a maximum or minimum height before using this attraction?
- Must guests be a maximum or minimum weight before using this attraction?
- Are certain types of apparel prohibited?
- Must guests use a certain body position (such as feet-first) with this attraction? Are certain body positions prohibited?
- Is there a time or distance requirement between users?
- Is equipment such as tubes or mats required for use of this attraction? Is equipment prohibited from use on this attraction?

The attraction manufacturer usually provides guidelines for use that answer these questions. Site-specific facility policies and procedures and industry best practices support these guidelines. In addition to signs, audio scripts played to guests in line can be an effective backup prevention strategy. You need to know the restrictions and rules for each area or attraction that you lifeguard and enforce these rules with all guests.

Consistency in rule enforcement is important. Consider an example from a guest's point of view: A child does not meet the height requirement, but the dispatcher allows him or her to go down a waterslide. The family plays in the waterpark and returns to the ride when a different dispatcher is on duty. The dispatcher checks the height and tells the child he or she cannot ride. What happens? The guest is upset, the rules seem not to matter, and the lifeguard doing her or his job looks like the bad guy—all of which could have been prevented by consistency. If you are unsure of what a rule is or how to enforce it, call for a supervisor.

Use of Life Jackets

Many waterparks require that children under a certain age or height, as well as all nonswimmers, wear life jackets in wave pools, lazy rivers, and deep-water areas. Laws in some locations require life jacket use. If you work at a facility with a life jacket requirement, you will need to be trained in the site-specific policy and procedure for life jacket sizing, distribution, and monitoring.

A loaner life jacket program can be an effective prevention strategy.

Sizing guidance may vary slightly depending upon the style and manufacturer recommendations, but basic sizing instructions include the following:

- First select the right size based on the person's weight. The lifejacket should have a weight range printed on the inside.
- Put the jacket on the person and clip all the buckles or close zippers.
- Adjust any straps, starting at the bottom to obtain a snug, but not too tight fit.
- Pull up on the shoulders. If the lifejacket rides up more than the width of two fingers, readjust the straps or select a smaller size.

Inspections

The facility where you work should have checklist forms for you to use if you are responsible for inspecting a water attraction. Inspections are usually conducted each morning before opening. Even if you know that the attraction has been inspected, stay alert for problems that may develop during the day. Look for and report to your supervisor any of the following:

- Cracks
- Loose bolts
- Missing or broken pieces
- Nonfunctioning parts
- Unusual noises
- Increased frequency of injury or patron complaints
- Anything different or unusual

The inspection may also include other items such as test riding the attraction to check water-flow levels, confirming working communication systems, and verifying that the attraction is operating correctly.

Besides knowing the rules for using waterpark attractions and inspecting them, you must also adjust your surveillance techniques when guarding in a waterpark.

Attraction Standard Operating Procedures (SOPs)

SOPs should be available to you for each attraction at your facility. The SOP outlines important information including but not limited to these requirements:

- Rider restrictions or requirements (physical and mental)
- Staffing
- Training
- Water flow
- Rider vehicles
- Signage and rules
- Inspections
- Safety procedures
- Emergency procedures

This information will usually be communicated to you through a facility handbook or site-specific training manual.

Surveillance Strategy at Waterparks

The specific features of a water attraction may affect your scanning pattern or posture. For example, the waterfalls and sprays of a children's play area may block your view from a stationary chair and make it necessary for you to walk or stand within the zone to scan. A sitting position at a wave pool may be adequate when the waves are off, but when the waves begin, a standing position may offer you a better view of the zone. The curves of a river-current attraction may make it necessary for you to walk the zone so that you can cover all areas. Let's look at four common kinds of water attractions and the way in which you should plan to guard them: waterslides, flowing-current features, wave pools, and other types of features.

Waterslide Considerations

Injury trends indicate that the large majority of injuries at waterparks happen on waterslides. The most common are impact injuries that involve any of the following:

- A rider's body hitting against a slide terminus at high speed
- Impact with other riders or objects
- A rider's tube flipping, causing the rider to hit the slide
- A rider slipping and falling while entering or exiting the slide area

Waterslide Ride Cycle

A guest's ride on a waterslide encompasses seven phases:

1. Entry to the attraction
2. Queue to the starting platform
3. Load at the slide start
4. Release into the slide flume
5. Ride
6. Landing at the terminus
7. Exit

The combination of prevention strategies in each phase, along with reinforcement and surveillance by the lifeguard at the top dispatch position and the lifeguard in the landing area at the exit, determine the safety of the ride for the guest.

Waterslide Terminus

When lifeguarding at the end (terminus) of waterslide, your zone will usually be the landing pool or run-out. Some waterslides, however, have sections of catch pools where riders briefly stop their descent until the flow pushes them into the next section of the ride. Depending on the manufacturer's recommendations, lifeguards may need to be placed at those catch pool areas.

Your responsibilities in a slide catch pool, run-out, or splashdown area may include the following:

- Helping guests regain balance or stand up after landing
- Observing riders and looking for injury, distress, or drowning symptoms
- Helping guests manage tubes as they make their way to the exit

- Directing guests out of the slide path
- Enforcing rules and reminding guests of ride procedures
- Scanning the zone and keeping nonriders out of the splashdown or catch pool area
- Communicating, by hand or flag signals, with the dispatch lifeguard or attendant

Figure 15.1 This lifeguard is at an in-water catch pool position and monitoring exit all the way to the stairs

If you are assigned to the catch pool, you are responsible for watching sliders enter the water and then following their path all the way to the exit. You are also responsible for scanning the catch pool to make sure that someone has not entered the water from the side or stairs rather than by coming down the slide.

The procedure at your facility will determine whether you guard from an in-water or on-deck position at a slide catch pool (see figure 15.1). Many slide catch pools can be effectively covered from a seated or standing position on the deck.

To provide surveillance for the zone, you must be positioned so that you can see the entire area, including the stairs and exit points. The amount of head turn necessary for you to see the entire zone will vary depending on your position and the size of the catch pool, but generally it will be less than that needed for scanning a traditional pool. You will also deal with only a few guests at a time, depending on how many sliders enter the catch pool, and for only the few seconds needed for them to exit the area.

If you are in the catch pool, your additional duties will include communicating with the dispatch lifeguard or attendant, enforcing slide rules and procedures, and keeping nonriders out of the catch pool.

Remember that your safety is always a consideration. If you stand too close to the direct slide path, you could suffer an injury from a collision with a slider. The current in the direct slide path is likely to be strong and could cause you to lose your balance or footing.

Waterslide Dispatch Considerations

Waterslides have a unique element of rider freedom, unlike a roller coaster in which a rider is strapped in. As a result, the dispatcher plays an important role in safety and prevention. Dispatch is the control of riders at the top of a slide. The length of time needed for guests to ride down the slide and then move out of the slide path determines dispatch timing. Usually, a lifeguard or attendant at the top of the slide who can see the lifeguard monitoring the catch pool or run-out area controls when riders start down the slide (see figure 15.2). If you are in charge of dispatch, you need to know the attraction rules, safety and operating procedures, communication signals, emergency response, and other site-specific knowledge and information about the attraction. Your duties may include the following:

- Monitoring and enforcing requirements for rider height, size, age, ability, or other rider criteria that the slide manufacturer or your facility has set (facilitated by height sticks, signs marked with the minimum requirement, and prescreening of guests to identify eligible riders with wristbands)

- Helping riders get into position on tubes or mats
- Observing riders and looking for injury, distress, or drowning symptoms
- Verbally instructing riders in proper body position for the slide or conducting demonstrations
- Issuing "go" commands when it is safe to dispatch and controlling dispatch timing
- Controlling the emergency stop (E-stop) to shut off water flow during an emergency
- Providing guest service
- Monitoring the area for severe weather or other safety considerations
- Monitoring water flow levels
- Monitoring ride vehicles (rafts, tubes, mats) for correct inflation or safety requirements
- Clearing guests from the slide tower in the event of severe weather or other emergencies
- Communicating, by hand or flag signals, with the catch pool lifeguard
- Responding according to the facility and attraction emergency action plan (EAP)

To communicate waterslide rules, do the following:

- Be clear and simple.
- Demonstrate when appropriate.
- Get confirmation of understanding from the guest.
- Ask the riders whether they have questions.

Figure 15.2 A lifeguard in a slide dispatch position.

Use safety-related rule enforcement phrases such as "For your safety . . ." or "According to slide manufacturer requirements . . ." and avoid using any type of demeaning words or comments related to weight or physical appearance of the guests.

The dispatch position also plays an important role in guest service. Because guests are usually excited to ride the waterslides, the dispatch position is at the height of that excitement. Think about the ride from a guest's perspective and be part of a great experience. When interacting with guests with disabilities, treat them with the same level of respect and communication you show all guests. Offer assistance, but don't assume it is needed, and know the options you have to make reasonable accommodations to ride the slide.

Communication Tools for Slide Dispatch

While in a dispatch position you will need to maintain communication with the lifeguard at the bottom of the slide, in addition to being able to contact a supervisor. Common communication methods include

- whistles,
- dispatch lights,
- flags,
- hand signals, and
- air horns.

You must know and use the expected communication tools, which may be different depending on the attraction or location within your facility.

Dispatch Rotations

A dispatch rotation occurs when two staff members switch positions and transfer care and responsibilities of the dispatch position. As with any lifeguard position, a rotation should be a smooth and professional process so that no gaps occur in the safety procedures. Here are suggested steps for an effective dispatch rotation:

1. The incoming dispatcher approaches the dispatch position.
2. The incoming and outgoing dispatchers brief each other.
3. Both dispatchers complete a single cycle of dispatch together.
4. The outgoing dispatcher confirms that the incoming dispatcher is all set.
5. The outgoing dispatcher leaves, and the incoming dispatcher continues.

The debrief discussion step of the rotation should be limited to relevant information about the attraction and guests. The dispatch rotation should take as much time as needed to maintain safety, but not more than three ride cycles. The outgoing dispatcher should leave by walking down the stairs, not sliding down, unless site-specific conditions make that method appropriate.

Format for Dispatching

The simple acronym "ELITE" will help you remember a format for dispatching riders the same way every time (StarGuard Elite 2018).

E – Engage. Use a greeting and a smile with each guest! An upbeat and positive attitude will help you control access to the slide. Use physical barriers if needed to keep the line of guests organized and prevent overcrowding in the dispatch area or rushing the slide entrance.

L – Look. Look at each rider to confirm that the person meets the physical requirements to use the slide such as height, weight, proper attire, and no loose items. Look at the slide to confirm that the water flow is correct. Look at each ride vehicle to check that it is functioning properly, with correct inflation, secure handles, and working straps. Look at the bottom lifeguard to confirm the catch pool or run out is clear.

I – Instruct. Every rider needs instructions, every time. Know the script (also known as a spiel) for each attraction. Speak respectfully, in a clear voice loud enough to be heard. For some attractions, the spiel may include a visual demonstration when possible. If the rider seems unsure, confirm that the instructions are understood. Be consistent with the spiel and rule enforcement. Treat riders with disabilities with respect by speaking to them directly to offer assistance without making assumptions. Know your options for offering reasonable accommodations.

T—Time. The most frequent cause of injuries on water slides is not enough time between riders – resulting in collisions. Each slide has different and specific requirements regarding adequate interval between riders. Some intervals are based on a time frame, others when a rider passes a certain point that can be visually confirmed, and others rely on a communication signal from the lifeguard at bottom of the slide confirming that the area is clear. Some slides have an automated green light or other visual signal to control dispatch. If signals of any type are used, be sure to know what each means. If a guest needs help when it is time to dispatch, keep yourself safe and out of the slide path and be sure to remain professional whenever providing personal assistance.

E – Evaluate. Once dispatched, evaluate that the rider is having a safe experience. Be prepared to act in the event of an emergency. Know your role in the attraction Emergency Action Plan (EAP), the location of the Emergency Stop (e-stop) button if present, and the location of emergency equipment. Keep your skills at a test-ready level so that you are competent to respond at any time.

Your employer may provide you with additional training and resources that are available for the ELITE dispatch program.

Flowing-Current Considerations

A zone on a lazy river or torrent river usually includes a length of the river. The lifeguard is located in the middle so that half of the zone is upriver and half of the zone is downriver. Because the river attraction is narrow, your scanning pattern will be from side to side. Even though the river is shallow, you should still scan the bottom and use changes in posture such as by alternating sitting, standing, and strolling to help you stay alert (see figure 15.3).

Figure 15.3 Surveillance on a flowing-current attraction.

The presence of tubes in a river-current attraction may limit your ability to see under the surface of the water. Pay particular attention to the entry and exit areas of the river where tubes may get jammed and could possibly trap small children underneath. Keep these areas free of tubes. Your responsibilities at a river-current attraction may include the following:

- Directing guests to enter and exit at designated points along the river (multiple or controlled entry and exit areas that minimize patron and tube congestion)
- Helping guests get in or out of tubes
- Enforcing rules and reminding guests of ride procedures
- Pulling out unused tubes

Wave Pool Considerations

A wave pool is essentially a flat-water pool part of the time and a flat-water pool with water movement when the waves are on. When lifeguarding in either condition, you will be assigned a specific zone that is your area of coverage. This area should be small enough that you can get to the farthest point in about 20 seconds and small enough and without obstructions so that you can scan the area within 10 seconds.

One difference between wave pools and regular pools is the sudden shift in patron use that commonly occurs. Most wave pools are equipped with a signal that gives a 15- to 30-second warning before the wave action starts. When the signal for the wave action begins, guests who do not want to be in the water when the waves are on will leave the wave pool, and guests who have been waiting for the waves to start will enter if they are not already in the pool. You need to be extra vigilant during these times.

The size of the wave pool, the crowded conditions, guests moving in and out of the water, and the wave action all combine to make scanning, targeting, and rescuing more difficult than at traditional pools.

Wave pools provide various types of waves depending on the equipment used. Some wave machines create a back-and-forth water movement on the surface; others create a series of realistic cresting waves that guests can surf. Your facility orientation should include a description of the types of waves your machinery generates, the water depth in the wave pool during waves and during calm, the timing of wave sequences, and the locations and use of the E-stop buttons that shut down the wave action.

Your wave pool responsibilities may include the following:

- Scanning for distress or drowning symptoms
- Monitoring the entrance and exit to the wave pool and restricting entrance and exit to the beach area only, not from the sides
- Monitoring and restricting use around or near wave chamber outlets or intakes
- Enforcing rules

Other Attractions

Inflatable slides, cable drops, rope challenges, climbing walls, and children's play structures are some of the attractions commonly found in aquatic facilities. Each of these attractions comes with the manufacturer's guidelines for use. Your facility may add its own specific rules or procedures. Learn the rules and prevention strategies for all the attraction areas at the facility where you lifeguard.

Your main priority will always be to scan for distress or drowning symptoms, target when you see symptoms, assess the situation, and decide to act. Let's now discuss how to adapt your response, rescue, and emergency care skills in a waterpark setting.

Response, Rescue, and Emergency Care at Waterparks

The currents, waves, noise, large spaces, dispatch platforms, and crowded conditions at aquatic attractions can all affect your response. Therefore, you must practice rescue scenarios in a variety of conditions at each attraction in the facility where you work. The more familiar you are with the conditions, the easier it will be for you to adapt your emergency care and rescue skills to meet the objective of the rescue.

An important consideration during an emergency at a waterpark is knowing how to stop water flow at an attraction, which is usually done with an E-stop button. E-stop stands for emergency stop. Pushing the button will immediately stop the attraction. After an E-stop is pushed, the attraction will need to be restarted from the power source; pulling the button out again will not work. An E-stop will be present for most attractions that have moving water such as waterslides, wave pools, and lazy rivers.

STAAR at Waterparks

The StarGuard aquatic rescue model (STAAR) can be used to illustrate what might need to be adapted at a waterpark or facility with play features so that you can effectively see and respond to an emergency.

- **Scan.** You should be aware of how the attraction affects your ability to see your zone. For example, when waves are on in a wave pool, scanning in a standing position might be necessary. The long, narrow zone of a river current will require a lot of head turning to scan the zone, whereas the catch pool of a slide might not require much head turning at all because the zone is small and right in front of you. The obstructions created by a play feature may require that you stroll the zone to see all areas. As you become familiar with each attraction at your facility, you will be able to identify positions and scanning patterns that work best.

- **Target.** To help you target potential emergencies, you should be aware of behaviors that might be unique to various attractions. For example, in a wave pool you might notice a patron get knocked over by an oncoming wave or get a mouthful of water when submerged by a wave. In a river current, you might notice a patron fall off a tube, struggle with a tube, or be motionless. In a slide catch pool, you might hear a person cough after getting a nose-full of water or notice a person struggling to stand. These kinds of behaviors could catch your eye and cause you to assess the situation. As you become familiar with each attraction at the facility where you work, you will notice patterns in patron behavior that will help you target unusual situations.

- **Assess.** You should be aware of what information you must acquire when you scan. When you assess the condition of guests at various water-play attractions, you are in essence asking yourself questions about the situation and deciding whether you need to act. For example, if you target a woman who gets knocked over by a wave or is unable to get her footing after exiting a slide, you might ask yourself, *"Can the woman get up on her own?"* If you assess that she cannot, then you decide to act. In a river-current attraction, you might ask yourself, *"Is this man relaxing and asleep as he floats by, or is he unresponsive?"* If you suspect he is unresponsive, then you decide to act. As you become familiar with each attraction at the facility where you work, you will develop the ability to assess the conditions of guests based on the circumstances.

- **Alert.** You should be aware of any additional actions needed at an attraction when you alert others that you have identified a distressed or drowning person. For example, at a wave pool you may need to push an E-stop button to stop the waves. At a slide you may need to signal to the dispatch person to stop the flow of riders. As you become familiar with each attraction at the facility where you work, you will know the procedure for alerting others and activating the emergency action plan.

- **Rescue.** You should be aware of how the conditions at an attraction might affect your ability to make a rescue and provide emergency care. For example, making a rescue in a wave pool when the waves are off may be different from making a rescue when the waves are on. Currents created at the bottom of slides may make in-water rescues more difficult. The only way to obtain this information is to practice rescue scenarios at each attraction at the facility where you work.

Let's look at some strategies that will be helpful in the various types of waterpark attractions.

Waterslide Considerations

- You may need to provide an assist, rescue, or first aid care in a slide run-out, in a catch pool, at the top of a slide, or in another unique location that is part of the attraction. Adapt the procedures to the conditions at the attraction to meet the objectives of care.

- Signal the dispatch guard or attendant to push the E-stop to prevent other guests from sliding into your rescue scene.

- Injury or sudden illness can occur inside the slide trough, in the catch pool and run-out area as well as on top or at the base of the slide tower. Practice rescue scenarios in these locations.

Flowing-Current Considerations

- The pull of the current may complicate a rescue in a river-current attraction. Try to avoid moving against the current.

- The water depth in river attractions is usually shallow; always enter feetfirst with an ease-in entry or compact jump from the side.

- When you make contact with the person, don't try to fight the current; instead, move with the water flow to a takeout point.

- To manage a rescue, hit the E-stop to turn off the water flow. Until the water stops moving, position yourself with your back to the current so that the water is flowing from head to toe to help support the guest's body.

- If the current is too strong, stop trying to stand on the bottom; float with the person while performing rescue breathing.

- If possible, your backup team should be prepared to follow you to an appropriate takeout point rather than making you fight the current to get to a designated spot.

Wave Pool Considerations

- Push the E-stop button as part of your alert response and point toward the intended location of your rescue.

- Because the wave action of the water may not stop right away, time your compact jump so that you enter the water at the height of the wave where the water is deepest rather than at the trough where the water may be shallow.

- Be prepared to swim around and through a crowd of swimmers and tubes.

- Be prepared for longer extrication times in a wave pool because of the large size of the area, crowded conditions, wave action, and other factors. When rescuing an unresponsive victim in the deeper area of the wave pool far from the entry point, you will probably not be able to extricate the person to the beach entry or deck within 30 seconds. Therefore, you should be prepared to begin rescue breathing in the water while you make progress to the safe point of exit.

- When placing the CPR mask on an unresponsive person drowning, make a good seal to prevent the wave action from pushing water into the person's nose and mouth.

- Because the wave action may not stop right away, practice rescues with the waves on to become comfortable with the movement and effort required to perform rescue breathing in the waves.

- Practice extrication methods that are practical for the zero-depth beachfront area, such as those described in chapter 16. Usually, the safest and most effective way to extricate a person from a wave pool is to exit at the beachfront zero-depth entry. The sides of a wave pool are usually very high, and the deck is often several feet (about a meter) from the water surface. Stairs may or may not be built into the side walls, but when side-wall stairs are present, they tend to be narrow and steep.

Emergency Care Considerations

Many large waterparks have supervisory or EMS personnel on site who respond to a call for emergency care such as CPR or spinal injury management. In these situations, your role is to be one of the support team. Therefore, you need to practice emergency care scenarios with the personnel who would respond in a real situation so that you can work together as a team and know your responsibilities before an incident occurs.

Now let's consider what you can expect, and what will be expected of you, at the waterpark workplace.

Waterpark Workplace Expectations

Maximizing the experience of your waterpark guests should be of primary importance to you and your team (Deines 2015). You are in a highly visible position to the crowds that visit waterparks and are often the person that provides the most guest services contact. The impression that the guests have of their experience will have a lot to do with how you present a professional image and serve as a role model to the guests in your care. Set a good example whenever you enjoy the water attractions at your facility. If you use the attractions, either during or outside operating hours, follow the rules and regulations as though you were a guest.

In some ways, lifeguarding at a facility with play features or waterpark attractions is easier than lifeguarding at a traditional pool. Maintaining a high level of anticipation and vigilance is easier when a lot of action is occurring. In other ways, lifeguarding at a waterpark is more difficult. A waterpark environment has many more distractions. The noise of the crowd, the noise created by the slides or waves, and the activity level can all entice you to watch the fun rather than your zone. Be prepared to deal with and tune out those distractions.

Waterparks usually have a large number of lifeguards on duty at any given time, and you will operate as part of a team. Because of the many attractions, in-service training will likely be on a continual basis and include site-specific operational procedures, customer service training, vigilance and scanning drills, rescue scenarios, and physical conditioning. In addition, you will likely participate in frequent reviews (audits) of your performance while you are on the job.

▶ VISIT THE WEB RESOURCE

You can reinforce your learning by visiting the web resource, where you can do the following in the interactive online learning activities based on chapter 15:

- ◆ Respond to simulated scenarios at a waterslide, a wave pool, and a flowing-current attraction.
- ◆ Identify scanning strategies for various waterpark features.
- ◆ Practice dispatching riders on waterslides.
- ◆ Test your knowledge and receive feedback.

CHAPTER SUMMARY

Key points	Best practices on the job
• At a waterpark you will operate as part of a team.	• Frequently inspect slides and play features for hazards.
• Waterpark features require additional prevention, surveillance, and response strategies.	• Know and enforce rules specific to each attraction.
• The large majority of injuries at waterparks happen on waterslides.	• Provide slide dispatch instructions the same way for every rider, every time.
• The attraction manufacturer usually provides guidelines for use.	• During slide dispatch, enforce height and weight rules, dispatch at correct intervals, enforce correct body position, and maintain communication with the exit area.
• Consistency in rule enforcement is important.	• Adapt strategies, techniques, and methods for the waterpark environment.
• You are in a highly visible position to the crowds that visit waterparks and are often the person that provides the most guest services contact.	• Know how to modify surveillance strategies and communication for each attraction.
	• Deliver quality customer service.
	• Plan and then practice scenario drills to determine the methods best suited to the physical conditions and recreational features at your waterpark.
	• Participate in regular audits and performance assessments.

Lifeguarding at Nonsurf Waterfronts

CHAPTER OBJECTIVES

This chapter

- identifies features of a nonsurf waterfront;

- identifies additional prevention, surveillance, response, rescue, and emergency care procedures for the waterfront setting; and

- reinforces workplace safety and performance expectations for the waterfront setting.

If you will work at a waterfront, you must complete the waterfront training module in addition to the basic StarGuard course. The waterfront module may be taught at the same time as your StarGuard course or presented as a separate training session. Each section of this chapter covers a StarGuard Risk Management Model component as it applies to lifeguarding at waterfronts. *Note:* The material presented in this chapter supplements the other chapters in this text.

Waterfront Features

A waterfront, for purposes of the StarGuard lifeguard training program, is a marked and restricted swimming area enclosed by lines, docks, or piers within an open body of water, and the accompanying beach. The waterfront designation applies to nonsurf bodies of water such as lakes, ponds, and rivers and does not include ocean lifeguarding.

Lifeguards who work at a surf or nonrestricted waterfront, such as an ocean beach with no enclosed swim area, must have additional open-water, surf rescue, and physical conditioning skills that are outside the scope of the basic StarGuard waterfront training program. Open-water or surf rescue training for beach lifeguards usually is conducted by the agency responsible for providing protection at the beach. Many agencies that operate surf beaches use StarGuard basic training as a prerequisite and then provide additional surf rescue training as the operating standard of care. If you work at a surf or nonrestricted waterfront, you must obtain additional and site-specific training.

Each waterfront has its own natural characteristics, but common features include the following:

- Turbid (dark) water that prevents a lifeguard from being able to see or identify anything under the surface

- Uncontrollable environmental conditions such as weather, temperature, wildlife, moving and turbulent water, varying water depths from tides or dams, unstable bottom conditions, and rocks and other submerged hazards

- Locations that may have long EMS response times

The unique features at a nonsurf waterfront require additional site-specific skills. Let's start by looking at ways to reduce risk at a waterfront setting.

Prevention Strategy at Waterfronts

Waterfront areas present unique risks that you must manage to provide a safe environment for swimmers. Some ways to manage risks are inspecting sites frequently and choosing appropriate areas for aquatic activities. Other prevention strategies include preparing participants for waterfront aquatic activities.

Site Inspections

Because hazards at outdoor water areas often change over time, you must check frequently for hazards. Depending on your location, your responsibilities for a site inspection may include the following:

- Clear the beach or swim area of debris, such as glass, cans, branches, hooks, food and drink containers, and human or animal waste.
- Check that appropriate rescue equipment is available, which for protected waterfronts may include rescue watercraft, masks, fins, snorkels, scuba gear, waterproof flashlights, search nets, and binoculars.
- Place equipment in a rescue-ready position. Determine the best rescue-ready position by conducting rescue scenarios. After each scenario, evaluate how long it took the rescue equipment to reach the scene and how practical it is to keep equipment in various locations.
- Check that appropriate communication equipment is available, which for protected waterfronts may include two-way radios, a bullhorn, a public address system, flags, cell phones (if service is available), or other means to communicate with patrons across open spaces.
- Make sure you can receive cell phone and radio signals before you need them in an emergency. Keep in mind that when dialing 9-1-1 from a cell phone in the United States, you may reach an emergency dispatch service in a different county than you expected.
- Monitor the environment. Post or announce weather and water conditions along with warnings about restricted areas.
- Swim and walk the area to identify holes, drop-offs, rocks, or other hazards.
- Identify currents.
- Identify underwater obstructions.
- Check the water level and depth.
- Check the depth under floating docks; the water depth at lakes linked to dam systems can change significantly from day to day.

Skills Testing Swimmers and Mandatory Life Jacket Use

When you can assign people to swimming areas of different depths, you should first assess their swimming abilities. You should also assess swimming ability during group outings to a water area before allowing people to participate in water activities in which the water is more than waist deep. Don't rely on a swimmer's assessment of his or her own swimming ability before testing. The purpose of skills testing is to identify participants who do not have the endurance or ability to keep their heads comfortably above water without a life jacket.

A skills test must reflect the skills needed for the activity and conditions. As an example of general skills testing, consider asking participants to demonstrate the ability to swim approximately 25 yards (or meters) and to tread water without using their hands for 1 minute. Your objective is to have each participant demonstrate to you in a measurable way a swimming ability appropriate for the activity. To conduct skills testing in a waterfront setting, follow these guidelines:

- Choose specific skills-testing activities appropriate for your environment. Your test must reflect the skills needed for the activity and conditions.
- Choose a testing area in which the water is no more than waist deep for the participants.
- The testing area should be free of sudden drop-offs or submerged objects such as logs or other debris.
- Conduct skills tests near the shoreline or along a dock.
- Participants should enter the water feetfirst.

Assign the swimmers, based on the results of the testing, to either a swimming area or a nonswimming (shallow) area. You might also require that nonswimmers use a life jacket. Document the results of the swim tests. Include the date, time, and each swimmer's name, age, and skills assessment outcome.

When managing large groups, consider using some type of identification that shows which people belong in which areas. In restricted waterfront settings, one way to do this is to provide a wristband or breakaway necklace to each patron who has completed skills testing. Use one color to designate a swimmer and another to designate a nonswimmer.

Buddy System and Buddy Check

Another useful surveillance strategy is to use a buddy system and call for frequent safety breaks, during which all patrons get out of the water for a short time. In a buddy system, pair swimmers by ability. If the ability of each of the pair is not equal, the less-skilled swimmer defines the swim area for that pair. Buddy swimmers must stay within sight of each other at all times. To identify which buddies are swimming and which have left the swim area, use one of the following methods:

- Keep a buddy board or swimmer chart on a notepad; buddy pairs must check in and check out with the specified staff person in charge of the chart.
- Designate two ball caps as "in" and "out"; swimmers place their names in the hat that designates their swimming status.
- Have each swimmer leave a similar article of clothing, such as a shirt or cap, in a designated area to indicate to staff which swimmers are in and out.

Besides using a buddy system, you may want to use a buddy check (also called a safety break) as well. Simply signal a check after a set amount of time, asking all participants to get out of the water. A buddy check takes less than 1 minute to implement and allows you to make sure that all participants are present and accounted for. Preassigned buddies or small groups account for each other.

Drowning Detection Technology

Because the cloudy water of a waterfront can make seeing a submerged swimmer almost impossible, the use of technology to track a swimmer's location can help. If the waterfront where you work uses a drowning detection system, it is a redundant safety measure, not a substitute for your vigilance!

Surveillance Strategy at Waterfronts

In most waterfront settings, you cannot scan the bottom because the water is turbid, so keeping nonswimmers in shallow water, having nonswimmers wear life jackets if feasible, and keeping track of all swimmers becomes even more important. Setting up clear boundaries for safe swimming and nonswimming areas, testing people to assess their swimming skills, and conducting buddy checks and safety breaks will help you account for all swimmers. In waterfront settings, having someone provide surveillance from a watercraft, floating dock, or platform may be helpful.

Depending on the layout of your waterfront, swimming areas and nonswimming areas may be marked using buoy lines or a combination of piers, docks, and lines. When possible, divide the water into areas for specific uses, such as swimming, diving, and sliding. Communicate to participants through signs, visual markings, and verbal safety briefings the clear boundaries between the swimming areas and nonswimming areas.

When you guard in a waterfront area, keep track of patrons by doing the following:

- If feasible, maintain a constant count of patrons in your zone with each scan or sweep.
- Watch patrons swimming to or from floating platforms and look for signs of distress.
- Allow only one diver or slider to enter the water at a time. Allow subsequent divers or sliders to enter only after you have seen the preceding diver or slider return to the surface and move out of the entry area.
- Do not allow prolonged underwater swimming or breath-holding games.
- If flotation devices such as rafts or noodles are allowed, pay particular attention to those using these devices and restrict their use to people who have passed the skills screening.

Guarding From a Rescue Watercraft

Guarding the area from a watercraft in the water is another way to keep track of swimmers at a waterfront. You can use watercraft at a waterfront to patrol the perimeter of a swim area or to serve as an anchored surveillance position. Watercraft can be human powered, such as a paddleboard, kayak, canoe, or rowboat, or motor powered, such as a personal watercraft (e.g., Jet Ski), inflatable boat, or small motorboat (see figure 16.1). Your facility should provide you with an orientation and instruction in safety practices for the specific watercraft you might use. You should also practice rescue scenarios using the watercraft.

For motor-powered watercraft, the ideal setup is to have two lifeguards on each craft—one serving as an operator and one providing surveillance. When this is not possible and the operator provides surveillance, having a good communication device, such as an air horn or radio, is important. Rescue watercraft should carry the following equipment:

- Life jackets for each occupant and at least one extra life jacket for a potential passenger
- Oars or paddles
- Lines (ropes)
- Flotation devices that can be thrown
- A rescue tube
- A bailer (except for a paddleboard, sit-on kayak, or Jet Ski)

Figure 16.1 Guarding from a sit-on kayak.

- A waist pack or kit with a ventilation mask, gloves, and first aid supplies
- Water or fluids for hydration
- Communication devices (e.g., whistle, air horn, radio, signal flags)

Depending on the size of the craft, in the United States the U.S. Coast Guard might require motor-powered craft to carry additional equipment such as an anchor and line and a fire extinguisher.

Guarding From a Floating Dock or Platform

Many waterfronts have floating docks or platforms that are for use by patrons and that also serve as a lifeguard station (see figure 16.2). A means of effective communication from this position to other lifeguards is important, especially if you need help

Figure 16.2 Guarding from a floating dock.

managing unruly or threatening behavior or need to enter the water to make a rescue. Practice your emergency whistle or air horn signals during times of peak use to be sure others on the waterfront can hear you. When feasible, a set of first aid, emergency response, and search equipment should be present on the station for quick access.

Be sure to prohibit patrons from swimming under the dock or platform or into areas where you cannot see them.

Response, Rescue, and Emergency Care at Waterfronts

Providing response, rescue, and emergency care may be more difficult at waterfronts than at pools because of the natural environment and the distance between the site and emergency help. But by preparing for rescues, developing emergency action plans and methods for search and rescue (and search and recover), and determining safe ways to perform rescues, your organization should be ready to deal with these circumstances.

At waterfronts, preparation should include training on the communication system that is in place and underwater search equipment such as a mask or goggles, fins, and a snorkel.

Communication System for Waterfront Lifeguards

Waterfront swimming areas can become noisy, and swimmers may be spread out over larger distances than in a pool setting. You need some means besides yelling to communicate with participants and other lifeguards or rescuers. Systems include hand or whistle signals or a combination of the two, megaphones, and other signaling devices such as flags, air horns, or two-way radios. You and the other lifeguards or rescuers must know what the signals mean.

Mask, Fins, and Snorkel

Wearing a swim mask will let you see better under the water when performing a rescue or conducting an underwater search. Here are some tips for using a mask:

- Be sure that the mask fits correctly, forming a watertight seal around your eyes to prevent leaking. If a mask is not available, goggles can help if you will be swimming underwater in shallow depths (under 10 feet, or 3 m) and for short periods. If you will be deeper, the water pressure against goggles may become uncomfortable, and you should consider using a mask.

- To prevent fogging, wipe the interior surface with an antifog agent or a small amount of saliva.

- To remove water from a leaking mask, tilt your head back slightly. Press the top of the mask faceplate toward your forehead; the bottom of the mask will move slightly away from your face. Exhale strongly through your nose to push the water out of the mask.

- To prevent or relieve mask squeeze (an uncomfortable pressure against your face and eyes when you descend), exhale small bursts of air from your nose. This air will equalize the pressure in the mask to that of the pressure in the water.

- To prevent or relieve pressure in your ears when you descend, you must equalize your ears. Choose a method that works for you: Blow gently against a pinched nose, pinch your nose and swallow, or pinch your nose and yawn.

Figure 16.3   Search swimming with a mask, a snorkel, and fins.

Using a snorkel allows you to keep your face submerged as you search (see figure 16.3). Use a snorkel keeper to secure the snorkel to the head strap of your mask or goggles. Place the mouthpiece in your mouth and hold it in place lightly with your lips and teeth. Breathe slowly and deeply. When you are ready to submerge completely and swim deeper, take a relaxed, deep breath and hold it, and pull yourself down under the water. Do not hyperventilate (by breathing rapidly several times and then holding your breath) before submerging.

When you surface, clear your snorkel by exhaling strongly with a short burst of air to force the water from the tube. Exhale to clear the tube only when you are sure you are at the surface and the top of the snorkel is no longer submerged. When the water has been expelled, inhale through your mouth and continue relaxed breathing.

Wearing fins will increase your propulsion through the water. Fins come in two styles: full heel and open heel, which usually requires you to wear booties. Whenever possible, put on your fins when you are in or at the edge of the water. If you have to walk with fins on, move sideways or backward to prevent tripping. When you swim, kick with slow, smooth kicks. The movement should come from your hips, and your knees should have a slight to moderate bend, depending on the style of fin.

While swimming with a mask, snorkel, and fins, keep your arms either in front or in a relaxed position along your sides. If you are performing a bottom search, keep your hands forward and sweep them toward the sides to feel for the victim. To surface dive while wearing a mask, snorkel, and fins, do the following:

1. Tuck your chin to your chest and press your head and shoulders forward.
2. Bend your hips to roll into a pike or tuck position.
3. Lift your legs to extend your body; this movement allows you to descend headfirst. Move your hands in front of your body into the search position, which will also protect you from submerged hazards.

Missing-Person Emergency Action Plan

A waterfront should have a specific emergency action plan (EAP) in place in case someone is reported missing. If a person is missing, search the water first. Customize the emergency action plan based on the site-specific waterfront and consider these factors:

- Number of staff available
- Number of bystanders likely to be present
- Response time of EMS or search and rescue or recover teams
- Water depth

- Water temperature
- Water clarity
- In-water hazards
- Search methods appropriate for the waterfront setting
- Equipment or watercraft available

Regardless of the circumstances, a missing-person EAP should include these elements:

- A specific communication signal to indicate a missing-person situation
- A designated staging area for all staff and bystanders
- Two groups of searchers—one water based to begin immediately and one land based

Those searching on land (while a water search is being conducted) should gather information about the person, including name, age, and description, and start the search in the immediate area, including the bathhouse, campsite, and parking lot. The search should then extend to the surrounding area, including woods, cabins, and outbuildings.

Search and Rescue Versus Search and Recover

Search and rescue refers to situations in which a missing person is likely to be found quickly enough that survival is possible. Search and recover refers to situations in which so much time has passed that survival is unlikely.

At a waterfront, enough lifeguards and other rescuers should be available that search and rescue is your initial protocol. Search the bottom of the swim area first because your window for performing search and rescue is relatively short. For this reason, it should take no more than 5 minutes to search the swim area completely. The specific conditions at your facility—including the number of staff, equipment, water depth, availability of bystanders, and search techniques—determine how large an area you can search within this period and should help in establishing appropriate swim area size.

Search and rescue efforts should begin near the place where the person was last seen. If possible, visually mark the spot where the person was known to have submerged by sighting, or lining up, the spot with a stationary object on the shore. Sighting from several positions and vantage points further helps pinpoint the area. If currents are present, begin the search downstream because it is likely that the person has been pushed to a different location by the moving water.

Search and rescue efforts by lifeguards and bystanders should continue until the person is found or until a search and recover dive team (usually EMS, fire, or police professionals) arrives. When EMS arrives, continue your search until the person directing the EMS effort directs you to stop or gives other instructions. Search strategies for restricted waterfront areas may include the following:

- **Dragnet search**. Use a weighted net that is pulled by two rescuers along the search area. One method of constructing a dragnet is to string a weighted net on a section of PVC. The rescuers use the PVC as a handle to pull the net. Another option is for rescuers to hold the top of the net at each end. Begin the search near the person's last known location and follow a predetermined pattern to move the net quickly across the bottom of the swimming area. You may walk or move the net while swimming as long as the net reaches the bottom.

- **Grid system**. Some waterfronts may have lines or markers anchored along the bottom to help when conducting an underwater search. The members of the search team, wearing masks, snorkels, and fins (or scuba gear, if trained to use such equipment), line up along each grid mark and move forward along the designated path.

- **Swimming search line**. This search method is similar to the grid system, but it lacks the benefit of physical markings on the bottom. In shallow water where the bottom can be clearly seen, the search team should swim in a line, shoulder to shoulder. In deeper water, the search team should combine surface dives with arm sweeps to look and feel for a victim on the bottom. The rescuers surface dive to the bottom, swim, and sweep with the arms for 10 to 15 feet (3 to 4.5 m), surface, back up approximately 3 to 5 feet (1 to 1.5 m), and repeat the process.

- **Walking search line**. The search team forms a line, facing the direction in which the search will begin, and hooks elbows. The line of rescuers moves forward while rescuers sweep the area in front and to the side with the feet and legs, until the shortest rescuer is in chest-deep water.

For all search strategies, if contact with the missing person is made, the rescuer immediately stops and signals to initiate the emergency action plan.

Performing search and recovery in a setting with murky water and moving currents may be more difficult, because these conditions make a point last seen indistinguishable from the surrounding area. Using quick dives, you and other rescuers must rapidly search where the victim was last seen. After these first few minutes have passed, the chances of a successful recovery and resuscitation decline. Drowning in cold water may be the exception to this rule, so continue recovery attempts for up to one hour or until the situation becomes unsafe for rescuers. When someone is reported missing in conditions of murky water or currents, follow these steps:

- Activate the emergency action plan.

- Ask people on shore to help fix the point last seen.

- Pick out a landmark on an opposing shore in line with the point last seen to help identify the appropriate search area.

- Identify the time of submersion.

- Initially search the point last seen with either an in-water search by wading and swimming; a surface search by surface swimming or using a watercraft; or an underwater search with goggles or a mask, fins, and a snorkel.

- In turbid water conditions, using a waterproof flashlight while performing underwater swim search procedures may increase visibility.

Rescue Approach and Entry Considerations

At a waterfront, you may need to swim a greater distance to make a rescue than you would in a pool. To save time, you may want to run down the shoreline to a position in line with the person and then enter the water. If the person is more than 30 feet (9 m) from you, swimming and trailing the rescue tube may be faster than holding it. Stop about 10 feet (3 m) from the person, pull your rescue tube into position, and then complete the rescue.

Depending on the circumstances and equipment available, a swimming water rescue may be your last choice. The phrase reach, throw, row, and go identifies water rescue options in order of preference:

1. **Reach.** Extend a rope, flotation device, or pole to the person.
2. **Throw.** Throw a rope or flotation device to the person.
3. **Row.** Use a rescue watercraft to row or motor to the person and use the boat as a rescue platform.
4. **Go.** Swim out and perform an in-water rescue.

Throwing a buoy or rope can be effective, but the person often has difficulty finding and maintaining contact with a thrown object. In addition, hitting the person with the device may cause injury. When throwing an object, aim behind and upwind of the person (and upstream in moving water). Then pull the object toward the person. If you aim in front and fall short, you will waste valuable time pulling in the line and rethrowing.

When making a water rescue, you must decide how to enter the water based on your distance from the person and her or his condition. Use a compact jump when you are jumping from a height into water of any depth where underwater obstructions may be present. Use a protected water entry when entering from water level (see figure 16.4).

The protected water entry is a modified belly flop, which will help you stay on the surface and protect your face and neck from possible injury. To perform this entry, do the following:

1. When you are about knee deep, push off with your legs and lean forward.
2. Arch your back and cross your arms in front of your face.
3. Your chest and abdomen should enter the water first. The more you are able to stay on the surface, the better you will be able to maintain a constant view of the person's position in the water.

Figure 16.4 Protected water entry.

Shoreline Extrication

Injured, ill, or unconscious people may need to be removed from the water or moved to another location away from the edge of the water. Always lift with your legs, keeping your back straight and bending your knees. Keep your center of gravity low and the weight of the victim close to your body. Factors that may affect the type of extrication method you choose include the following:

- Presence and size of waterfront obstructions, such as rocks and trees
- Size of the victim
- Whether or not you will use spinal injury precautions
- Height from the water to the shore
- Equipment available
- Number of people available to assist

Do the following after you reach the shoreline:

- On a sloping beach, kneel with your back to the water so that you can evaluate the victim better and will not fall on him or her.
- Pull the victim far enough on shore to avoid incoming waves.
- Place the victim parallel to the waterline so that the head is at the same level as the rest of the body. This position reduces the risk of vomiting.

One-Rescuer Assist

Use this method if a person is responsive and can walk. Place the person's arm around your shoulders and your arm around her or his waist. Provide support and assistance as needed as you walk out. A second rescuer can move to the other side of the injured person to provide additional support.

Seat Carry

This method requires two or three rescuers. Use it if a person is conscious but cannot walk. Two rescuers are at the person's upper body and place the person's arms around their shoulders. If only two rescuers are available and the injured person's size allows, rescuers can create a seat by joining hands under the person's upper legs and lifting (a). If a third rescuer is available, he or she can hold the person's legs and help carry the person out.

Cradle Carry

Use the cradle carry for a responsive or unresponsive person. Hold the person just above the knees. Cradle your arm around the middle of her or his back (b).

Two-Person Extremity Carry

Use this method for a responsive or unresponsive person. One rescuer gets behind the person and prepares to lift by grasping under the person's arms. The second rescuer stands at the person's feet, between the legs, facing away from the person. This rescuer grasps the person's ankles and pulls them into his or her body for support *(c)*. For a larger person, the rescuer backs up and holds under the knees. Both rescuers lift the person at the same time and walk forward, with the rescuer at the feet leading the way.

Beach Drag

One or more rescuers use this extrication method if a person is unresponsive. The rescuer holds the person under the armpits and walks backward out of the water and up on to the beach *(d)*.

Emergency Care Considerations

Conditions specific to waterfront areas may affect how you manage an unresponsive drowning victim. You must be prepared for a potentially long EMS response time and be able to extricate an unresponsive drowning victim at a shoreline. The equipment you have available and the number of rescuers or bystanders you have to help will determine the techniques you use to get an unresponsive drowning victim on to land to begin emergency care.

In rural waterfront areas where delayed emergency medical system response times can be expected, you must plan your emergency procedures accordingly. For example, if your emergency oxygen equipment is capable of administering 15 minutes of oxygen and you can expect a 20-minute response, you should have an extra tank or two on site.

Here are additional considerations when working in a waterfront setting:

- Consider the effects that the shoreline may have on rescue equipment. For example, sand will stick to a CPR mask placed on the ground and will be difficult to remove quickly.
- Continue CPR as long as possible for a victim who has drowned in cold water. Survival, even after long submersion times, has been reported in circumstances when the water was cold.
- Continue CPR and rescue breathing as long as possible for people who have been struck by lightning.
- Collect a sample of the water from all drowning events that require resuscitation. The water may be needed to determine whether contamination was present, which can be helpful for postresuscitative care.

Waterfront Workplace Expectations

Be aware of how cold water, which is often present in waterfront areas, can affect your endurance and swimming skills. Wear a wetsuit during training activities to prevent hypothermia. Maintain your physical conditioning through regular exercise.

Protective footwear is a necessity when working in a waterfront setting. If the waterfront workplace is remote, no guests may present during certain times of the day. You need to remain vigilant and perform best practices, even if you and other lifeguards are the only people present.

If the waterfront has recreational features such as platforms, waterslides, trampolines, or inflatable structures, you should know and understand the risks associated with those attractions. The manufacturer will usually provide the safety and operating guidelines. Your employer will be responsible for establishing site-specific rules and training you on this important information.

▶ VISIT THE WEB RESOURCE

You can reinforce your learning by visiting the web resource, where you can do the following in the interactive online learning activities based on chapter 16:

◆ Identify hazards and establish zones in a virtual waterfront setting.

◆ Evaluate scenarios and identify how to adapt skills to the waterfront setting.

◆ Test your knowledge and receive feedback.

CHAPTER SUMMARY

Key points	Best practices on the job
• Conditions can change quickly at a waterfront. • Turbid water means water that is not clear and looks dark. • Prevention strategies should focus on access control, particularly for nonswimmers or weak swimmers. • Surveillance and scanning are difficult in turbid water, as you cannot see if a person is submerged. • Different communication devices and rescue equipment may be needed at a waterfront.	• Frequently inspect waterfront swimming areas for hazards. • Adapt scanning strategies for turbid water. • Conduct a bottom search first if a person is missing. • When feasible conduct swim tests and restrict nonswimmers to water that is less than waist deep or require them to wear life jackets. • Plan and then practice search and rescue drills to determine the methods best suited to the physical conditions and recreational features at your waterfront.

APPENDIX: EMERGENCY OXYGEN

Drowning causes a forced respiratory arrest (breathing stops). With each heartbeat, oxygen is removed from the blood until it is essentially zero, at which time cardiac arrest occurs (heart stops), and eventually irreversible brain damage develops.

In drowning casualties, especially children, the primary cause of cardiac arrest is hypoxic respiratory arrest. Therefore, when available, treatment should be to treat this underlying cause with emergency supplemental oxygen. The use of emergency supplemental oxygen is not recommended for routine use in other first aid situations.

It is reasonable to provide emergency oxygen for a responsive drowning victim who has been pulled from the water before going into cardiac arrest, but has symptoms from hypoxia. Symptoms of hypoxia include:

- cough,
- foam at the mouth or nose,
- low oxygen saturation (as measured by a pulse oximeter), and
- altered mental status.

For the drowning victim who is not breathing, emergency oxygen fed into a barrier mask during CPR enriches the oxygen concentration of the breath being blown into the victim by the rescuer. In either case, the amount of oxygen available to the victim is greatly increased.

Oxygen in Emergency Care Versus Medical Care

Over the years there has been confusion about the legal regulations in the United States concerning the use of emergency oxygen and the need for a prescription. All oxygen cylinders are filled with what is known as medical-grade oxygen, as established by the United States Pharmacopeia (USP). The type of equipment that is attached to the cylinder and the intended use determine any restrictions or prescription requirements.

Oxygen equipment intended for emergency use (see figure A.1) can be purchased over the counter (OTC) without a prescription, and anyone properly instructed in the use of emergency oxygen can administer it. Requirements for emergency-use equipment are as follows:

- Emergency oxygen is in a portable cylinder with a regulator that provides oxygen for a minimum of 15 minutes.

This appendix is reprinted and adapted, by permission, in part from American Safety and Health Institute with Human Kinetics, 2007, *Complete emergency care* (Champaign, IL: Human Kinetics). Updated information is licensed from the American Safety and Health Institute which is based on the latest international evidence-based science and treatment recommendations.

- The device has a constant fixed-flow rate of not less than 6 liters per minute.
- A content indicator gauge is present to determine how much oxygen is in the cylinder.
- The device is labeled "emergency" and has operation instructions.
- A mask with a connection for oxygen tubing is supplied for oxygen administration.

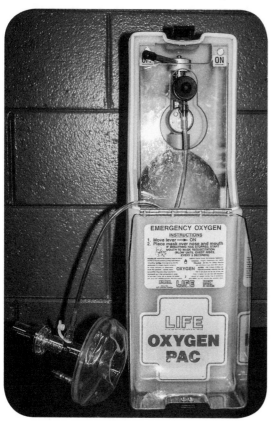

Figure A.1 Emergency oxygen system.

The U.S. Food and Drug Administration (FDA), the regulatory agency for medical gases, requires that labeling for all oxygen equipment bear the following statement: "WARNING: For emergency use only when administered by properly trained personnel for oxygen deficiency and resuscitation. For all other applications: CAUTION: Federal law prohibits dispensing without prescription."

Even though the regulations at the federal level in the United States allow the use of emergency oxygen without a prescription, your local requirements may vary. Check the regulations that govern oxygen equipment or use in your location.

If oxygen equipment is not intended for emergency use and is capable of providing less than 6 liters per minute, it requires a prescription. The Food and Drug Administration requires a doctor's prescription for use of oxygen in medical applications, such as for people with chronic lung disease or other conditions that require a varied flow and dosage of oxygen supply under the direction of a medical professional. The physician's staff or other personnel (e.g., EMS) may administer it as prescribed by the physician. Oxygen for medical use has a flow rate of 0 to 25 liters per minute that is controlled at the discretion of the operator.

The training you receive as part of lifeguard training is general in nature. To be considered properly trained to administer emergency oxygen, you must also have specific knowledge of the equipment you will use. You will need to become familiar with the manufacturer's directions and instructional materials provided with your system.

Components of an Emergency Oxygen System

An emergency oxygen system consists of these main components:

Figure A.2 An oxygen cylinder gauge.

- The *cylinder* holds the oxygen under pressure.
- The *regulator* controls how fast the oxygen flows from the cylinder.
- The *gauge* indicates how much oxygen is in the cylinder (see figure A.2).
- The *tubing* carries the oxygen to the delivery point.
- The *delivery mask* is placed on the person's face so that oxygen can enter the person through the mouth, nose, or both.
- The *case* safely secures the cylinder and other components.

Cylinder

The cylinder is constructed of steel or aluminum and is painted green for easy identification. Cylinders come in various sizes, identified by a letter such as C, D, or E. The size determines how much oxygen the cylinder can hold. Most emergency systems use a C-size cylinder, which provides about a 40-minute supply of oxygen.

A valve stem located on top of the cylinder is where the regulator is attached so that oxygen can safely flow out or where a filling device is attached to put oxygen back in. The valve stem has a special pin mount to prevent the cylinder from being filled with anything other than USP medical-grade oxygen. A washer is located at the connection point to help maintain a good seal; the washer is made of plastic, Teflon, nylon, or rubber with a metal ring.

The valve stem is used to turn the oxygen flow on and off. A handle may be built in, or a handle wrench may be needed. The handle wrench is supplied with the unit and should be securely attached with a chain.

When the oxygen supply runs out, most cylinders are refillable, although some are designed for one-time use and are disposable.

Regulator

A regulator is a device that attaches to the valve stem and decreases the content pressure to a safe delivery rate. Delivery rate is expressed in liters per minute (LPM or L/M). The regulator is tightened against the valve stem by turning a T-handle at the side of the regulator, and the oxygen flows out of the regulator through a tapered hose barb. You should know about and recognize the various types of regulators available so you can select the one that is appropriate for your level of training. In the United States, emergency oxygen systems must use a fixed flow regulator.

Regulators come in three types:

- *Fixed flow* is the required regulator for use with emergency oxygen. Depending on the setting (6 or 12 LPM), such a system delivers a fixed flow of oxygen at a precise rate that cannot be adjusted. The oxygen constantly flows out at the fixed rate until it is turned off.

- *Variable flow* is the most common regulator used by medical professionals. It requires the user to set the amount of oxygen delivered from 0 to 25 LPM based on the patient's need, the delivery device used, and protocol. The oxygen flows out constantly at the adjusted rate until it is turned off.

- *Demand regulators* deliver oxygen only when the person breathes in or, if fitted with a mechanical ventilator, when the provider pushes a button (similar to the function of a scuba regulator). This delivery system is highly efficient but requires specialized training and is for use by licensed medical professionals or specialized rescue personnel.

Gauge

The gauge indicates how much oxygen is available, but all gauges don't measure the same way. Become familiar with how the gauge on your system indicates the content level. The most common indicators are an empty-to-full scale, the pressure level inside the cylinder, or the time remaining in minutes.

If the gauge is built into the valve stem, it will read even when the flow is turned off. If the gauge is located on the regulator, the oxygen system must be turned on before the gauge will activate.

Tubing

The oxygen flows from the regulator to the delivery mask through crimp-proof plastic tubing. The tubing is attached to the regulator by slipping it over the hose barb, and it is attached to the delivery mask by slipping it over an oxygen inlet port.

Delivery Mask

Several types of oxygen delivery masks are available. You must know about and recognize the various types so you can choose the delivery mask appropriate for your level of training and the condition of the victim.

- Barrier *(CPR)* mask. The device most commonly used with emergency oxygen systems is a *barrier mask* with an oxygen inlet and one-way valve. The barrier mask is the same one you use for CPR, but it is fitted with a port or inlet to which the oxygen tubing attaches. It is the ideal mask for delivering oxygen to either a breathing or nonbreathing victim. Sold under many brand names (Rescue Mask, Pocket Mask, SealEasy, to name a few), this mask is the one to consider for all emergency oxygen administration. Advantages of using a barrier mask with an oxygen inlet to deliver emergency oxygen include it is easy to teach and learn its use—simply attach the tube from the oxygen system to the port on the mask, it eliminates direct contact with the nonbreathing victim's mouth or nose, and it is easy to seal and to deliver rescue breaths supplemented with emergency oxygen to the nonbreathing victim.

- Nasal cannula or simple face mask. A *nasal cannula* or *simple face mask* is included with some emergency oxygen systems and is designed for use with victims who are breathing. A nasal cannula is a section of tubing that fits around the head and administers small quantities of oxygen directly into the nose. A simple face mask usually has an elastic strap that fits around the head and large ventilation holes in the mask that allow the oxygen flow to be diluted with air. Advantages of a nasal cannula or simple face mask to deliver emergency oxygen include the device can be held in place without assistance, it doesn't cause claustrophobia by covering the mouth and nose, it is nonthreatening, and it is used for victims who are breathing with mild to moderate respiratory distress.

- Bag-valve mask. A *bag-valve mask* requires specialized training that is included in CPR courses for health care providers and professional rescuers. It is used only with nonbreathing victims to administer artificial ventilations. When connected to a supplemental oxygen source capable of delivering high-flow oxygen, the device stores oxygen in a bag that is filled from an oxygen reservoir. One rescuer holds the mask in place, and another rescuer squeezes the bag to deliver the oxygen. Advantages of bag-valve-mask to deliver emergency oxygen include when connected to a high-flow (12 to 15 LPM) oxygen source, it delivers close to 100 percent oxygen and it eliminates the need for any mouth-to-mask contact.

- Nonrebreather mask. A *nonrebreather mask* requires specialized training and is to be used in a clinical setting by a licensed medical professional. Lifeguards should not use a nonrebreather mask to deliver emergency oxygen.

Case

Keep your emergency oxygen system in a case to protect the components from damage and to provide easy access during an emergency. The most common types of cases

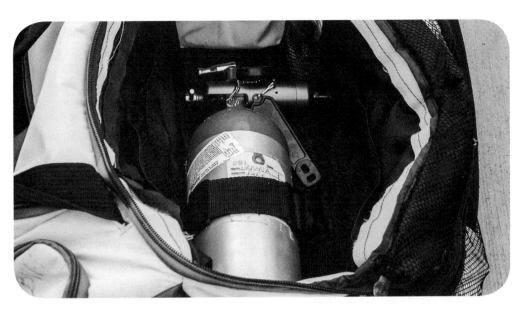

Figure A.3 You can store your oxygen in a fabric response bag, so you have quick access to it when executing your emergency action plan.

are a wall-mounted hard case, a portable hard case, and a fabric bag with a carrying strap (see figure A.3).

Assembly of Emergency Oxygen

Keep your oxygen system assembled and ready for immediate use. The only time you should take the system apart is for refilling, cleaning, or replacing parts. Follow these general steps when you want to remove the cylinder from an emergency oxygen system:

1. Turn the system off.
2. Loosen the regulator.
3. Lift the regulator off the valve stem.

Follow these steps when you assemble the components of an emergency oxygen system:

1. Remove the protective seal on the cylinder valve stem (if present).
2. Connect the handle wrench, if the handle is not built in.
3. Quickly open and close the valve to test the flow, and clean out any debris around the valve. Be sure the exit port (where the oxygen comes out) is directed away from you.
4. Check to make sure the sealing mechanism (gasket or washer) is in place on the regulator or at the connection to the tank stem.
5. Attach the regulator to the cylinder valve stem. Hand-tighten only.
6. Attach one end of the tubing to the hose nipple of the regulator.
7. Attach the other end of the tubing to the oxygen nipple or port of the mask.
8. Turn the system on and listen for oxygen flow.
9. Turn the system off and store for use.

Oxygen Safety

Emergency oxygen systems have three main safety concerns:

1. Oxygen inside the cylinder is compressed and highly pressurized.
2. Oxygen is chemically reactive and can interact with other chemical substances.
3. Oxygen supports combustion when a source of flame or spark is present.

Although oxygen cylinders are durable and safe under normal use, they are susceptible to damage from unprotected falls or inadvertent strikes. For example, if an oxygen cylinder should fall from a height and strike a hard surface, the valve head might break, causing rapid release of the contents (2,000 pounds per square inch [psi] or greater). The cylinder could "rocket," causing significant damage and personal injury or death depending on the contents' pressure.

Although oxygen is not flammable, it can react with other chemicals and create enough heat to initiate combustion or, in some cases, explosions. Oxygen also feeds a fire, substantially increasing the rate at which flammable materials burn.

In the United States, the Occupational Safety and Health Administration (OSHA), Compressed Gas Association (CGA), and other regulatory agencies have the same specific regulations for safe handling, use, and disposal of **all** compressed gas cylinders. Carefully read the material safety data sheet (MSDS) that accompanies the product. For locations outside the U.S., follow the international regulations that apply to safe handling, use, and disposal.

Improper use of plastic gaskets or washers has been proven to be a major factor in cases where regulators used with oxygen cylinders have burned or exploded, in some cases injuring personnel. The plastic crush gaskets commonly used to create the seal at the cylinder valve or regulator interface should **never** be reused. Reuse can deform the plastic gasket, increasing the likelihood that oxygen will leak around the seal and ignite. Also take the following general safety precautions:

- Always "crack" cylinder valves (open the valve just enough to allow gas to escape for a very short time) before attaching regulators in order to expel foreign matter from the outlet port of the valve.
- Always follow the regulator manufacturer's instructions for attaching the regulator to an oxygen cylinder.
- Always use the sealing gasket specified by the regulator manufacturer.
- Always inspect the regulator and seal before attaching it to the valve to ensure that the regulator is equipped with only one clean sealing-type washer (reusable metal-bound rubber seal) or a **new** crush-type gasket (single use, not reusable, typically nylon) that is in good condition.
- Always be certain the valve, regulator, and gasket are free from oil or grease. Oil or grease contamination can contribute to ignition in oxygen systems.
- Tighten the T-handle firmly by hand; do not use wrenches or other hand tools that may overtorque the handle.
- Open the post valve slowly. If gas escapes at the juncture of the regulator and the valve, quickly close the valve. Verify the regulator is properly attached and the gasket is properly placed and in good condition. If you have any questions or concerns, contact your supplier.
- Reports have been made of patients and their bedding being set on fire during

defibrillation when oxygen was in use. The oxygen concentration necessary to produce ignition will typically extend less than a foot (30 cm) in any direction from the oxygen source and will quickly disperse when removed. Therefore, you should remove the mask from the victim's face, place it several feet from the victim, and shut off the oxygen flow when delivering shocks. Leaving a device that continues to discharge oxygen near the victim's head before defibrillation is dangerous.

Other Safety Guidelines

Read and follow the specific maintenance, safety, and operating instructions provided with your system. These warnings apply to all oxygen systems:

- Never use oil, grease, adhesive tape, or other petroleum products on or near an oxygen cylinder or its components. A violent reaction can occur.
- Never smoke or use a match or lighter near oxygen systems.
- Turn off the oxygen flow and remove the oxygen system when delivering a shock with an automated external defibrillator (AED).
- Emergency oxygen systems are not designed to be used in rescue situations as an air supply to the rescuer.
- Do not use emergency oxygen systems in oxygen-deficient atmospheres as a respirator or an air supply.
- Do not use emergency oxygen systems in a fire situation. Remove the victim from such dangers before using oxygen.
- Do not use emergency oxygen systems in hazardous or explosive environments. Remove the victim from such dangers before using oxygen.

Safe Storage Requirements

Here are some guidelines for storage of emergency oxygen:

- Do not place containers where they might become part of an electrical circuit or arc.
- Do not expose compressed gas cylinders to extreme temperatures (more than 125 degrees Fahrenheit, or 51.6 degrees Celsius).
- Keep valve protection caps on cylinders at all times except when cylinders are secured and connected to dispensing equipment.
- Do not store containers near readily ignitable substances or expose them to corrosive chemicals or fumes.
- Do not store containers near elevators, walkways, building entrances or exits, or unprotected platform edges or in locations where heavy moving objects may strike or fall on them.
- Secure all compressed gas cylinders in service or in storage at user locations to prevent them from falling, tipping, or rolling. Store and use them valve end up.
- Secure compressed gas cylinders with straps or chains connected to a wall bracket or other fixed surface or on a cylinder stand.
- All compressed gases **must** be stored in areas away from heat, spark, flame sources, and explosive environments. If your facility maintains an extra supply of emergency oxygen cylinders, store them in a manner consistent with the guidelines described previously. Label the areas for **full** and **empty** cylinders.

Maintenance of Emergency Oxygen

Emergency oxygen systems are relatively maintenance free, but they need to be inspected on a regular basis to ensure the systems are ready for emergencies. After use during an emergency, the cylinder will need to be refilled (unless it is a disposable cylinder), and the components will need to be properly cleaned.

Inspections

Make inspection of your emergency oxygen system a regular part of your safety routine. Document your findings in a log. Conduct a visual inspection at least monthly that includes the following:

- See that no damage is visible to cylinders, regulators, or other components. Report damage to your safety or department manager immediately.
- Examine the content indicator gauge. Report cylinders that have not been used but that read "low" on the content indicator gauge as possibly having a leak. This helps ensure there is an adequate supply on hand when needed.
- Make sure the mask is present and that the one-way valve is attached and secure.
- Check that the tubing is not crimped and is securely attached to the hose barb on the regulator and the oxygen inlet on the mask.
- Ensure that any necessary handles or pins are present and attached to the device.
- Make sure the components are clean and dry.
- Check the stability of the unit mount, rack, or holders.
- Conduct an operational inspection when you first obtain your emergency oxygen system and after reassembly, or at least every six months. Be sure to turn the system on, confirm oxygen flow, and turn the system off and store it for use.

Refilling and Testing

When the gauge on your emergency oxygen system indicates less than half full, it's time to refill the cylinder. Any medical or industrial gas distributor that uses CGA's #870 pin-indexed universal coupling for oxygen can refill cylinders. Look for these distributors in your phone directory under *welding equipment* and *gases*. Another option for refilling is to contact your local fire department or hospital and ask if they offer refill service for emergency oxygen systems.

Federal regulations in the United States and most countries require that an oxygen cylinder be visually inspected (internally and externally) and pressure tested every five years or at any time the cylinder shows evidence of dents, corrosion, cracked or abraded areas, leakage, thermal damage, or any other condition that might render it unsafe for use. After a successful pressure test and inspection, a date is stamped into the cylinder. A cylinder is checked for a valid test date before it can be refilled. Federal regulations also require those who perform these cylinder tests to be currently approved to do so. Disposable cylinders do not have this requirement, but they **must not** be refilled under any circumstances.

Cleaning

When an emergency oxygen system is used to provide care, the components are considered contaminated and must be replaced or cleaned. Cleaning procedures should follow bloodborne pathogen exposure and decontamination guidelines.

As with any item contaminated with blood or other potentially infectious material, a reusable oxygen cylinder or oxygen delivery device (mask, tubing, cannula) or other component that is visibly contaminated must be handled by a trained person who is wearing proper personal protective equipment. The cylinder or component can be initially surface-cleaned using warm, soapy water. It must be cleaned and disinfected with at least a 1:100 bleach-and-water solution or a commercial solution approved for use against biohazards.

Dispose of blood-soaked disposable components as biohazardous waste, or disinfect them as described previously in chapter 3 and dispose of them as regular waste. Consider asking EMS personnel if they will dispose of any contaminated materials for you. Have a policy in place for how you intend to dispose of these materials.

Now that you know how to operate an emergency oxygen system, let's explore how to integrate its use during an emergency.

Considerations for Oxygen in an Emergency Action Plan

You must answer at least these questions in order to be prepared to administer emergency oxygen:

- How much oxygen should be kept on hand?
- Where should the emergency oxygen unit be mounted or stored?
- Who will bring emergency oxygen to the scene?
- When will emergency oxygen be used?

Answer these questions **before** an emergency occurs, then practice your emergency action plan regularly. You don't want an emergency situation to be the first time you've put your plan to the test.

When you are deciding how much oxygen to keep on hand, a good rule is to determine the average EMS response time to your facility and have enough to last twice as long as the response time. In most circumstances, 30 minutes' to 1 hour's supply is sufficient. Also have an extra full cylinder to replace any that are off site being refilled or tested.

When you are deciding where the emergency oxygen unit should be mounted or stored, start with the storage guidelines listed previously in this appendix. Then identify a location that meets these guidelines and is easily accessible at all times. Do not store your emergency oxygen system in a locked closet. If it is necessary to lock up the system overnight, be sure that part of your daily opening procedure is to bring the system to a predetermined accessible location.

When you are deciding who will bring the emergency oxygen to the scene, you must consider the number of people who will likely be present should an emergency occur. If you are the only trained person who will respond, you will either have to take the emergency oxygen with you when you first recognize an emergency or ask bystanders to bring the emergency oxygen to the scene. If another trained person will usually be on site to respond, you must consider how an emergency situation will be communicated so that person will bring the emergency oxygen.

When you are deciding your protocol for when to use emergency oxygen, here are two good general rules to follow:

1. Use emergency oxygen any time a person has been submerged and is experiencing signs of respiratory distress, and any time a person has been submerged and requires rescue breathing or CPR.

2. Use emergency oxygen as soon as reasonably possible under the circumstances.

Chapter 11 explains how to integrate emergency oxygen into an unresponsive drowning person rescue response.

BIBLIOGRAPHY AND RESOURCES

All Chapters

U.S. Centers for Disease Control and Prevention. 2014. Model aquatic health code (MAHC): An all-inclusive model public swimming pool and spa code. Available: http://www.cdc.gov/mahc/currentedition/index.html

U.S. Centers for Disease Control and Prevention. 2014. Model aquatic health code (MAHC) annex. Available: http://www.cdc.gov/mahc/currentedition/index.html

Chapter 1

Branche C, Stuart S (eds). 2001. *Lifeguard effectiveness: A report of the working group.* Atlanta, GA: Centers for Disease Control and Prevention, National Center for Injury Prevention and Control.

Schwebel D, Jones H, Holder E, Marciani F. 2010. Lifeguards: A forgotten aspect of drowning prevention. *Journal of Injury and Violence Research.* 2(1): 1-3. http://www.ncbi.nlm.nih.gov/pmc/articles/PMC3134895/

Wendling R, Vogelsong H, Wuensch K, Ammirati A. November 2007. A pilot study of lifeguard perceptions. *International Journal of Aquatic Research and Education* 1(4): 322-328.

World Health Organization. 2014. Global report on drowning: Preventing a leading killer. Available: http://www.who.intl

Chapter 2

Aquatic Safety Research Group. 2011. Note & float: Free lifesaving program for aquatic facilities. Available: http://www.aquaticsafetygroup.com/NoteAndFloat.html

Biswick C, Mattucci, M. 2011. Vested interest: One facility's experience with a life-jacket required policy shows why it's worth consideration–and the fringe benefits that can result. *Aquatics International.* Available: www.aquaticsintl.com/2011/may/1105_rm.html

Centers for Disease Control and Prevention. 2016. Unintentional drowning: Get the facts. www.cdc.gov/homeandrecreationalsafety/water-safety/waterinjuries-factsheet.html

Fielding F, Pia F, Wernicki P, Markenson D. November 2009. Scientific review: Avoiding hyperventilation. *International Journal of Aquatic Research and Education* 3(4): 432-49.

Griffiths T. June 2016. The language of drowning: a look at the terms "hypoxic blackout" vs. "shallow water blackout". *Aquatics International.* http://www.aquaticsintl.com/facilities/the-language-of-drowning_o

Hsiao R. February 2009. An analysis of risk management implementation in aquatic centers in Taiwan and a review of selected law cases. *International Journal of Aquatic Research and Education* 3(1): 38-65.

Hsiao R, Kostelnik R. August 2009. Are university swimming pools safe? A model to predict the number of injuries in Pennsylvania university swimming pools. *International Journal of Aquatic Research and Education* 3(3): 284-301.

Langendorfer S. February 2010. Lightning risk and indoor pools. *International Journal of Aquatic Research and Education* 4(1).

Morgan P, Lunt H, Tipton M. 2015. Oral presentation. Intentional hyperventilation prior to breathhold and submersion – hypoxia or arrhythmia as the killer? In *World conference on drowning prevention program and proceedings*, J. Scarr, editor. 311.

Petrass L, Blitvich, J. February 2012. The nature of caregiver supervision of young children in public pools. International Journal of Aquatic Research and Education 6(1): 11-23.

Chapter 3

American Safety and Health Institute. 2016. *Bloodborne pathogens.* Eugene, OR: Health and Safety Institute.

American Safety and Health Institute with Human Kinetics. 2007. *Complete emergency care*. Champaign, IL: Human Kinetics.

Centers for Disease Control and Prevention. 2016. 12 steps for prevention of recreational water illnesses (RWI's) for pool and aquatics staff. Available: http://www.cdc.gov/healthywater/swimming/pools/twelve-steps-for-prevention-rwi.html

Centers for Disease Control and Prevention. 2016. Fecal incident response recommendations. Available: http://www.cdc.gov/healthywater/pdf/swimming/pools/fecal-incident-response-recommendations.pdf

Centers for Disease Control and Prevention. 2016. Vomit and blood contamination of pool water. Available: http://www.cdc.gov/healthywater/swimming/pools/vomit-blood-contamination.html

Centers for Disease Control and Prevention. June 1997. Preventing allergic reactions to natural rubber latex in the workplace. Available: http://www.cdc.gov/niosh/docs/97-135

Centers for Disease Control and Prevention. 2011. Recreational water illness. Available: www.cdc.gov/healthywater/swimming/rwi

Health and Safety Commission and Sport England. 2003. *Managing health and safety in swimming pools* (HSG 179). Sudbury, UK: HSE Books.

Hlavsa M. 2009. Three state programs that helped prevent outbreaks. 2009 World Aquatic Health Conference, Recreational Water Illness (RWI) Prevention Seminars.

International Life Saving Federation. 1999. Statement on communicable diseases. Available: http://www.ilsf.org/sites/ilsf.org/files/filefield/medicalpolicy02.pdf

Sackett D, Lachocki T. 2006. Preventing recreational water outbreaks. *Recreation Management*. Available: http://recmanagement.com/200607gc01.php

Chapter 4

Avramidis S. August 2007. The 4W model of drowning. *International Journal of Aquatic Research and Education* 3(1): 89-100.

Avramidis S, Butterly R, Llewellyn D. February 2009. Drowning incident rescuer characteristics: Encoding the first component of the 4W model. *International Journal of Aquatic Research and Education* 3(1): 66-82.

Avramidis S, Butterly R, Llewellyn D. August 2009. Where do people drown? Encoding the third component of the 4W model. *International Journal of Aquatic Research and Education* 3(3).

Avramidis S, Butterly R, Llewellyn D. August 2009. Who drowns? Encoding the second component of the 4W model. *International Journal of Aquatic Research and Education* 3(3): 224-235.

Griffiths T. 2007. Disappearing dummies and the 5-Minute Scanning Strategy. *Lifeguard vigilance training DVD*. Champaign, IL: Human Kinetics.

Lanagan-Leitzel, L. August 2012. Identification of critical events by lifeguards, instructors and non-lifeguards. *International Journal of Aquatic Research and Education* 6(3); 201-214.

Hawkins S, Sempsrott J. 2015. Use of the terms near, dry, delayed, and secondary drowning. *Position Statement 15-1 of the Starfish Aquatics Institute* 15(1) Available: http://bit.ly/saipositionstatement15-1

Sempsrott J, Schmidt A. 2012. Drowning: an update. *Medscape*. www.medscape.com/viewarticle/722180

Van Beek E, Branche C, Szpilman D, Model J, Bierens J. November 2005. A new definition of drowning: Towards documentation and prevention of a global public health problem. *Bulletin of the World Health Organization* 83(11): 801-880.

Witman D. November 2008. Invited review: U.S. adoption of the uniform definition of drowning. *International Journal of Aquatic Research and Education* 2(4).

Chapter 5

Branche C, Stuart S (eds). 2001. *Lifeguard effectiveness: A report of the working group*. Atlanta, GA: Centers for Disease Control and Prevention, National Center for Injury Prevention and Control.

Brener J, Oostman M. May 2002. Lifeguards watch, but they don't always see. *World Waterpark Magazine*. Available: http://poseidon-tech.com/us/pressArticleWWA0205.pdf

Doyle, B. 2015. Oral presentation: Surveillance errors by lifeguards - comparison of results 2007-2014: Have we improved? In *World conference on drowning prevention program and proceedings*, J. Scarr, editor. 213.

Griffiths T. 2007. Disappearing dummies and the 5-Minute Scanning Strategy. *Lifeguard vigilance training DVD*. Champaign, IL: Human Kinetics.

Griffiths T. February 2008. Invited review: Reaction to Hunsucker and Davison's "Vision and signal detection." *International Journal of Aquatic Research and Education* 1(1).

Griffiths T. 2011. Oral presentation: The supervision myth. In *World conference on drowning prevention program and proceedings*, J. Scarr, editor. 127.

Griffiths T, Fenner P, Oostman M, Pia F. 2006. Lifesaver surveillance and scanning: Past, present and future. In *Handbook on drowning*, J Bierens, editor. Berlin Heidelberg, Germany: Springer-Verlag.

Hunsucker J, Davison S. February 2008. Invited review: How lifeguards overlook victims—vision and signal detection. *International Journal of Aquatic Research and Education* 1(1).

Hunsucker J, Davison S. August 2013. Scan time goal with analysis of scan times from aquatic facilities. *International Journal of Aquatic Research and Education* 7(3). 227-237.

Lanagan-Leitzel, L. August 2012. Identification of critical events by lifeguards, instructors and non-lifeguards. *International Journal of Aquatic Research and Education* 6(3); 201-214.

Mills P. Lifeguard vigilance and drowning detection systems. January/February 2005. *Recreation*. Available: www.imspa.co.uk/recreation/documents/REJan05pp36-39Lifeguard.pdf

Pia F. 1984. The RID factor as a cause of drowning. First published in *Parks & Recreation*, June: 52-67. Available: www.pia-enterprises.com/RID.pdf

Poseidon Technologies. September 2001. Executive summary: Bibliographic study on lifeguard vigilance. Available: http://poseidon-tech.com/us/vigilanceStudySummary.pdf

Poseidon Technologies. September 2001. Lifeguard vigilance bibliographic study. Available: http://poseidon-tech.com/us/vigilanceStudy.pdf

Smith T. November 2006. Seeing is believing; a technique called vigilance voice can help your lifeguards identify problems at your pool. BNet: The CBS Interactive Business Network. Available: http://findarticles.com/p/articles/mi_m1145/is_11_41/ai_n27079997

United States Lifeguard Standards Coalition. 2011. United States lifeguard standards: an evidence-based review and report by the United States lifeguard standards coalition. *International Journal of Aquatic Research and Education* 5(1). Available at: http://scholarworks.bgsu.edu/ijare/vol5/iss1/8

Chapter 6

American Safety and Health Institute with Human Kinetics. 2007. *Complete emergency care*. Champaign, IL: Human Kinetics.

Doyle B, Webber J. 2015. Oral presentation: Errors by lifeguards in emergency situations: How to improve team performance while under duress. In *World conference on drowning prevention program and proceedings*, J. Scarr, editor. 222.

European Emergency Number Association. 2011. What is 112? Available: www.eena.org/view/en/About112/whatis112.html

National Emergency Number Association. 2011. 911 tips and guidelines. Available: www.nena.org/911-tips-guidelines

Spengler J, Anderson P, Donnaughton D, Baker T. 2009. *Introduction to sport law*. Champaign, IL: Human Kinetics.

Szpilman D, Webber J, Quan L, Bierens J, Morizot-Leite L, Langendorfer SJ, Beerman S, Løfgren B. 2014. Creating a drowning chain of survival. *Resuscitation*. 85(9): 1149-52.

Szpilman D. 2015. Oral presentation. How can lifeguards apply reasoning and decision making to work more effectively? In *World conference on drowning prevention program and proceedings*, J. Scarr, editor. 230.

Chapter 7

International Life Saving Federation. 1999. Statement on who needs further medical help after rescue from the water. Available: www.ilsf.org/sites/ilsf.org/files/filefield/medicalpolicy05.pdf

Leclerc T. February 2007. A comparison of American Red Cross and YMCA preferred approach methods used to rescue near drowning victims. *International Journal of Aquatic Research and Education* 1(1): 34-42.

Chapter 8

American College of Emergency Physicians. January 2015. ACEP policy statement: EMS management of patients with potential spinal injury. Available: http://www.acep.org/Physician-Resources/Policies/Policy-Statements/EMS-Management-of-Patients-with-Potential-Spinal-Injury/.

Boissy, P., Shrier, I., Brière, S. et al. 2011. Effectiveness of cervical spine stabilization techniques. *Clinical Journal of Sport Medicine*. 21: 80–88

Dixon M, O'Halloran J, Hannigan A, Keenan S, Cummings N. Confirmation of suboptimal protocols in spinal immobilisation? September 2015. *Emerg Med J*. 32(2):939-945. Available: http://emj.bmj.com/content/early/2015/09/11/emermed-2014-204553.full

Dworkin GM. 2001. Responding to Aquatic Emergencies. Emergency Medical Services Magazine. The need for collaborative agreements between fire and rescue agencies and aquatic recreation and lifeguard agencies. Available: www.lifesaving.com/issues/need-collaborative-agreements-between-fire-and-rescue-agencies-and-aquatic-recreation-and-lif

Hauswald M. 2013. A re-conceptualisation of acute spinal care. *Emerg Med J.* 30(9):720-3.

Hsieh J. August 2015. Is it time to stop immobilizing kids? Available: http://www.ems1.com/ems-products/neonatal-pediatric/articles/3035178-Is-it-time-to-stop-immobilizing-kids/

Kwan I, Bunn F, Roberts J. 2001. Spinal immobilisation for trauma patients. Cochrane Database Syst Rev. (2):CD002803.

Morrissey J. 2013. Research suggests time for change in prehospital spinal immobilization. *Journal of EMS.* 38(3).

National Association of EMS Physicians, American College of Surgeons Committee on Trauma. 2013. EMS spinal precautions and the use of the long backboard. *Prehosp Emerg Care* 17:392-3.

Quinn R, William J, Bennett B, Stiller G, Islas I, McCord S. 2014. Wilderness Medical Society practice guidelines for spine immobilization in the austere environment: 2014 update. *Wilderness Environ Med.* 25(4):S105-S117

Shafer JS, Naunheim RS. 2009. Cervical spine motion during extrication. *West J Emerg Med.* 10(2):74-78.

White C, Domeier R, Millin MG. 2014. EMS spinal precautions and the use of the long backboard - resource document to the position statement of the National Association of EMS Physicians and the American College of Surgeons Committee on Trauma. *Prehospital Emergency Care* 18(2):306-14.

Chapter 9

American Heart Association. 2015. 2015 American Heart Association and American Red Cross international consensus on first aid science with treatment recommendations. *Circulation* 122:S934-S946 (supplement 2). Available: http://circ.ahajournals.org/content/122/16_suppl_2/S582.extract

American Safety and Health Institute. In press. *Basic first aid.* Eugene, OR: Health and Safety Institute.

ASTM International. 2009. Standard guide for defining the performance of first aid providers in occupational settings. ASTM Standard F2171-02.

Hood N. 2015. Oral presentation. Overview of the ILCOR process and first aid treatment recommendations relevant to the aquatic first aid, rescue and resuscitation environment. In *World conference on drowning prevention program and proceedings*, J. Scarr, editor. 306.

Singletary E, Zideman D, De Buck E, Chang W, Jensen J, Swain J, Woodin J, Blanchard I, Herrington R, Pellegrino J, Hood N, Lojero-Wheatley L, Markenson D, Yang H; on behalf of the First Aid Chapter Collaborators. 2015. Part 9: first aid: 2015 international consensus on first aid science with treatment recommendations. *Circulation.* 132(suppl 1):S269–S311.

U.S. Department of Labor, Occupational Safety and Health Administration. 2006. Fundamentals of a workplace first-aid program. OSHA 3317-06N.

Chapter 10

American Heart Association. 2015. 2015 American Heart Association guidelines update for cardiopulmonary resuscitation and emergency cardiovascular care. *Resuscitation* 132: S313-S589.

American National Standard. 2009. Criteria for accepted practices in safety, health, and environmental training. ANSI Standard Z490.1.

American Safety and Health Institute. In press. *Basic life support.* Eugene, OR: Health and Safety Institute.

ASTM International. 2009. Standard guide for defining the performance of first aid providers in occupational settings. ASTM Standard F2171-02.

Australian Resuscitation Council. 2008. Guidelines of the Australian resuscitation council: Any attempt at resuscitation is better than no attempt. Available: http://www.resus.org.au/arc_compression_only_cpr_advisory_statement.pdf

Bhanji F, Finn J, Lockey A, Monsieurs K, Frengley R, Iwami T, Lang E, Ma M, Mancini M, McNeil M, Greif R, Billi J, Nadkarni V, Bigham B; on behalf of the Education, Implementation, and Teams Chapter Collaborators. 2015. Part 8: education, implementation, and teams: 2015 international consensus on cardiopulmonary resuscitation and emergency cardiovascular care science with treatment recommendations. *Circulation.* 132(suppl 1):S242–S268.

International Liaison Committee on Resuscitation. 2010. 2010 international consensus on cardiopulmonary resuscitation and emergency cardiovascular care science with treatment recommendations. *Resuscitation* 81:E1-E330.

Nolan J, Nolana J, Soarb J, Zidemanc D, Biarentd D, Bossaerte L, Deakinf C, Kosterg R, Wyllieh J, Böttigeri B, on behalf of the ERC Guidelines Writing Group. 2010. European resuscitation council guidelines for resuscitation 2010. *Resuscitation* 81:1219-1276. Available: www.cprguidelines.eu/2010

Travers A, Perkins G, Berg R, Castren M, Considine J, Escalante R, Gazmuri R, Koster R, Lim S, Nation KJ, Olasveengen T, Sakamoto T, Sayre M, Sierra A, Smyth M, Stanton D, Vaillancourt C; on behalf of the Basic Life Support Chapter Collaborators. 2015. Part 3: adult basic life support and automated external defibrillation: 2015 international consensus on cardiopulmonary resuscitation and emergency cardiovascular care science with treatment recommendations. *Circulation.* 132(suppl 1):S51–S83.

Vanden Hoek TL, Morrison LJ, Shuster M, Donnino M, Sinz E, Lavonas EJ, Jeejeebhoy FM, Gabrielli A. 2010. Guidelines for cardiopulmonary resuscitation and emergency cardiovascular care. 2010 American Heart Association. *Circulation.* 122: S829-S861.

Chapter 11

American Heart Association. 2015. 2015 American Heart Association guidelines update for cardiopulmonary resuscitation and emergency cardiovascular care. *Resuscitation* 132: S313-S589.

Australian Resuscitation Council. 2015. The ARC Guidelines. Available: http://www.resus.org.au/guidelines

Australian Resuscitation Council. March 2014. Guideline 9.3.2 Resuscitation of the drowning victim. Available: http://resus.org.au/glossary/drowning-guideline-9-3-2/

Bhanji F, Finn JC, Lockey A, Monsieurs K, Frengley R, Iwami T, Lang E, Ma MH, Mancini ME, McNeil MA, Greif R, Billi JE, Nadkarni VM, Bigham B; on behalf of the Education, Implementation, and Teams Chapter Collaborators. 2015. Part 8: education, implementation, and teams: 2015 international consensus on cardiopulmonary resuscitation and emergency cardiovascular care science with treatment recommendations. *Circulation.* 132(suppl 1):S242–S268.

Bierens J, Lunetta P, Tipton M, Warner D. 2016. Physiology of drowning: A review. *Physiology.* 31(2): 147-166.

Bierens J, Berden H. 1996. AIDS: are volunteer lifesavers prepared for a storm? *Resuscitation* 32: 185-91.

Brennan R, Braslow A. 1998. Skill mastery in public CPR classes. *Am J Emerg Med* 16:653-7.

Chamberlain D, Smith A, Woollard M, Kern K. 2002. Trials of teaching methods in basic life support

(3): comparison of simulated CPR performance after first training and at 6 months, with a note on the value of re-training. *Resuscitation* 53:179-87.

Chin K, Galea P, Goel K. 1980. Secondary drowning in children. *British Medical Journal.* 281(6251):1351.

Eberle B, Dick W, Schneider T, Wisser G, Doetsch S, Tzanova I. 1996. Checking the carotid pulse check: diagnostic accuracy of first responders in patients with and without a pulse. *Resuscitation.* 33:107-16.

Farr K, Camp E, Yusuf S, Shenoi R. 2015. Vomiting is not associated with poor outcomes in pediatric victims of unintentional submersions. *The American Journal of Emergency Medicine.* 33(5):626-30.

Gregorakos L, Markou N, Psalida V, Kanakaki M, Alexopoulou A, Sotiriou E, Damianos A, Myrianthefs P. 2009. Near-drowning: Clinical course of lung injury in adults. *Lung.* 187:93.

Idris A, Berg R, Bierens J, Bossaert L, Branche C, Gabrielli A, Graves S, Handley A, Hoelle R, Morley P, Papa L, Pepe P, Quan L, Szpilman D, Wigginton J, Modell J, Other Contributors, Atkins D, Gay M, Kloeck W, Timerman S. 2003. Recommended guidelines for uniform reporting of data from drowning: "The Utstein Style". *Circulation.* 108:2565-2574

International Liaison Committee on Resuscitation. 2010. 2010 international consensus on cardiopulmonary resuscitation and emergency cardiovascular care science with treatment recommendations. *Resuscitation* 81: E1-E330.

International Life Saving Federation. 1999. Statement on automatic external defibrillation use by lifesavers and lifeguards. Available: www.ilsf.org/sites/ilsf.org/files/filefield/medicalpolicy03.pdf

International Life Saving Federation. 1999. Statement on who needs further medical help after rescue from the water. Available: www.ilsf.org/sites/ilsf.org/files/filefield/medicalpolicy05.pdf

International Life Saving Federation. 2001. Statements on in water resuscitation. Available: www.ilsf.org/sites/ilsf.org/files/filefield/medicalpolicy07in-waterresuscitation.pdf

International Life Saving Federation. 2003. Statement on critical CPR skills for lifesavers. Available: www.ilsf.org/sites/ilsf.org/files/filefield/medicalpolicy10. pdf

International Life Saving Federation. 2003. Statement on positioning a patient on a sloping beach. Available: www.ilsf.org/sites/ilsf.org/files/filefield/medicalpolicy09.pdf

International Life Saving Federation. 2003. Statements on the use of oxygen by lifesavers. Available: www.ilsf.org/sites/ilsf.org/files/filefield/medicalpolicy08.pdf

International Life Saving Federation. 2010. Statement on compression-only CPR and drowning. Available: http://www.ilsf.org/es/news/articles/new-medical-position-statement-compression-only-cpr-and-drowning

Lapostolle F, Le Toumelin P, Agostinucci J, Catineau J, Adnet F. 2004. Basic cardiac life support providers checking the carotid pulse: performance, degree of conviction, and influencing factors. *Acad Emerg Med* 11:878-80.

Leclerc T, Canabal J, Leclerc H. February 2008. The issue of in-water rescue breathing: A review of the literature. *International Journal of Aquatic Research and Education* 2(1).

Liberman M, Lavoie A, Mulder D, Sampalis J. 1999. Cardiopulmonary resuscitation: errors made by prehospital emergency medical personnel. *Resuscitation* 42:47-55

Lopez-Fernandez Y, Martinez-de Azagra A, de la Oliva P, Modesto V, Sanchez J, Parrilla J, Arroyo J, Reyes S, Pons-odena M, Lopez-Herce J, Fernandez R, Kacmarek R, Villar J. 2012. Pediatric Acute Lung Injury Epidemiology and Natural History Study: Incidence and outcome of the acute respiratory distress syndrome in children. *Critical Care Medicine*. 40(12):3238-3245.

Lumb A. 2010. *Nunn's applied respiratory physiology*. 7th ed. Oxford: Churchill Livingstone.

Manolios N, Mackie I. 1988. Drowning and near-drowning on Australian beaches patrolled by lifesavers: A 10-year study, 1973-1983. *The Medical Journal of Australia*. 148:1657.

Mejicano G, Maki, D. 1998. Infections acquired during cardiopulmonary resuscitation: Estimating the risk and defining strategies for prevention. *Annals of Internal Medicine*. 129: 813-828.

Milne S, Cohen A. 2006. Secondary drowning in a patient with epilepsy. *British Medical Journal*. 332(7544): 775-6.

Monsieurs K, Nolan J, Bossaert L, Greif R, Maconochie I, Nikolaou N, Perkins G, Soar J, Truhlář A, Wyllie J, Zideman D. 2015. European resuscitation council guidelines for resuscitation 2015. *Resuscitation*. 95: p1-312, e1-262.

Moule P. 2000. Checking the carotid pulse: diagnostic accuracy in students of the healthcare professions. *Resuscitation* 44:195-201.

Noonan L, Howrey R, Ginsburg C. 1996. Freshwater submersion injuries in children: a retrospective review of seventy-five hospitalized patients. *Pediatrics* 98:368-371.

Nyman J, Sihvonen M. 2000. Cardiopulmonary resuscitation skills in nurses and nursing students. *Resuscitation* 47:179-84.

Papa L, Hoelle R, Idris A. 2005. Systematic review of definitions for drowning incidents. *Resuscitation*. 65(3):255-64.

Pearn J. 1980. Secondary drowning in children. *British Medical Journal*. 281(6248):1103-5.

Perkins G, Stephenson B, Hulme J, Monsieurs K. 2005. Birmingham assessment of breathing study (BABS). *Resuscitation* 64:109-13.

Pratt F, Haynes B. 1986. Incidence of "secondary drowning" after saltwater submersion. *Annals of Emergency Medicine*. 15(9):1084-7.

Rivers J, Lee G, Orr H. 1970. Drowning: its clinical sequelae and management. *British Medical Journal*. 2:157-161.

Ruppert M, Reith M, Widmann J, Lackner C, Kerkmann R, Schweiberer L, Peter K. 1999. Checking for breathing: evaluation of the diagnostic capability of emergency medical services personnel, physicians, medical students, and medical laypersons. *Annals of Emergency Medicine*. 34:720-9.

Saule H. 1975. Sekundares Ertrinken. *Klin. Padiat*. 187:346-349.

Schmidt A. June 2012. Drownings present as hypoxic events. *Journal of Emergency Medical Services*. http://www.jems.com/articles/print/volume-37/issue-7/patient-care/drownings-present-hypoxic-events.html

Schmidt A, Szpilman D, Berg I, Sempsrott J, Mogan P. 2016. A call for the proper action on drowning resuscitation. *Resuscitation*. http://www.resuscitationjournal.com/article/S0300-9572(16)30043-0/pdf

Schmidt A, Sempsrott, J, Hawkins S, Arastu A, Cushing T, Auerbach P. 2016. Wilderness Medical Society issues official guidelines for the prevention and treatment of drowning. *Wilderness & Environmental Medicine*. 27(2): 236-251. http://www.wemjournal.org/article/S1080-6032(16)00003-X/fulltext

Sempsrott J, LaMar H, Nelson D, Owens J. Oral presentation Team focused, "pit crew" drowning resuscitation" case reports and a novel approach for pre-hospital providers. In *World conference on drowning prevention program and proceedings*, J. Scarr, editor. 309.

Szpilman D, Bierens J, Handley A, Orlowski J. 2012. Drowning. *NEJM* 366:2102-2110.

Szpilman D. 1997. Near-drowning and drowning classification: A proposal to stratify mortality based on the analysis of 1,831 cases. *Chest.* 112(3):660-665.

Szpilman D, Soares M. 2004. In-water resuscitation: Is it worthwhile? *Resuscitation.* 63:25.

Tibballs J, Russell P. 2009. Reliability of pulse palpation by healthcare personnel to diagnose paediatric cardiac arrest. *Resuscitation.* 80:61-4.

Travers A, Perkins G, Berg R, Castren M, Considine J, Escalante R, Gazmuri R, Koster R, Lim S, Nation KJ, Olasveengen T, Sakamoto T, Sayre M, Sierra A, Smyth M, Stanton D, Vaillancourt C; on behalf of the Basic Life Support Chapter Collaborators. 2015. Part 3: Adult basic life support and automated external defibrillation: 2015 international consensus on cardiopulmonary resuscitation and emergency cardiovascular care science with treatment recommendations. *Circulation.* 132(suppl 1):S51–S83.

Vanden Hoek T, Morrison L, Shuster M, Donnino M, Sinz E, Lavonas E, Jeejeebhoy F, Gabrielli A. 2010. Guidelines for cardiopulmonary resuscitation and emergency cardiovascular care. Part 12: Cardiac arrest in special situations. 2010 American Heart Association. *Circulation.* 122: S829-S861.

Yarger L. May 2008. Emergency oxygen: Use in aquatic and recreation facilities is overdue. *International Journal of Aquatic Research and Education* 2(2).

Chapter 12

Avramidis S. February 2009. Lifeguard leadership: A review. *International Journal of Aquatic Research and Education* 3(1): 89-100.

Centers for Disease Control and Prevention. 2016. Recommendations for prevention pool chemical injuries. Available: http://www.cdc.gov/healthywater/swimming/pools/preventing-pool-chemical-injuries.html

Human Kinetics. 2008. *Safe chemical handling for lifeguards and pool operators.* Champaign, IL: Human Kinetics.

International Life Saving Federation. 1999. Statement on sun dangers for lifeguards. Available: www.ilsf.org/sites/ilsf.org/files/filefield/medicalpolicy04.pdf

Park District Risk Management Agency. 2011. Aquatics policy and training guide: 3 points of contact (pamphlet). Wheaton, IL: Park District Risk Management Agency.

Skin Cancer Foundation. 2011. The Skin Cancer Foundation's response to the release of the FDA's final regulations on sunscreens. Available: http://www.skincancer.org/the-skin-cancer-foundations-response-to-the-release-of-the-final-fda-monograph.html

U.S. Food and Drug Administration. 2012. FDA sheds light on sunscreens. www.fda.gov/forconsumers/consumerupdates/wcm258416.htm

Wendling R, Vogelsong H, Wuensch K, Ammirati A. November 2007. A pilot study of lifeguard perceptions. *International Journal of Aquatic Research and Education* 1(4): 322-328.

World Health Organization. 2002. Global solar UV index: a practical guide. www.who.int/UV/publicatins/en/UVIGuide.pdf

Chapter 14

Bramblett D, White B, White J. 2007. *StarGuard triathlon and open water race manual.* Savannah, GA: Starfish Aquatics Institute.

Fawcett P. 2005. *Aquatic facility management.* Champaign, IL: Human Kinetics.

Griffiths T. 2012. *Safer beaches.* Champaign, IL: Human Kinetics.

Grosse S. 2014. *Children with challenges.* Port Washington, WI: DSL Ltd.

Lepore M, Gayle W, Stevens S. 2007. *Adapted aquatics programming.* Champaign, IL: Human Kinetics.

Pound R, Cassidy S, Cliff H, Rodeo S, Rose E. April 12, 2011. Open Water Review Commission recommendations. Available: www.usaswimming.org/_Rainbow/Documents/7446603a-b37d-44eb-b8c2-18b5eece7ca3/Open%20Water%20Review%20Commission%20Recommendations.pdf

Seghers G. 2015. Oral presentation. Making open water swimming safe. *World conference on drowning prevention program and proceedings*, J. Scarr, editor. 186.

Chapter 15

Beard E. Autism policy do's and don't's for waterparks. *World Waterpark.* Available: http://edition.pagesuite-professional.co.uk//launch.aspx?eid=76ce6e56-a26c-4b76-aa5d-84a7c1cf82dc

Centers for Disease Control and Prevention. Water plan areas and interactive fountains. Available: http://www.cdc.gov/healthywater/swimming/pools/water-play-areas-interactive-fountains.html

Deines G. February 2015. Overcoming the 5 areas of guest complaints. *World Waterpark*. Available: http://edition.pagesuite-professional.co.uk//launch.aspx?eid = 22a20fc3-fd0a-41af-ab0d-d800e3548196

International Association of Amusement Parks and Attractions. 2011. Waterpark safety. Available: www.iaapa.org/safety/WaterParkSafety.asp

Kidd, S. 2018. Elite dispatch training program. Unpublished internal document and multimedia presentation. IAM StarGuard Elite LLC.

Rowland K. Implementing a lifeguard video training program. *World Waterpark*. Available: http://edition.pagesuite-professional.co.uk//launch.aspx?eid = c6a9f5a1-97f6-4016-88c1-a0f005158aa2

Saferparks. 2009. Injury trends for waterpark attractions. Available: www.saferparks.org/safety/injuries/byrt_waterpark_attractions.php

Chapter 16

American Camp Association, Scheder C. 2010. *Camp waterfront management*. Monterey, CA: Healthy Learning.

Griffiths T. 2012. *Safer beaches*. Champaign, IL: Human Kinetics.

Starfish Aquatics Institute, Padgett J. In press. *Wilderness lifeguarding*. Savannah, GA: Starfish Aquatics Institute.

ABOUT THE CONTRIBUTORS

Justin R. Sempsrott, MD

Dr. Sempsrott has served as a Medical Director for Starfish Aquatics Institute (SAI) since 2011. A graduate of the University of South Florida College of Medicine, he completed his residency in emergency medicine at the University of Nevada, School of Medicine. In 2006, he founded *Lifeguards Without Borders,* a non-profit NGO dedicated to reducing the global burden of drowning morbidity and mortality. A frequent lecturer across the globe, Dr. Sempsrott also publishes widely on the topic of drowning. He has won numerous awards and honors from educational institutions and conferences, such as the World Conference on Drowning Prevention in Da Nang, Vietnam in 2011, the 2015 National Drowning Prevention Alliance's Lifesaver of the Year, and the 2015 National Water Safety Congress Presidents Award. Dr. Sempsrott is a member of the American College of Emergency Physicians and a member of the American Academy of Emergency Medicine. He currently works as an EMS, flight, and emergency medicine physician in Nevada.

Seth Collings Hawkins, MD

Dr. Hawkins is board-certified in both EMS and emergency medicine and has served as Medical Director for SAI since 2011. He is a graduate of Yale University with a degree in medical anthropology and UNC-Chapel Hill with a doctorate in medicine. He completed his residency in emergency medicine at the University of Pittsburgh. Academically, he is currently an assistant professor of emergency medicine at Wake Forest University and the executive editor of *Wilderness Medicine Magazine.* Clinically, he works as an emergency physician at Catawba Valley Medical Center in North Carolina and is EMS medical director of Burke County EMS and the North Carolina state parks system. Dr. Hawkins is the first physician ever named a Master Fellow of the Academy of Wilderness Medicine, and is also a fellow of both the Academy of Emergency Medicine and the American College of Emergency Physicians. He also serves as the medical director for Landmark Learning, which developed the Wilderness StarGuard training now administered by Starfish Aquatics Institute. He publishes and speaks extensively on wilderness and emergency medicine, with a special interest in drowning prevention and treatment. When not working, he is a competitive swimmer in the US Masters Swimming program.

Lake White

Lake White has experience in all aspects of the aquatics industry. He is a faculty member for the Starfish Aquatics Institute's StarGuard, Starfish Swimming, and AquaTech programs. He has served as SAI's director of the StarGuard program and as director of quality assurance and improvement. He is currently on the executive staff team for StarGuard Elite. Lake has developed and led "train the trainer" instructor development programs around the globe and has conducted a wide range of risk management and safety assessments for swimming pools, waterparks and waterfronts. A frequent speaker at aquatic industry conferences, Lake was recognized by the World Waterpark Association (WWA) with a conference "Best Speaker" award in 2014. He has served on industry leadership committees and been involved in local drowning prevention initiatives, including development and implementation of the first Make-a-Splash project in Atlanta through USA Swimming. He has experience coaching swimming, and was himself a high school all-American competitive swimmer and triathlete. He lives in Savannah, Georgia with his wife and three children.

ABOUT THE AUTHOR

Jill White founded the Starfish Aquatics Institute (SAI) in 1999 and cofounded StarGuard Elite in 2016 with the mission to reduce drowning and save lives. She has consistently been named one of the Top 25 Most Influential People in Aquatics by *Aquatics International* magazine and has been the recipient of the prestigious Al Turner Memorial Commitment to Excellence Award from the World Waterpark Association. In the fall of 2014, White was inducted into the World Waterpark Hall of Fame.

She has authored textbooks on lifeguarding, lifeguarding instruction, and swim instruction for the National Safety Council, Jeff Ellis & Associates, and SAI, and served as the aquatic education division director for Human Kinetics. She has firsthand experience in training, supervising, and managing lifeguards and has personally taught thousands of lifeguards and hundreds of lifeguarding instructors. White has collaborated in drowning prevention and standards development initiatives and is a frequent speaker at national and international conferences.

White lives in Savannah, Georgia.

Take your facility operations to the next level with StarGuard Elite

StarGuard Elite is a comprehensive suite of services that builds upon the SAI StarGuard certification. Waterpark and aquatic facility owners and operators can now receive unprecedented support:

- **Operational standards and practice guidelines for a turnkey aquatic risk management system.** The system will help you verify zones, establish a comprehensive safety plan, and guide daily operations at the highest level to meet (and exceed) the CDC's Model Aquatic Health Code (MAHC).
- **Accountability and recognition through a lifeguard license layered over the StarGuard certification.**
- **An exceptionally professional and innovative audit program.** You'll receive an annual facility risk-assessment visit and unannounced audits, and can also conduct unlimited in-house audits of lifeguards and facility operations using the same easy-to-use forms and methods.
- **Continuing education and networking.** Learn from ongoing risk-management alerts and an annual client-only CAMP (Conference for Aquatic Management Professionals).
- **Additional training and certification.** Receive specialized training for lifeguard supervisors, waterslide dispatch, extremely shallow water attractions, and other specific needs.
- **Customized online portal.** Track certifications, preservice and in-service training, rescue reporting, audit results and corrective actions, and more!
- **An assigned client partner.** Get personalized access to leaders in the industry.
- **Incident support.** Have access to the most experienced professionals in the industry to help you and your staff navigate through a crisis.

Join the growing international list of StarGuard Elite facilities today.

For more information: http://bit.ly/StarGuardelite